D1569842

LATINA POLITICS, LATINO POLITICS

LATINA POLITICS, LATINO POLITICS

Gender, Culture, and Political Participation in Boston

CAROL HARDY-FANTA

Temple University Press
Philadelphia

Temple University Press, Philadelphia 19122
Copyright © 1993 by Temple University. All rights reserved
Published 1993
Printed in the United States of America

⊗ The paper used in this publication meets the minimum require-
ments of American National Standard for Information Sciences—
Permanence of Paper for Printed Library Materials, ANSI
Z39.48-1984

Library of Congress Cataloging-in-Publication Data
Hardy-Fanta, Carol, 1948–
  Latina politics, Latino politics : gender, culture, and political
participation in Boston / Carol Hardy-Fanta.
    p. cm.
  Includes bibliographical references and index.
  ISBN 1-56639-031-1 (alk. paper). — ISBN 1-56639-032-X
(pbk. : alk. paper)
  1. Hispanic American women—Massachusetts—Boston—Political activity. 2. Hispanic Americans—Massachusetts—Boston—Politics and government. 3. Boston (Mass.)—Politics and
government. 4. Political participation—Massachusetts—Boston.
I. Title.
F73.9.S75H37 1993
323.1′168074461—dc20   92-27093

To my daughters, Allison and Carly,
for the women you will become.

Somos la vida, la fuerza, la mujer
Julia de Burgos

Contents

Preface

I did not plan to write a book about Latina women and politics. In fact, when I began this project in 1987, I had developed an elaborate proposal to study broad questions of Latino political participation. At that time, I was interested in factors that would explain the relatively low voter participation rates among certain Latino groups in the United States and the supposed role of culture in political participation. I was particularly curious whether Latinos suffer from "political apathy" or whether their political participation is constrained to a greater extent by structural obstacles within the sociopolitical system.

While all these topics represent valid areas for research, my focus changed as I began listening to Latinos in the Boston community and as I began participating in community events. I began to hear themes that forced me to reevaluate the project. From the first day of interviews and community observations, and consistently throughout my more than two years of fieldwork, a pattern emerged—a pattern of gender differences in how Latina women and Latino men in Boston perceive politics and how their different perceptions inform their ways of mobilizing the community. What also emerged was that Latina women play a very active political role, a finding that challenges the invisibility of Latina women as political actors so prevalent in current political science literature. As these and other themes became apparent, I realized I had to write a different kind of book. What follows, therefore, is a book about Latina women, Latino men, and gender differences in how they define politics, how they develop political mobilization strategies, and how they conceive political participation.

Above all, this is a book about people: Latino people who shared with me their political experiences, opinions, and life stories. Interviews and community events took me from the Massachusetts State House and Boston City Hall to housing projects and community centers. I met influential Latino men like Edwin Colina, Juan Maldonado, Pedro Contreras, and Armando Meléndez—who, in many cases, hold positions in city or state government. I also met influen-

tial Latina women—activists like Andrea del Valle, Blanca Schoolman, and María Ramírez—who are influential less for the positions
they hold and more for the hours they spend talking to neighbors,
colleagues, friends and strangers about getting involved in solving
community problems.

Antonio Rojas, Felipe Aviles, Nelson Merced, and Marta Rosa
have all run for elected office: Merced and Rosa won; Rojas and
Aviles lost—but all were eloquent about their long struggle to get
something for Latinos in Boston. Merced, Aviles, Rojas, Jesús Carrillo, Juanita Fonseca, and Catalina Torres are all influential Latinos—members of what might be called the "political elite" of the
Latino community. Fonseca is one of *las pioneras* (the pioneers) of
early efforts to gain bilingual, culturally appropriate social services
for Latinos in Boston.

In most studies of Latino politics, and of politics in general, the
focus is on influential individuals: community leaders, activists, and
politicians—the political elite. Equally important, if not more so, are
the stories of noninfluential Latinos, if only because they are the targets of the mobilizers. What are the reasons behind the political activity or inactivity of these "ordinary" Latinos—the common folk,
the masses, or as is said in Spanish *la gente del pueblo*?[1] These are the
apparently apathetic masses that form the puzzle of Latino political
participation in the United States.

Carlos García, for example, is a house painter from Puerto Rico.
Francisco Salamanca and Juan Betances are Dominicans who work
as mechanics; all three have set their sights less on politics and more
on work and making a living. But Jaime Romero, a young Puerto
Rican, and Tito Morales, an older man who is also from Puerto
Rico, are very involved in community political efforts. Silvia Barajas,
a Dominican woman who works in a factory, and Dalia Ruiz, a
Puerto Rican woman who is enrolled in an English as a second language program, are very politically aware; they express concern
about socioeconomic conditions in the Latino community and would
like to see more community action. Sonia Cardona, in contrast, came
here three years ago from Puerto Rico with her young child. She
seems thoroughly uninvolved in any aspect of American politics: she
is training to become a cosmetologist and is preoccupied with school
and her child. In designing this study, I wanted to understand the
political experiences of *la gente del pueblo* in their home countries
and their experiences in the United States. These experiences might
explain what led them to choose or reject political involvement.

María Luisa Soto, Tito Morales, Inez Martínez, Aracelis Guzmán,
Marta Correa, and Josefina Ortega are Latinos who bridge the gap

between the common folk (*la gente del pueblo*) and the influential Latinos and government officials (*la gente profesional*, the term commonly used to describe these individuals). Soto, for example, is an older Puerto Rican woman with two grown children. She has been a force in Latino organizing around housing issues for many years and is comfortable working in political campaigns and party politics as well as in community efforts for local action. Her name is well known in the community because she has remained connected to the community despite her public prominence.

Guzmán is a Mexican American in her late forties who lives with her two children in a run-down apartment on a street that has struggled to rid itself of drug pushers. She works full time as a clerical assistant and wants to go back to school. She finds the time to talk to her neighbors, to encourage them to join a Latino parents' organization for better education. Her vision of politics is very personal—a one-to-one interaction between equals struggling for a better life for women and the community.

At Mujeres Unidas en Acción (Women United in Action), an organization established to teach English to Latina women, politics is blended into everyday life. For women there, politics is about the development of the self through working with others. Community issues forums abound to encourage an exchange of ideas on a variety of social issues—from AIDS and domestic violence to citizenship. Women become participators by being active in the running of the organization; they take on new roles and develop new capabilities (Young and Padilla 1990). The provision of child care assures attendance at group events. Politics for these women is working together to achieve change.

Two years of fieldwork, over sixty interviews, and almost one hundred hours of participant observation in the Latino community produced a wealth of data about Latino political participation in Boston, Massachusetts. The most gratifying aspect of the project was the response of the community. Not one of the people I approached to be interviewed refused to participate; virtually everyone expressed enthusiasm for the topic and stressed the need to understand the factors that stimulate political participation. Many thanked me, in one form or another, for bringing the story of Latino community struggles to light. Latina women, in particular, wanted their contribution to politics acknowledged.

The rationale for using a qualitative, exploratory research design is that such a design has distinct advantages when breaking new ground. First, surveys and other quantitative methods obscure forms of participation that have not been observed before precisely *because* they measure only previously measured behavior.[2] Second, to understand the role of Latina women in politics requires a research design not biased by gender and culture. Finally, qualitative methods permit the definition of "What is political?" to be determined by Latino community members, not by Anglo or Latino researchers.

The answers to the question "What is political?" and to questions related to gender, culture, and political participation were generated from interviews with influential Latinos in the city of Boston; interviews with the common folk, *la gente del pueblo*; and participant observation of community events—protests, electoral campaigns, conferences, community forums, and informal interactions.[3]

Using a combination of reputational and snowball sampling, I generated a list of influential Latinos. This list included community leaders, community activists, and people active in electoral politics. In general, I followed Luker's (1984, 251–252) model of snowball selection, in which every activist or influential Latino had to be "nominated" by at least two or more other people. At the end of each interview I asked, "Who do you feel draws other Latinos into political participation?" Occasionally the process was more informal; for example, some influential Latinos identified others using phrases like: "I assume you have talked to Antonio Rojas and Jesús Carrillo," or "Have you spoken with Juanita Fonseca yet?"

The names of the women and men who bridge the gap between *la gente del pueblo* and *la gente profesional* emerged in interviews with influential and noninfluential Latinos. These people (referred to hereafter as the "*gente*/influentials")—María Luisa Soto, Marta Correa, Tito Morales, Inez Martínez, Aracelis Guzmán, and Josefina Ortega—are able to draw Latinos into participating at community events.

Selection of *la gente del pueblo* occurred in two ways. First, some were volunteers I met at various Latino community centers. For example, at the end of an interview with Josefina Ortega, a woman in her sixties who plans cultural events for children and is active in electoral politics, she invited me to come to the Latino lunch at a local community center located in the Mission Hill neighborhood. I went, and I found her cooking and leading a group in traditional Latin American songs. Clara Ybarra, a Latina co-worker at the center that day, sat and chatted with me. She promptly pulled me over to a table where five or six people were sitting and said, "Come on over; tell them what you're doing." At the discussion that ensued—interrupted only by lunch being served—the group gave their opinions, expounded upon the reasons for low political participation of Latinos here, talked about their participation in their home countries and about the political situations in Cuba and Nicaragua, and commented on the problems facing Latinos in Boston. At the end I asked for volunteers, and Juana Oviedo, a Puerto Rican, and Octavio González, a Guatemalan, indicated willingness to meet with me in their homes. We ended with the exchange of telephone numbers.

A staff member at El Centro Católico (the Catholic Center) in the South End referred seven persons to me: Sonia Cardona, Luis Hernández, Jaime Romero, Carlos García, Marta Torrijos, Juan Betances, and Francisco Salamanca. I met six others through Mujeres Unidas en Acción in North Dorchester: Julia Santiago, Dalia Ruiz, Aurelia Rivera, Marisela Pena, Ana Crespo, and Silvia Barajas. Ivelisse Rodríguez volunteered at a meeting of the Familias Latinas de Boston, an organization of Latino parents. In all, I interviewed twenty-two individuals of *la gente del pueblo*.

There were distinct advantages to selecting people who had some association with a specific community center.[4] Given that I was not attempting a random sample, I felt it important not to spread myself all over the city of Boston selecting isolated individuals who, because of their disparate experiences, would provide scattered, impressionistic results. In addition, the three centers were located in the three different Latino neighborhoods. I therefore had access to the more recent arrivals and the poorer, less established residents of the North Dorchester/Roxbury area; the more "savvy," longtime residents of Jamaica Plain; and members of the South End, with its established Latino services and history as "the Puerto Rican community."[5]

Interviews with activists and influential Latinos began with an opening invitation, "Tell me what you do politically," followed by five topic areas: the ways they work to mobilize Latinos in Boston, their views of politics and political participation, activities they have been involved in, successes and failures of community mobilization, and the source of their own political involvement.

For *la gente del pueblo*, the opening invitation was: "Tell me a story of your migration to the United States." Each Latino coming to the United States has a migration story; the story represents an essential part of his or her social and political experience. In telling the story, we explored the person's expectations and aspirations upon migrating, whether the aspirations were fulfilled, overall satisfaction with life in the United States and Boston, and level of attachment to this country. Subsequent topics included politics as a problem-solving process (Nelson 1979), relationships with Latino agencies and government institutions, and both traditional and alternative political efforts to address personal and community issues such as crime, housing, education, employment, and poverty.

Interviews lasted from one-and-one-half to three or more hours. All the interviews with *la gente del pueblo* were conducted entirely in Spanish; those with influential Latinos were in English or Spanish.

Findings generated by a qualitative study such as this are suggestive, not conclusive. They form the basis for future hypothesis testing and for theory building. I feel a certain kinship with Robert Coles in responding to the objection of a small sample in one city: "I claim no definitive conclusions about what any 'group' feels or thinks. I don't even claim an exclusive say about what the limited number [of, for me, Latinos] . . . I've gotten to know 'really' think. . . . One can only insist on being as tentative as possible, claiming only impressions, observations, thoughts, reflections, surmises, speculations, and in the end, a 'way of seeing' " (Coles 1986, 17). Thus, I cannot say that the people I interviewed "speak" for all Latinos in Boston, let alone Latinos in different states.[6] What I can say is that through this research a new way of looking at Latino politics is opened up to view, a way that does not ignore the role of Latina women, and a way that challenges existing theories of political participation.

Understanding how Latinos view politics did not come from interviews alone. Joining the community group Familias Latinas de Boston allowed me to gain an in-depth understanding of one community group over an extended period. Participating in formal, organized political activities such as manning the phone banks at the campaign office of a Latino candidate and attending political banquets, public forums, and conferences and workshops provided another means of observing how gender and culture interacted to stimulate—or suppress—political participation. I also joined protest marches and rallies and tracked down voter registration information in Spanish for a group at Mujeres Unidas en Acción. In addition, I learned much from informal interactions: at groups on domestic violence, during lunch at Latino community centers, and during spontaneous conversations with Latinos from many countries and diverse backgrounds. As I talked to people in community settings and observed how they interacted politically, the political roles of Latina women and the gender differences in how politics is defined emerged. Thus, multiple observations were available to check what I was hearing in the interviews about how to stimulate Latino political participation, and how Latina women and Latino men act politically.

Several aspects of this book need to be discussed, especially the inclusion of Spanish quotes and the use of fictitious names. The people I interviewed and interacted with during the course of fieldwork spoke in Spanish as well as in English. All quotes given in Spanish were spoken in that language. English quotes were spoken in English.

It should be noted that, in general, I translate all Spanish quotes as faithfully as possible. This does not always mean a literal translation. In any quotes where I have strayed from a literal translation, I will indicate so by a note. I have included quotes in Spanish (with translations for non–Spanish-speaking readers) for two reasons: accuracy and politics. The original Spanish language captures subtle meanings that may be lost in translation. In addition, the right to maintain language and cultural integrity has been a political issue for Latinos in the United States. This *is* a book about Latino politics, and I believe, as do many Latinos, that what we say about politics, how we say it, and *what language we say it in* frames the conclusions we draw. Regarding accents, I have generally followed established rules of Spanish language *except* in the case of certain proper names. When a person I interviewed indicated that she or he no longer uses an accent, I did not accent her or his name. In addition, prior to the computer age, with its easy use of a variety of fonts, accents, and symbols, typewritten and published materials rarely included accents on foreign words; therefore, when I cite works by Latino authors whose names in publication did not retain the appropriate accents, I was faithful to the published work, even though by rules of grammar an accent is required. Finally, certain words (e.g., *tú* as a personal pronoun) technically require an accent, but this rule is generally not followed in the Americas; I therefore do not use an accent in these cases.

Most of the names of people and community groups used in this book are fictitious. The exceptions are the names of public figures like mayors Flynn and White, governors Dukakis and King, and notables like former state representative and candidate for mayor Mel King and candidates for elected office Carmen Pola and Diana Lam. Other exceptions are Latino elected officials, like Marta Rosa and Nelson Merced, whom I interviewed. In addition, one group, Mujeres Unidas en Acción, asked to be known by its real name, in recognition of the role it has played in bringing women together for change. A full list of those who wished to have their contribution acknowledged by name is provided below.

Interviews and community observation field notes were transcribed into *The Ethnograph*, a computerized text analysis program. The transcripts were coded according to themes and patterns and analyzed qualitatively. In addition, the program generated frequencies with which women and men discussed certain themes. These frequencies are included not so much to provide statistical proof for my findings but to highlight the gender differences and the relative weight women and men gave to the different themes.

This book represents a personal odyssey. I met Latinos from many countries and from many walks of life. I was struck by the contrasts and diversity that is the Latino community. Some days, I sat in offices at City Hall and looked out windows at a view of Boston Harbor. Other days, I had coffee in living rooms where the noise of trucks rumbling by made holding a conversation difficult. The rewards were great: wherever I went, I was with people.

The people I met and the experience itself have left a permanent imprint. I spoke with men and women from Puerto Rico, the Dominican Republic, and many countries in Central and South America. As they shared their stories of coming to America, I traveled in memory with them. Weaving their stories into this book was a challenging experience.

The people who offered to speak to me and who opened up their homes, organizations, and meetings to me provided innumerable opportunities to understand something about Latino politics in Boston. All were generous with their time, recollections, experiences, and opinions. To all those who contributed so much time and so many experiences: ¡Se lo agradezco mucho!

The following is a list of individuals whom I interviewed formally. Names given are real names except when, due to a request for anonymity, the name is marked with an asterisk. Titles, where provided, are those held by the contributor at the time of the interview. This list gratefully acknowledges the contribution of all these people and the many others who contributed information informally. I apologize for any omissions or errors in spelling or titles: Maria Aguiar, Coordinator, Latino Women's Health Services; Felix Arroyo, Director of Personnel, City of Boston and cofounder, Latino Democratic Committee; Silvia Barajas*; José Bautista; Beatriz Bustillo*; Pablo Calderón, Vice-President, Design Housing, Inc.; Yohel Camayd-Freixas, independent research consultant and cofounder, Latino Democratic Committee; Sandra Centero, dental hygienist; Javier Colón, lawyer, META; Marta Correa*; David Cortiella, Executive Director, Fair Housing Office, Boston City Hall; Zoila R. Cueva, outreach worker and bookkeeper; Annette Díaz, Martha Elliot Health Center; Jovita Fontanez, Assistant Director, Neighborhood Services, Boston City Hall; Carlos García*, house painter; Clara García, Executive Director, Inquilinos Boricuas en Acción; Tania García, Special Assistant on Minority Affairs, Massachusetts Commission for the Blind; Charlene Gilbert, Campaign to Elect Nelson Merced; Octavio González*, office cleaner; Aracelis Guzmán*; Peter Hardie, Campaign to Elect Nelson Merced; Luciano Herrera, janitor; Rita Gonzales Levine, Director, West Boston/Brookline Local Service Center, Massachusetts Department of Mental Retardation; Inez Martínez*; José Massó, Deputy Director of Marketing, MBTA; Nelson Merced, State Representative, Fifth Suffolk District; Antonio Molina, General Manager, Radio Continental and businessman; Margarita Muñiz, Principal, Rafael Hernández School; George "Chico" Muñoz; Julia Ortiz; Felicita Oyola; Mariwilda Padilla, teacher; Pedro P. Posada, Director, Youth Services, Inquilinos Boricuas en Acción; Luis Prado, Executive Director, La Alianza Hispana; Antonio Prieto, Director, Parker Hill Neighborhood Service Center; José M. Ramos; Delfina Rentas; Diego de Ribadeneira, journalist, *Boston Globe*; Aurelia Rivera*; Iris Rivera; Alex Rodriguez, Director, Massachusetts Commission Against Discrimination; Jaime Rodríguez, National Congress for Puerto Rican Rights and researcher, William Joiner Center, University of Massachusetts, Boston; Mirna Rodríguez, legislative aide; Mayra Rodríguez-Howard, Administrator, Department of Public Welfare; Marta Rosa, Chelsea School Committee Member; Francisco Salamanca*, mechanic; María Sánchez, probation officer, Juvenile Court; Miguel Satut, President, Associated Grantmakers; Juanita Sosa, Coordinator of Support Services, Mujeres Unidas en Acción; Consuelo Gonzales Thornell, Vice-President, Bell Associates, Inc.; Marta Torrijos*, human services worker; José Antonio Vincenty, lawyer; Beatriz McConnie Zapater, Director of Education, Hispanic Office of Planning and Evaluation.

I particularly wish to acknowledge all the women of Mujeres Unidas en Acción for opening up their organization to my view. The following are the names of women who participated in the *charla* at Mujeres Unidas en Acción and who wished to have their contribution acknowledged by name: Santa Beata, Margarita Cruz, Madeline Cortes, Isabel Ferreira, Ana Julia Martínez, Virgen M. Oquendo, and Margarita Pacheco. Special thanks go to Juanita Sosa for introducing me to many of the women at Mujeres Unidas en Acción and for facilitating the discussions about politics that took place. Mujeres Unidas deserves recognition for the many opportunities it provides for the full development of Latina women.

In addition, numerous community groups opened up their doors to me for the purposes of this research. I would like to acknowledge, in particular, the following organizations: Padres Latinos de Boston; the Campaign to Elect Nelson Merced; the Marta Rosa Campaign; Hispanic Office of Planning and Evaluation; the community forums at the University of Massachusetts, Boston; the Mauricio Gastón Institute for Latino Community Development and Public Policy, University of Massachusetts, Boston; the Fifth National Congress for

Puerto Rican Rights; legislators and legislative aides at the Massachusetts State House; the Latino Democratic Committee; Inquilinos Boricuas en Acción; and Action for Boston Community Development—Parker Hill Neighborhood Service Center. I would particularly like to thank Juan Carlos Ferrufino at the Cardinal Cushing Center and Antonio Prieto at the Parker Hill Action for Boston Community Development—their personal introductions to clients and members of their staff made many interviews possible.

My professional mentors were a constant source of challenge and support. I wish to thank Dr. Deborah Stone for urging me on intellectually and professionally. She consistently encouraged me to achieve my highest goals; without her support, this book would not have been possible. Thanks also go to Dr. Dale Rogers Marshall and Dr. James Jennings, who were remarkable in their ability to combine constructive suggestions, incisive observations, and warm support whenever we talked. I also wish to thank Dr. Hillard Pouncy for his detailed comments on the implications of my research for the understanding of political participation. His suggestions enabled me to reevaluate and reexamine my assumptions at many critical junctures.

I traveled the road to this point in the company of friends and family. It would have been impossible to live through the research and writing process without the support of the women in my dissertation group: Robin Gregg, Jennifer Jackman, Maggie Martin, and Beth Miller. I thank you for believing in what I was doing even when I was doubtful, I thank you for listening when I was confused, I thank you for letting me laugh and cry. I wish to thank Robin, especially, for the *hours* we spent on the phone while writing our Ph.D. dissertations and for her continued encouragement since then, despite being separated by the Atlantic Ocean. Jennifer deserves special thanks for lending me all her books on politics and feminism and for sharing her experiences in the "real world" of politics. Thanks also to Maggie, who showed us all how to produce great research, and to Beth, who understands the joy and pain of combining motherhood, research, and long hours of writing.

I also wish to thank my friends Sue Sand and María Luisa Portuondo. Thank you Sue, for saying many times, "If anyone can do it, you can." A special thanks goes to María Luisa for the *endless* hours we spent together developing, refining, and practicing the Spanish version of the interview guide. Even more, however, I thank you for the emotional support and friendship you have given me for years. To my good friend Sara Zall—thank you for all the long walks and long conversations about children, marriage, and personal goals. Your expressions of support and, even, admiration have sustained me through the many miles we have walked together. I thank my parents, Sue and Eldon Hardy, for providing the opportunity to experience another country as home, for the educational preparation that made this book possible, and, especially, for their love over the years.

A special acknowledgment goes to my husband, Chris, and my daughters, Allison and Carly. You suffered through the years as I wrote my Ph.D. dissertation and then, without much hesitation, geared yourselves up to support me again as I wrote this book. I especially thank my husband, who gave it his all: for the weekends you took the kids to the Cape so I could work in quiet, for the nights you listened to my struggles, and for taking care of *everything* more times than I can count. I can honestly say, "I couldn't have done it without you." To Allison: Since I started this project you have gone from learning to write the alphabet to being able to write your own research projects. You are now a competent schoolgirl with whom I can talk about interviewing projects and about editing our writing. Your smiles often keep me going. To Carly: Ever since you were a baby, you've seen me working up to this book. You started out crawling around under the computer; now you can write your own stories on it. When I tried to explain what a Ph.D. was, I said, "It's like a *doctor of books*"; now you have turned into a lover of books, too. Your love of learning inspires me. Thank you, Chris, Allison, and Carly, for all the love and support you have given me throughout the years.

Thanks are extended to Rosita Colón, Gladys Rivera, Annette Macaudda, and the women at ASAP Typing, Inc., for their faithful transcription of the hundreds of hours of interviews. I would also like to thank my friend Jolie Rossing, of Jolie Rossing Advertising, for once again coming to my rescue: she produced beautifully clear maps first for my dissertation and then, when the 1990 data became available, for this book. Rolf Goetze, of the Boston Redevelopment Authority Research Department, deserves a special acknowledgment as well for generously contributing his time to generate the data for Map 2. A special thanks goes to Miren Uriarte, Director of the Mauricio Gastón Institute for Latino Community Development and Public Policy at the University of Massachusetts, Boston, for her time, encouragement, and support. I would like to show appreciation to María de los Angeles Torres at DePaul University for her helpful review and suggestions—and to my editor at Temple University Press, Doris Braendel, for her enthusiastic support. Finally, I thank Richard Gilbertie and Carole Brown for their skill in guiding the book through the editorial and production process.

LATINA POLITICS,
LATINO POLITICS

Introduction

Q: *Tell me what you do politically.*
A: Well, it depends on what you mean by politics.
　　　　　　　—*Andrea del Valle, Puerto Rican community activist*

"What is political?" is always a fundamental question of politics.
　　　　　　　—*Benjamin Barber,* Strong Democracy

"¡Ay! ¡Me encanta *la política!"* ("Oh! I *adore* politics!") exclaims Silvia Barajas, a recent arrival in Boston from the Dominican Republic. For her, politics is reaching out to other women and improving their living conditions. Jesús Carrillo, a Cuban-American activist, talks about politics as creating political organizations and increasing Latino electoral representation. The voices ring in my ears, Latina women and Latino men talking about their visions of politics and Latino political participation in Boston. I hear María Luisa Soto, a Puerto Rican who moved to Boston many years ago from New York City, talk about the years she has devoted to mobilizing Latinos in Boston. Then there is Octavio González, a recent immigrant from Guatemala, who is afraid of political authority; he is too grateful for the better life he has found here to even question the political decisions that affect him. Women like Inez Martínez talk about politics as drawing people together; she came here twenty-five years ago from Mexico and has worked to organize fellow tenants in her housing project. Luis Hernández, a Puerto Rican, focuses on elections and on his efforts to encourage Latinos to vote.

This book is a study in contrasts—a multitude of voices in Span-

1

ish and English—threads in a story about the nature of politics for Latina women and Latino men in the United States. The goal of this book is to tie these voices together in a way that will shed light on the interaction of gender, culture, and political participation.

Two themes emerged from this study. First, contrary to their invisibility in mainstream political and social science literature, Latina women are political actors in Boston's Latino community. Puerto Rican women, Dominican women, and women from Central and South America are not passive about politics. On the contrary, they are active in all areas of traditional politics including running for office, promoting voter registration, acting as links between city officials and the community, and providing political education.

Latina women make up the majority of the participants and activists at political events. For example, at meetings of the Comité de Familias Latinas de Boston (Latino Families of Boston Committee), a group formed to tackle issues of educational inequities for Latino students; at a march down Dudley Street to protest state budget cuts; at community forums hosted by Latino agencies; and in the election campaigns of Nelson Merced and Marta Rosa, Latina women made up more than half of the participants. Even more important, they led meetings, rallied protesters, marched, acted as community spokespersons, and mobilized Latino community residents. I found that Latina women have been the force behind mass mobilization efforts and political protests throughout the history of the Latino community in Boston.

Second, the way Latina women in Boston *talk* about politics reveals a very different vision of "What is political?" than that of Latino men—a vision that goes beyond voting, elections, and office holding. In addition, how Latina women view the meaning of politics and political participation informs their mobilization strategies and makes them more effective than Latino men in mobilizing the Latino community. As women, they reflect a more participatory vision of democracy than one based only on male models of politics. This participatory vision of politics is more effective in part because it is more in tune with cultural expectations and it overcomes many of the structural constraints on Latino political participation in this country.

Gender and the Nature of Politics

As I try to recapture the moment at which a study about Latino politics evolved into a book on gender, culture, and political partici-

2

pation, I recall my first interview with Andrea del Valle. Her name had come up many times in interviews with other Latino activists as someone who is "good at organizing Latinos." We met in a room at the local health clinic where she worked. The clinic was quiet in the after-hours hush of a warm summer evening, and we settled in, making small talk as we became acquainted. I began the formal interview with my usual invitation: "Tell me what you do politically." Without hesitation, she responded, "Well, it depends on what you mean by politics."

What she went on to talk about was a vision of politics and political participation as *making connections*: connections between people, connections between private troubles and public issues, and connections that lead to political awareness and political action. Del Valle is not alone in envisioning a broader, more participatory model of political life. Another woman, Carla Gardner, a campaign worker, also stresses that politics is more than voting: "What's important is what will follow the campaign, pulling people into a community effort, making people feel a part of politics, that they count and can affect the outcome, affect the process, affect their lives. Hispanics vote when there's something to vote for, but there's more to politics than just voting." Gardner echoes other Latina women activists who, in one way or another, claim that politics is more than elections and voting. Politics for women like Gardner, del Valle, and for Josefina Ortega and María Luisa Soto—two older Puerto Rican women who have worked for decades to draw Latinos into community action—is an *interactive process*, embedded in their daily lives and culture.

When these women talk about their political lives, their vision of politics as interpersonal connections and an interactive process is in sharp contrast with the image of politics presented by the Latino men I interviewed. Juan Maldonado, Jesús Carrillo, and Felipe Aviles, all influential Latino political leaders, talk about politics very differently: politics is elections, politics is access to government positions. Like many men, Armando Meléndez, a prominent Puerto Rican businessman, defines politics as electoral representation: "Politics, per se—we have one state representative in the whole state when there are over three hundred thousand Hispanics. . . . So that shows me there isn't very much Latino politics in the state."

Carrillo epitomizes the male emphasis on political positions as *the* definition of politics. When I said: "Tell me what you do politically," he turned to his computer and printed out a list of official positions he has held, campaign awards, speeches—his political accomplishments. And Maldonado, a Puerto Rican in his early forties who is prominent in Latino politics in Boston, spent his entire interview describing Latinos moving in and out of various government positions; he called this political participation.

What about Latinos who are not activists or influential within the Latino community? They too perceive politics differently depending on their gender. After leaving her home in Puerto Rico, Julia Santiago lived in New York City. There she had been on welfare; in Boston she works as a counselor. She told me her story of rising from an oppressed life to one of political consciousness. Santiago feels that her first political act took place when she left an abusive husband: "Taking a stand—taking a stand—*es algo, tu sabes—muy político*" ("Taking a stand—taking a stand—is something, you know—very political").

Luis Hernández, in contrast, *assumed* that what I wanted to talk about was the politics of elections, the politics of the vote. Hernández is forty years old and came here almost eighteen years ago from a small town in Puerto Rico. He has a seventh-grade education and worked in a restaurant for many years. His employers let him go after an illness kept him away from his job too long; he now works as a janitor in one of the local Latino agencies. I began our interview with an invitation to tell his migration story and his view of the problems that face Latinos in Boston. He seemed to become somewhat impatient; after a relatively short time he queried, *"Pensaba que esto iba a ser algo sobre la política"* ("I thought this was going to be something about politics"), and moved right into how he is frustrated when he tries to get Latinos to vote. He was typical of the men in his quick assumption that politics means elections.

Ivelisse Rodríguez is thirty-four years old, and also from Puerto Rico. She arrived here on a one-way ticket with her two children and two suitcases. Her first act was to challenge the Travelers Aid Society, which wanted to "help" her by giving her a one-way ticket back to Puerto Rico. Because she left Puerto Rico to escape a situation of abuse involving her husband and her older daughter, she refused the agency's "help" and eventually settled in a Latino neighborhood in Boston. Rodríguez shared stories of other struggles. For example, she battled the criminal justice system, which erroneously arrested her second husband. She also brought a legal suit against the mental health department when a local hospital said they could not treat her daughter's psychiatric problem because they did not accept Medicaid, when in fact they did.

Rodríguez was perfectly comfortable discussing these confrontations in an interview about Latino politics. In fact, when I tried to move to explore traditional political behaviors such as voting and community organization leadership, she quietly but firmly said, *"Pues, para terminar esto . . ."* ("Just let me finish this . . ."),[1] and continued her account of her battles for justice.

*Latina** politics in Boston, even in the nonactivist population represented by Ivelisse Rodríguez, dispels myths about female passivity and Latino political participation. On the surface, Rodríguez appears to be very traditional and very passive; she describes herself as very submissive. She is a member of the Pentecostal church, which generally suppresses participation in "worldly affairs" (including politics).[2] Nevertheless, the ease with which Rodríguez moved from the story of her private struggles with government institutions to traditional electoral politics indicates the wide range of activities she considers political acts. The critical difference between Ivelisse Rodríguez and Luis Hernández is that Hernández *assumed* politics meant elections, whereas Rodríguez, like most of the other women, sensed a broader answer to the question "What is political?"[3]

Assumptions about the nature of Latino politics and political participation thus differ by gender. Gender differences in how politics is defined are the focus of this book, but the role of gender, culture, and political participation cannot be understood without first understanding the sociopolitical context of Latinos in Boston.

The Sociopolitical Context: Latinos in Boston

The Latino community in Boston is not large: Latinos now make up 11 percent of the city's population (Rivera 1991, 8). It is also a relatively recent community. While a few Latinos were in Boston as early as a hundred years ago, the Puerto Rican and Cuban community consisted of only about 2,000 individuals in the 1950s and early 1960s. The most rapid growth occurred between 1960 and 1970: the population grew from 2,104 to almost 18,000. The population then doubled to 36,430 in 1980 and grew by 70 percent to 61,995 in 1990 (Uriarte 1992, 4).

Boston's Latino community is also characterized by considerable diversity. In any book purporting to shed light on the Latino experience in the United States, it is crucial to clarify the term *Latino* and to say why an examination of an ethnically diverse, northeastern city such as Boston is relevant to the study of political participation. I use

*The term *Latina* is shorthand for Latina women. The term *Latino* is a more inclusive term that means either men or women. Since *Latina* can refer only to women, it is sometimes used alone, as in "Latina politics," "a Latina said . . ." or "many Latinas did. . . ." Since *Latino* may mean men or women, the term *Latino men* is used if I am speaking specifically of men.

the term *Latino* to include people who are Puerto Rican, Mexican American or Chicano, Cuban, Central and South American, and Dominican. In earlier years, Latinos have been referred to as "Hispanic" or "Spanish origin," especially by non-Hispanics. The shift to "Latino" reflects a sense on the part of the people who come from these groups to choose their own ethnic identifier. In addition, the development of ethnic consciousness as a "Latino community" discussed by Padilla (1985) in reference to Chicago's Mexican Americans and Puerto Ricans, is applicable to Boston, where members of all the Latino ethnic groups are attempting to "build community."

Because of the small number of Mexican Americans in the Northeast, I specifically focus on non-Mexican-American (i.e., non-Chicano) politics in this book. While a considerable amount has been written on Chicano politics, and Puerto Rican politics has begun to receive attention,[4] few studies have examined participation within multiethnic Latino communities. Most Latino communities on the East Coast of the United States are now made up of diverse Latino ethnic groups.

What is critical to understand from this complicated discussion of the meaning of ethnic names, the process of choice, and the percentages of different Latino groups that make up the Latino community in Boston is that, as Antonio Rojas says, "It's not monolithic." In addition, the ethnic differences stem from different *national* origins. The Latinos in Boston do not share one home country, and, as Rojas says, "You'll find Latinos tend to be *very* nationalistic. Puerto Ricans are Puerto Ricans, Cubans are Cubans, Dominicans are Dominicans, Mexicans are Mexicans, Argentines are Argentines." Although during the early years of the Latino community Puerto Ricans dominated both in terms of population size and political leadership, by 1990 only 42 percent of the Latino population was Puerto Rican.[5] The rest of the community is made up of Central and South Americans (29.8 percent), a rapidly increasing Dominican population (13.1 percent), Cubans (3.5 percent), Mexican Americans (3.5 percent), and "others" (Osterman 1992).[6]

The "Latino community" in Boston is therefore a vibrant mix of people who would identify themselves first as Puerto Ricans, Dominicans, *Guatematecos*, *Salvadoreños*, Chicanos. The self-designation "Latino" depends on many individual and structural factors. Individual factors include the recency of migration, the extent of an individual's involvement in Latino community life, and legal status; structural factors such as the impact of U.S. foreign policy, international relations, racism, and economic opportunities or obstacles also affect the Latino ethnic identity. I use the term *Latino* with all these cautions in mind; it is a shortcut, a way of discussing people who have an overall language in common, who often live in certain neighborhoods together, and who, when talking about socioeconomic and political needs, use the term *la comunidad latina* (the Latino community) to describe their common identity. In keeping with the reality of a multiethnic community, I interviewed thirty-two Puerto Ricans, ten Central Americans (four of Mexican-American origin, two from Guatemala, two from Ecuador, one from Honduras, and one from Colombia), four Dominicans, three Cubans, and four individuals of mixed or non-Latino origins. Twenty-nine of the individuals interviewed formally were women; twenty-four were men.

Neighborhood residence affects political participation by either concentrating ethnic groups into politically powerful blocs or by diffusing political potential through residential dispersion. As can be seen in Map 1, Latinos are dispersed throughout the city.

Although there are three neighborhoods where Latinos traditionally have constituted substantial portions of the population—the South End, Jamaica Plain, and North Dorchester/Roxbury—these neighborhoods are geographically separated from each other. In addition, data from the 1990 Census indicate that residential dispersion of Latinos in Boston is increasing rather than decreasing. Traditionally Latino districts such as the South End and Jamaica Plain show only modest growth, while the Latino population in, for example, East Boston has increased over 500 percent. Two neighborhoods (East Boston and Roslindale) that in 1980 had very few Latino residents are now over 10 percent Latino. Other neighborhoods such as Allston/Brighton are approaching the 10 percent mark.[7] Building community is harder when distance must be traveled; electoral representation is even harder to attain when electoral districts cut through such concentrations of Latinos that do exist. The increasing dispersion of Latinos throughout the city of Boston and the lack of contiguous boundaries between areas of greatest concentration create practical obstacles to developing political power through redistricting.[8]

Latinos migrating to the United States at this time face a very different economic structure than that which faced earlier waves of (predominantly European) immigrants. In addition, the international context creates very different political conditions from those faced by earlier immigrants. Despite the prejudice, antagonism, and ambivalence that confronted European immigrants during the great waves of immigration at the turn of the century, those early immigrants arrived in the United States at a time of economic expansion. Manufacturing jobs and jobs requiring little education or skills were plentiful, especially in comparison with the desperate economic situation of

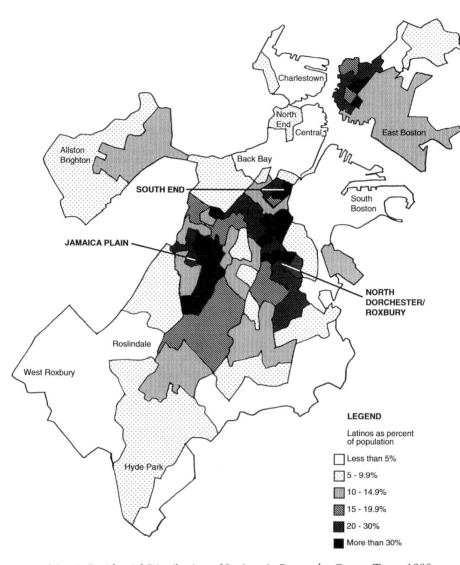

Map 1. Residential Distribution of Latinos in Boston by Census Tract, 1990. *Source:* 1990 Census; data courtesy of Rolf Goetze, Boston Redevelopment Authority Research Department (Goetze 1991).

their home countries. In addition, for the most part, those immigrants came from countries with which the United States had friendly or at least protective international relations.

Latino immigrants today, especially those migrating to the North-

8

east, face a very different economic and political reality in the United States. The economic structure has deteriorated: jobs are being lost, and the jobs available even during the boom years of the 1980s were low-wage service jobs offering little hope of advancement or opportunity to develop skills that could later be traded in for higher-level employment. Manufacturing—a sector that offered employment and opportunities for advancement at the turn of the century—is in deep decline. And while the Irish, Italians, Greeks, and Germans, to mention a few of the ethnic groups represented in earlier immigrant waves, certainly faced prejudice, current animosity toward immigrants is exacerbated by racism against Latinos, many of whom have darker skin and who are somehow held to blame for taking the increasingly scarce jobs that do exist at the lower end of the economic ladder.

A different set of international relations and the effects of U.S. foreign policy contribute as well to a very different political context for today's immigrants. Compared to the Irish, who were fleeing the potato famine and *British* domination, the Central and South Americans and the Caribbean Latinos are fleeing the economic and political consequences caused by the very country they are fleeing *to*: the United States.

At a discussion on politics and Latina women held at Mujeres Unidas en Acción (Women United in Action), an impassioned discussion began about U.S. intervention in countries like El Salvador, Nicaragua, the Dominican Republic, and Cuba. Amalia Mercado and others decried "Yankee imperialism": "*La verdad es que los Estados Unidos han aplastado a nuestros pueblos*" ("The truth is that the United States has crushed our countries"). She went on to recite a poem by Pablo Neruda to illustrate the antagonisms—and despair—created by the actions of the United States against the Dominican Republic (Dominicans often refer to their country as Santo Domingo). The poem begins lyrically, as do many by Neruda: "*Perdón si les digo unas locuras / en esta dulce tarde de febrero / y si te va el corazón caminando hasta Santo Domingo*" (Neruda 1966)[9] but goes on to lament the despots and tyrants who have dominated the political history of Santo Domingo, the thirty-year-long support of dictator Rafael Trujillo by the United States, and the U.S. invasion of 1965.

Some countries, like Puerto Rico, were colonized by the United States; their economic status and means of production were controlled (and, in the case of agriculture, destroyed) by the U.S. government. In the cases of Cuba and Nicaragua, the relationship was somewhat different: U.S. efforts to bring down the communist and socialist regimes created favored groups of Latinos, many of whom, such as the early waves of Cubans, migrated to more favorable conditions than those facing Latinos arriving today. Residents of many countries in South America, such as El Salvador, Guatemala, and Chile, as well as Nicaragua prior to the Sandinistas, saw the United States supporting dictators and armies that oppressed the people of those countries. The lower rates of naturalization and the apparently lower rates of political participation—as measured by voting—are, at least for some, a political decision determined by anger at U.S. policies in the Caribbean and Central and South America. Many women in the Mujeres Unidas en Acción discussion group echoed what many Latinos feel: they are unwelcome, and little is being done by the U.S. government to address their needs either in their home countries or here.

The changed economic conditions and the impact of foreign policy on immigration patterns affect many of the socioeconomic factors generally correlated with political participation. Poor people, young adults, and people without stable residences vote less. The lack of jobs with adequate wages and the flight of young Latinos from economic and political hardship in their countries mean that Latinos in Boston are poorer, younger, and more transient than their non-Latino counterparts.

The average household income of Latinos in Boston in 1990, for example, was substantially lower than that of white residents ($25,609 compared to $41,852; blacks had an average income of $29,750). The individual poverty rate for Latinos in Boston was 33.9 percent, compared to 13.9 percent for whites and 24.2 percent for blacks (*Boston Globe* 1992b). In 1990, 46.7 percent of Latino children under the age of eighteen were poor. Among whites the rate was 18.1 percent, and among blacks it was 33.8 percent (*Boston Globe* 1992a). The percent of Latinos over 25 years of age who did not graduate from high school was 47.2 percent compared to 18.5 percent for whites and 33.3 percent for blacks (*Boston Globe* 1992b).[10] Data also suggest that, indeed, the Latino population is substantially younger than the non-Latino population in Boston (Camayd-Freixas and Lopez 1983, 44; *Boston Globe* 1991b). Residential instability and the lack of legal status pose additional problems for Latino immigrant communities. It appears that the average length of residence in Boston for Latinos historically has been less than that of non-Latinos (Camayd-Freixas and Lopez 1983, 30).[11]

Virtually all the Latinos interviewed agreed that poverty, especially when combined with residential dispersion and residential instability, has suppressive effects on developing communal ties, communicating about issues and candidates, and registering to vote. Poverty constrains political participation in many ways. "Just surviving" takes all the energy of poor Latinos in Boston and leaves few resources for political participation. Juanita Fonseca, a Puerto Rican activist for many years, says simply, "I think if you're worried about food, shelter—a roof over your head—you're not going to get involved. You've got to have—to somehow feel that it's a piece of you—that it does make a difference. And that's hard." Rosa López, a Mexican-American woman in her forties, explains how not having money means less time for meetings:

> Even if they have the bus fare, cab fare, even if they have the babysitting money . . . *when you're poor, your time goes to surviving*. It's not a one-hour shopping trip to the supermarket where you go and leave your $120 this week. *You* go and get in your car and you shop and you leave your $120, and you get back in your car and you go home. That's not what a shopping trip is for a person who is poor. What takes me an hour will take someone half a day [first emphasis added].

She goes on:

> So the community is under a tremendous amount of stress just surviving, just getting through, making it and getting up. Putting everybody to bed with a babysitter so they can go out to a meeting? It's just not the lifestyle. . . . There are just tremendous barriers.

Although the Latino population is increasing in Boston (and the state), Latinos remain a relatively small minority. Their small population, coupled with the residential dispersion, ethnic diversity, and other problems discussed above, make challenging the extant power structure extremely difficult. The small size of many Latino, and black, communities often poses a barrier to political power in the United States (Browning, Marshall, and Tabb 1984, 1990; Travis 1990).

Two other aspects of the sociopolitical context shape Latino politics: (1) the Irish challenge to Yankee rule and subsequent dominance by the Irish of Boston politics and (2) the state of minority (especially black) politics in Boston today. The Irish have dominated Boston city politics since 1884. Of the seventeen men who have been mayor since 1884, ten have been Irish. In fact, "since 1901 the Irish have controlled the mayor's office for all but 10 years" (Eisinger 1980, 30). A similar pattern exists at all levels of city government.

What this means is a remarkably hostile environment for minority politics. After many years of Yankee paternalism, which tolerated the

11

black presence, the Irish actively excluded blacks from Boston politics (Travis 1990). Irish dominance continues today throughout all levels of city government; it, together with severe residential segregation of the black population, virtually precludes the election of blacks to citywide office. Blacks have been elected to the school committee, city council, and state legislature but have not been incorporated into the power structure and have limited ability to affect policy (Travis 1990). The major challenge by a black mayoral candidate was the Mel King campaign in 1983, a topic discussed in Chapter Four. Districtwide elections have provided more opportunities for blacks to be elected to the Boston School Committee and City Council; nevertheless, at the present time only two blacks are on the Boston City Council, although blacks currently make up almost 24 percent of the population (Rivera 1991, 8). The Boston School Committee was recently changed from an elected board to a board appointed by the (Irish) mayor. The combination of Irish dominance and the "ineradicable residues of racial prejudice and the racial caste system" (Eisinger 1980, 32) creates major obstacles to the development of political power for the black and Latino communities in Boston.

Gender, Culture, and Political Participation

A key debate in current feminist political theory concerns whether gender differences exist in political life. Is it true, as Chodorow (1974), Gilligan (1982), Tannen (1990), Miller (1991), and Surrey (1991) suggest, that women see the world in more relational terms while men are more concerned with positions and hierarchy? What are the implications of any such differences for politics and political mobilization? Do these differences, if true, exist across cultures— for Latina women and Latino men—or are they unique to white women?

A subset of questions implicit in this debate concerns the way the public and private dimensions of politics seem linked to gender. Do men define politics as activities in the public realm of life? If so, do the gender differences cross cultures? In other words, do Latino men view politics in public terms like their non-Latino counterparts while Latina women incorporate a more private vision, as is suggested by feminist political theory?

The examination of gender, culture, and politics in the Latino community in Boston addresses an even deeper debate in American politics. Central to any study of political life in America are fundamental questions of the way we define politics. Traditional theories focus on representative forms of government: voting, elections, political parties, interest groups. An alternative vision of politics—participatory politics (Pateman 1970, Mansbridge 1983, Barber 1984)—seems to entail more collective activities, more community ties, and a more informed, self-governing citizenry.

In addition, participatory democracy is seen by many as a potential antidote for the apparent decline in political participation by the American electorate (Burnham 1979, 1982, 1987; Barber 1984). What seems to be missing from these broad theories of participation is the attention to gender and cultural differences in the striving for participatory democracy. The study of white males in politics seems to lead to a view of politics and participation heavily weighted toward male perceptions of politics (Bourque and Grossholtz 1974). What happens to our vision of participatory democracy when we include gender and culture? I found that, in the Latino community in Boston, women embody the participatory aspects of political participation. Women focus on *participation* rather than on power, on connecting people to other people to achieve change.

What lessons may be learned from a study of the Latino community in only one city: Boston, Massachusetts? This book builds on a long tradition in the United States of examining "immigrant politics." All over the country, newspapers and other media are reporting the large growth in the Latino population in the United States. Between 1980 and 1990, Latinos grew from 6.4 percent to 9 percent of the population and are predicted to become the largest ethnic group in the United States by the year 2010 (Rivera 1991, 3). However, Latino population growth has not translated into proportionate political participation or into political power. Thus, attention to the process of how Latinos are drawn into politics, who mobilizes Latino communities most effectively, and how to increase political participation in communities like Boston are critical issues that need to be addressed.

Groups such as Puerto Ricans and Mexicans have some of the lowest voter participation rates of any groups in the United States, and virtually nothing is known about a group that is increasing rapidly in the Northeast: the Dominicans. The political incorporation of these groups is impossible without understanding how their members view American politics and how activists within their communities work to increase participation. The Latino community of Boston is a microcosm of Latinos in the eastern and midwestern parts of the United States. Latino communities outside of the West and Southwest are, as in Boston, made up of diverse groups of Latinos: Puerto Ricans, Dominicans, Cubans, Central and South Americans, and others.

13

This book also draws on a tradition of political scientists who generated some of the most influential theories of political participation and political consciousness from single-city studies (Hunter 1953, Dahl 1961, and Lane 1962, 1969).[12] The flaw in their studies lies not in their geographical limitations but in the fact that they present *as true* a vision of political participation and political consciousness drawn almost exclusively from the study of white males. Gender and culture are, for the most part, ignored. In this book I attempt to redress the pervasive problem—the lack of attention to gender and culture—inherent in most traditional immigrant political studies. I not only *include* women, but I carefully examine gender as a factor whose importance in Latino politics is as great as culture. I also point to the contribution of Latina women in efforts to increase political participation beyond their customary role in the socialization of children.

This book, then, is a book on Latina women and Latino politics in Boston. It reexamines political participation through the lens of gender as well as culture and finds that Latina women focus on the participatory part of participatory democracy. In it I suggest that Latina women in Boston have much to contribute, not only by stimulating political participation in Latino communities, but also by broadening our understanding of the nature of politics. I suggest that the current emphasis on representative forms of government may be a gendered construct and that efforts to make America more participatory require an examination of the role of women, including Latina women, if we are to counteract the cynicism and disaffiliation of the electorate in America today.

ONE

Discovering Latina Women in Politics: Gender, Culture, and Participatory Theory

Too many people have the image of Latina women—on welfare, staying at home—and I want people to know there are Latinas like me—who have worked for the community and who didn't get anything out of it for themselves.
—*María Luisa Soto, longtime Puerto Rican community activist*

You can have ten women, but if there's one man, "Oh, he must be the president!"
—*Andrea del Valle, Puerto Rican activist*

To talk about "discovering" Latina women in politics is a little like Columbus "discovering" America: just as the land already existed for its original peoples, Latina women know they have been active politically in Boston for years. Latina women in Boston demonstrate the full range of traditional political roles: running for office, mobilizing voters, mobilizing communities for concrete benefits, and providing political education for new members of the community. In addition, when the definition of "What is political?" is expanded beyond the traditional behaviors of electoral politics, Latina women consistently are the force behind political participation and mobilization in the Latino community. In this chapter, I challenge the invisibility of Latina women as political actors, a common perception in mainstream political science literature, first by revealing their numbers in traditional political roles and then by examining the ways Latina women's politics broaden the definition of the nature of politics. I then discuss the three central issues that frame my study of the political life of

15

Latina women and Latino men in Boston: the gender differences in the way politics is conceptualized, the tension between representative and participatory models of democracy, and the interaction of culture and gender in political mobilization.

Latina Women in Traditional Political Roles

Latina women in Boston have run for office more than their white female counterparts. Three of the six Latino candidates who have run for office in Boston (in elections with a Latino candidate) were women—Carmen Pola, Grace Romero, and Diana Lam. In fact, the first Latino to run for mayor of Boston was not a man but a woman: Diana Lam in 1991. While her candidacy was extremely short lived, the *Boston Globe* declared that she would have presented the most serious challenge to the incumbent.[1] Thus, Latina women have constituted 50 percent of the total number of Latino candidates in Boston. The overall percentage of candidates who are women is much smaller. For example, in the 1990 state primary elections in Massachusetts, only 15 percent of all candidates were women.[2] As path breakers, Latina women are noteworthy.

Latina women in Boston also participate in party politics. María Luisa Soto and Josefina Ortega frequently attend the State Democratic Convention and have served as convention delegates, yet they maintain strong relationships with people in the Latino community.[3] In addition, women are extremely active in leadership roles in the Latino Democratic Committee, a committee founded to assert Latino interests within the Democratic Party. Juanita Fonseca and Marisa Robles, for example, have served as co-chairs of the committee.

Efforts to mobilize Latinos to register and vote is another way women have contributed to increasing political participation in Boston's Latino community. Rosa López, for example, is a Mexican American who runs a major (non-Latino) government program. She is one of the editors of the bylaws for the Latino Democratic Committee and is very active in ward politics in her neighborhood. When López identifies key Latino ward workers, she names women in equal proportion to men.

> I went back to Jamaica Plain, where I had an already active core group of people like Camila Alvarado, like Julio Rojas, Pedro Contreras, like Marisol Quiñones. . . . Marisol Quiñones—she's a *terrific* person and we all knew each other, we lived in Jamaica Plain, were active in other things together, and we went back and we developed a Jamaica Plain Latino Democratic Committee. This was our local effort as part

16

of the overarching organization, the Latino Democratic Committee. We raised some money, Dukakis came to our fund raiser.

This core group of three Latina women and two Latino men was the most effective Latino political-organizing group in the state, according to López. She recalls: "We were the stars—we were the stars."

Rosa López is just one of many Latina women who have been involved in voter registration drives. Others are Marta Rosa, herself a candidate who was extremely active in voter registration, and Marisa Robles. In addition, María Ramírez and Beatriz Bustillo, in their roles as legislative aides for Anglo state legislators, work to get out the Latino vote in their districts. Men such as Felipe Aviles, an influential Puerto Rican with substantial experience in registering Latinos, acknowledge the contribution of Latina women to voter registration. Aviles volunteers, "I think that women have participated in politics in terms of being active and registering more voters than men have in the Latino community."

Many of these women who are active in voter registration are influential, professional Latinas in their early thirties and forties. However, older Latina women whose roots are with *la gente del pueblo* (the common folk) likewise work to register eligible Latinos; for example, Josefina Ortega, a sixty-two-year-old Puerto Rican, María Luisa Soto, fifty-four years old, from Puerto Rico, and Marta Correa, from Ecuador, who is also in her fifties. What these three have in common are their humble roots, their community and electoral activism, and their network of relationships within the Latino community. Of course, there are activists who are of *la gente del pueblo* (Aracelis Guzmán, Julia Santiago, and Inez Martínez, for example) and who, unlike Ortega, Soto, and Correa, are not active in *electoral* politics. I will discuss their political roles later; my point here is to demonstrate how both influential women and women of *la gente* contribute to Latino voter registration efforts.

Soto, Correa, and Ortega are typical of the *portavoces* or *alcadesas* of the community. In English, a *portavoz* is literally a megaphone, but the term is used to refer to a spokesperson; an *alcadesa* has come to mean the female form of *alcalde*, "mayor"—this term connotes a woman of great influence.[4] In an anecdote shared by Correa, one of these *portavoces* used a *portavoz* mounted on top of her car to publicize election day and rally the Latino neighborhood to get out and vote.

Another of the ways Latina women contribute to traditional politics in the Latino community of Boston is through their role of connector—providing a link between City Hall and the community.

17

When politicians want a Latino presence at a rally, they call on certain key women. When the mayor's office needs support, for example, these women are called. Correa explains how it works:

> Han tenido reuniones en el State House, y Juan [the mayor's Hispanic liaison] me llamó . . . y también, cuando iban a dar nombramiento a [Mayor] Flynn, y querían que hubieramos muchos hispanos—me llamaron.

> There have been meetings at the State House, and Juan [the mayor's Hispanic liaison] called me . . . and also, when they were going to honor [Mayor] Flynn, and they wanted a group of many Hispanics—they called me.

Correa recalls another time when Mayor Flynn's office called her: in an effort to gain visibility and votes in the community, the mayor wanted to hand out toys to Latino children at Christmas time. His connection to the community was a Latina woman—Marta Correa.

Correa, along with the other women who work within the system of electoral politics as well as those who operate more at the grassroots level, is able to "deliver" large numbers of Latinos to show support for candidates and to increase voter registration. She is candid about the fact that the (male) officials are getting the Latino people there to demonstrate that they have support within the Latino community. In this role, she knows she is serving the interests of the establishment; nevertheless, she is also working to draw her neighbors into politics.

Contrast this presence and activism in traditional political roles with the invisibility of Latina women as political actors, as evidenced in the mainstream social and political science literature. While there has been some writing on the life experiences of Latina women following migration,[5] some mention of Latina community leaders or elected officials,[6] a few references to the fact that Latina women tend to vote in higher percentages than Latino men,[7] and some recent attention to Mexican-American women in community organizing efforts,[8] little research includes an explicit goal of exploring Latina women and politics. What are their political views, opinions, attitudes, and, most important, their experiences in the political world? What do they think politically, and what is the nature of their political activities? Is it different from that of Latino males and from traditional models of women's political participation?

Mainstream social science research tends to restrict the study of women in general, and of Latina women specifically, to their social roles. Most writing on Latina women focuses on women in the labor force, as victims of poverty, and, predictably, in relation to children. Other writing discusses Latina women's physical and mental health.[9] In general, Latina women are portrayed in this literature as "three times oppressed"—by racism, sexism, and cultural traditions (Mirandé and Enríquez 1979, Barragán 1980, and Melville 1980). The stereotype of Puerto Rican and Mexican women, in particular, is that of passivity and submissiveness. *Marianismo*, the feminine correlate to and opposite of *machismo*, derives from the image of the Virgin Mary—meek, mild, and supportive of men. Assertiveness in social, public, and political arenas by Latina women supposedly runs counter to these cultural traditions. Garcia and de la Garza (1977) refer to a Latino tradition of "strong women," but these women are mythical figures; from these examples one would have to conclude that mainstream social and political science is comfortable with women only in their reproductive roles—or as goddesses. The political lives of Latinas are virtually ignored. The reasons are complex and range from commonly held assumptions to the male dominance of most political science research.

One explanation for the invisibility of Latina women in political science writing is provided by Andrea del Valle, a thirty-four-year-old Puerto Rican—a feminist and an indefatigable community organizer in Boston. She described some of the activities of the Puerto Rican Organizing Resource Center in Boston. I asked her if I should speak to Tomás Pachón, who I had heard was the president of the organization. She replied: "I don't know how people got the idea that it's a man, I think it's more in people's minds how they perceive things. You can have ten women, but if there's one man, 'Oh, he must be the president!'"

Del Valle attributes the invisibility of women in politics, specifically as leaders, to a particular mindset: leaders must be men. Del Valle herself holds no lofty position and is not acclaimed in the Anglo press as a "leader"; she works to organize others politically. Her politics is not the politics of positions and public speeches; who is president is less important to her than achieving change. Instead, she leads in the truer sense, that of engendering in others a passion for social action and social change. Her work, and the work of other women like her, is rendered invisible by the mindset of researchers who look at public, official, and titular politics.

Aviles, gives another explanation; he says, "Men are more easy to spot—and I told you that there are less men active in politics—although we make more noise than women." According to del Valle, Aviles, and researchers such as Pardo (1990), the male drive for pub-

19

lic prominence in political life overshadows the mobilizing work of Latina women. Since the mainstream academic press (and the public news media) focuses on people in positions, the politics of women, especially in political roles outside of official positions and without official titles, are rendered invisible.[10] Pardo (1990, 3) discovered a similar process when she examined the political organizing of Mexican-American women in Los Angeles. She found that the Latina women mobilized Latino men "by giving them a position they could manage. The men may have held the title of 'president,' but they were not making day-to-day decisions about work, nor were they dictating the direction of the group. . . . *This should alert researchers against measuring power and influence by looking solely at who holds titles*" [emphasis added].

A second explanation for the invisibility of Latina women in mainstream political science literature is that women in general—not just Latina women—have traditionally been left out of political analysis. Male political scientists such as Hunter (1953), Dahl (1961), and Lane (1962, 1969, 1972) have influenced the field of politics for decades; however, throughout their research they either have ignored the role of gender in political theory or have generalized to the population as a whole from the study of (typically white) men.

For example, Dahl's (1961) *Who Governs?* and Hunter's (1953) analysis of community power structure simply assume that "the people you study are men" (Bourque and Grossholtz 1974, 252). Others, like Robert Lane's works on "political man" (1972), political consciousness (1969), and political ideology (1962) imply knowledge about people in general but are drawn from interviews conducted exclusively with white men.

In other cases, women have been present in the research, but the role of gender is ignored. For example, when Wilson and Banfield "revisited" the political ethos theory in 1971, they interviewed male homeowners in Boston. They mention only in a footnote that a full 35 percent of the black homeowners and 32 percent of the Irish homeowners were actually women (1050).[11] However, Wilson and Banfield discuss neither the possible impact of gender differences on political ethos nor the fact that *these gender differences correlate directly with the ethnicity variable* that is the major focus of their research.

The research on nonwhite women is likewise deficient. Research is conducted on women as a minority group, but *minority* women in politics are less likely to receive attention. For example, Bayes's (1982) book on minority politics in the United States includes chapters on the politics of the black minority and the Chicano minority.

When she addresses women in politics, however, the subject becomes women *as a minority*, not minority (nonwhite) women in political life. Research on Latino political participation seems to follow the mainstream model of being a male preserve of knowledge—Latina women in political roles are ignored or dismissed. Most books on Latino politics include no mention of women in their chapter titles or indexes, or they ignore women completely (Jennings and Rivera 1984, Garcia 1988, Villarreal, Hernandez, and Neighbor 1988, Gómez-Quiñones 1990, Hero 1992). Women appear only in tangential ways—when they do appear at all—as wives of candidates (Foley et al. 1977), for example, or their contribution is reduced to a few sentences and paragraphs dispersed throughout an entire book (Gómez-Quiñones 1990).

In other cases, women as political actors are at once noted—and then dismissed. Guzmán, (1976, 165) for example, identifies Chicana women as important reputational leaders within Mexican-American communities and states that scholars have neglected these women in their role as community leaders. He fails, however, to remedy this neglect when he devotes only two paragraphs in his book to this subject (60). Guzmán does include a discussion on barriers to the political socialization of Mexican-American women (231–234); but by discussing women as *blocked* from participating, he contributes to their invisibility in activist roles. And although Santillan (1988a, 337) mentions the "increased visibility and participation of Hispanic women in the electoral process," in a later article he dismisses the Latina contribution to politics by saying that women suffer from political discouragement due to social inequality in the labor market and males appointing themselves as leaders. Santillan concludes that "the near total absence of Latinas in community politics seems almost to guarantee the delay of any substantial social progress in these urban communities for the present" (1988c, 474).

Even research on broad topics, such as Portes and Bach's (1985) *Latin Journey*, continues the pattern of generating conclusions based on research conducted only on men. *Latin Journey* presents an analysis of the labor market experience of Latino immigrants in the United States as if it were generalizable to all Latinos. One has to search to find the one sentence that reveals that the data are drawn from Latino men only. Portes and Bach later admit briefly that this is a flaw in their research, but what is their remedy? They directed at the men in their sample questions about other family members "including wives" (Portes and Bach 1985, 95). Latina women's own experiences and their roles beyond those of wives are ignored.

21

A final explanation for why Latina women are invisible in mainstream literature may be found in the very way politics is defined. When gender differences are scrutinized, researchers typically compare women to men on those behavioral measures of politics that either are dominated by men or defined by men as politics: organizational membership, voting rates in elections, and attitudes about political participation (see, for example, Baxter and Lansing 1981, Powell 1981, Rule 1981, Welch and Secret 1981, Klein 1984, Christy 1987). While there is nothing inherently wrong with such a comparison, an understanding of the political life of women is constrained by male definitions of politics.

Ignored—or rendered invisible—Latina women have been denied recognition of their political roles in the mainstream literature. One might ask at this juncture why I am focusing so much attention on Latina women in political roles that reflect traditional conceptions of political life, especially if one of my major points is that the definition of politics in these terms is a gendered construct, as I will discuss shortly. There are two answers to this question.

First, my point here is *not* that what Latina women do as candidates, as ward leaders, or as promoters of Latino voting is necessarily different from non-Latina women, or even from men (although gender differences in these roles do exist). My point here is "simply" that Latina women are political actors in Boston. They are participating in traditional political roles with great enthusiasm, effectiveness, and dedication.

The fact that Latina women demonstrate activism in electoral politics—traditional politics—is not really a simple point, however. It runs counter to the prevailing view of the apolitical Latina woman, the passive and submissive Latina woman. These are *Latina* women—the very women who are identified in the literature as submissive, passive, subordinated, and oppressed. Puerto Rican women, Dominican women, Mexican-American women, and Central American women in Boston—with their actions, their words, and their perspective on politics—challenge the ingrained image of the apolitical Latina woman. We cannot underestimate the importance of rendering visible the contribution of these women to the political mobilization of Latino communities.

Second, what is more important for this discussion of Latina women and the nature of politics is that, in addition to their activism in *traditional* political roles, Latina women were identified by both men and women as being the driving force for pulling Boston's Latinos into political participation. In addition to their roles as connectors between City Hall and the community, Latina women are connectors among members of the community to help the community solve its problems. As several Latinos said, "There's more to politics than just voting." If politics is more than elections and public office—if politics is about people joining together participating at all levels of community and government life— the role of Latina women in mobilizing Latinos becomes more visible. If "the challenge is to envision the human future and then to inspire a passion in others for that vision" (Barber 1984, 170), the question to be asked is: If there is more to politics than electoral politics—that is, the politics of representation—then how do gender and culture shape our understanding of this alternative?

Gender and the Construction of "What is Political?"

How does gender limit or enhance the definition of politics? One is reminded of Simone de Beauvoir's observation that men "describe the world from their own point of view, which they confuse with absolute truth" (1952, 133; quoted in Ferguson 1987, 210). Some suggest that part of the reason politics is defined in terms of public behaviors and formal organizations is that public life *is* the male life, and so politics has become defined in masculine terms as the public politics of elections, office holding, and political party (Ferguson 1987). In other words, the classical theory of politics as self-interested, atomistic, and, above all, public is, in reality, a theory based on masculine experiences that stress self-interest, public forums, and hierarchical struggles for self-advancement. In the context of this theoretical framework, then men rule.

Within the "absolute truth" of politics as constructed by men exists the essentially hierarchical ladder of representative government, in which a few are elected to represent the interests of the many. And within much of current political theory there exists a parallel hierarchy of political behaviors in which electoral politics is identified as "politics" while a whole wealth of political life is called a variety of other names: community organizing, community politics, and grassroots politics, to name a few. Above all else, the male image of politics is a politics of public life, of hierarchical representation, and of measurable behaviors, such as the vote.

A vision of participatory democracy is very different. Participatory democracy is firmly rooted in beliefs about community, collective organization, self government, and, above all, opportunities for participation by the many, not restricted to the elite few. Empirical examples of such participation in action, and how an increase in participatory experiences is brought about, are rare.[12] Another limitation of

existing theories of participatory democracy is that the role of gender, again, receives little attention.

The term *grassroots politics* is often used to reflect a more com-
munity-focused type of politics that involves greater opportunities for
self-government and self-direction and that increases participation by
connecting private problems to public issues. One of the major splits
in how politics is defined is between "politics" and "grassroots politics" or "community organizing." Political participation in a participatory model, however, is the politics of local efforts to achieve
change. The tension between local efforts on local issues and efforts
to elect representatives to tackle larger issues is a false tension in
participatory theory. In contrast to Schattschneider's (1975) hierarchical view of "experts" and "ignorants" is a vision of people becoming self-governing at all levels of government and in the workplace through the act of participating.

Latina Women and Participatory Theory

This alternative vision of blending self-government, grassroot community efforts, and personal/private issues with public issues plays a
central role in current feminist political theory. In particular, the political lives of women, and of Latina women specifically, are examined with a less biased eye in the feminist press. Women's vision of
politics includes a stronger sense of community, cooperation, and
collective processes of organization. Ferguson (1987) summarizes key
gender differences in how women view political participation:[13]

> Women, on the whole, are more embedded in (and more aware of
> their embeddedness in) social relations than are men; women, as a
> group, are more inclined toward a morality of responsibility and care-
> taking, while men, as a group, give more allegiance to an ethic of
> rights and obligations; women's experience tends to incline them to-
> ward greater appreciation of the concrete and the relational, while
> men give greater credence to that which is abstract and disembodied.
> (213)

Feminist theorists[14] explore the meaning of political participation and
help define the nature of politics in ways that male theorists such as
Schumpeter (1943), Sartori (1962), Schattschneider (1975), and
Verba,[15] who worried about global stability (and Anglo-American hegemony) do not.

Feminist perspectives on the politics of Latina women reveal a
broader definition of politics as well. Pardo (1990) and Rose (1990),

for example, examine the activism of Latina women in the United Farm Workers movement and in community organizing. MacManus, Bullock and Grothe, (1986, 606–611), although they concentrate on the registration and voting rates of Mexican-American women in Texas, note that Latina women have a role as revolutionaries and that Latina mothers are agents for social change. Unfortunately, for those who are concerned with multiethnic communities, most of this literature is on Chicana politics. Only a few articles focus on Puerto Rican women in political roles; these include works by Cerullo and Erlien (1984) on Latina women in the Mel King campaign in Boston, Bonilla-Santiago (1989) on Latina legislative activities in New Jersey, and Pantoja and Martell (1989–90) on Latina politics in New York City. A few writers examine Mexican-American and Puerto Rican women working together: Bonilla-Santiago (1991) discusses Latina leadership roles in the United States, and Carr (1989) describes group consciousness-raising projects in the multiethnic Latino communities of three Illinois cities.[16]

In their efforts to mobilize the community, Latina women in Boston embody key elements of a more participatory vision of political life. The methodology of the research conducted for this book (described briefly in the Preface and in greater detail in Hardy-Fanta 1991a) demonstrates that the ability to generate Latino political participation is linked to gender. When I developed a list of reputational leaders to interview that emphasized people in the news and individuals with official titles, 60 percent of the names were men. However, when these individuals were asked, "Who draws Latinos into participation?" the lists reversed themselves to 60 percent women. In fact, when the list excluded agency directors and people who hold jobs in city or state government, the vast majority (over 75 percent) of the people considered able to influence or draw people into the political process were Latina women.

Latina women in Boston provide empirical evidence of a broad expanse of political activism at the grassroots level. Julio Rojas, for example, is a community activist and an organizer of the Puerto Rican National Congress Convention that took place in Boston in May 1989. He describes the presence of women at the grassroots level of politics in Boston: "I say that women have been a major force at the grassroots level in the Hispanic community—from the day we came here, from the day we came to the United States." Nelson Merced, the first Latino state representative in Massachusetts, states that Latina women are just as crucial at the electoral level of politics but ties the women's political skills to their relationships within the community.

25

I think, more than anything else, women have a lot more potential; Hispanic women have a lot more potential for getting elected. They're more involved in the community, they're organized—they're better organizers. I don't want to make these general statements, but they communicate better with people, they're there in the community, they're in the trenches all the time, they deal with the children, they deal with the household and they may work, but they have—I think they have a stronger network, where men have—sort of—these networks, but I think they're weaker, whereas the women have a stronger network.

It would be impossible to include all the ways the Latino men and women I interviewed lauded these women; a few quotes will have to suffice. "If you look at our community, you will see—if you look through the gamut and count numbers, there are more women working into the politics of empowerment of the community than there are men," states Tamara González, a woman in her thirties who advocates for Latinos in a variety of human service programs. Teresa Andrade, who is active with Latino health care and other issues facing Latina women and their children, attests to the strong presence of Latina women in community politics—women who overcome the constraints of sexism and male concerns over power and turf: "The pecking order is such that it takes women awhile to get involved, but usually when they get involved, they get more involved than men. But around community-based struggles, I have *never* seen one where the women were not *extremely* involved."

One of the central debates in feminist theory, with implications for the present study of politics, is the question whether women see the world in ways different from men—in more relational terms (Gilligan 1982, Dietz 1989, Flanagan and Jackson 1990). Gilligan (1982), for example, reexamines women's moral base and brings to light the caring and relationship orientation of women in resolving social and personal issues. She argues that women view the world differently from men. The apparent differences between an ethics of care and an ethics of justice has implications for the interactive aspects of politics. Chodorow (1974) and Tannen (1990) claim that, for women, personal interrelationships and connection are more important than for men. They also suggest that men view the world in positional terms, in terms of personal status rather than connections and intimacy. The question may be raised whether such differences are rooted in biology, or whether they are socially constructed.[17] Regardless of the source of these apparent differences, however, the implication for political mobilization is that if political mobilization

26

is more likely to occur when interpersonal relationships rather than access to hierarchically determined positions are the basis for politics, then how women view politics is an essential element in any struggle for a more participatory America.

In suggesting that gender differences stressing relationships (for women) and positions and status (for men) exist, the question remains, then, whether these differences represent the *result* of gender construction or whether they represent a *normative prescription* for a more democratic society. As evidenced from the stories recounted throughout this book, the experiences of Latina women in Boston suggest that a more personally connected politics and a vision of politics as an interactive process based on personal relationships *are* more effective in mobilizing the Latino communities than a male vision of politics as access to power, positions, and formal structures.

A second debate that frames the issue of gender differences and participatory theory is the permeability of the boundary between private and public politics. Juanita Fonseca, in her office at City Hall, said to me, "The personal is political. . . . What happens every day is politics. What's going on right now—whether I agreed to meet you today—is politics." And Carmen Gómez, a South American who runs a social service agency, quietly declared: "Everything is political." These views support Evans's (1980) contention about personal politics—that the distinction between the personal and the political is artificially constructed.

These views are not supported, however, in most writings by male theorists. Even Barber (1984), in *Strong Democracy*, finally comes down on the side that politics must be considered to be public, not private (although he admits the boundary between the two is frequently hard to distinguish). Public politics, private politics, the personal and the political is one of the theoretical themes that permeates the definition of politics discussed in this book, and gets at the heart of my next point.

For Latina women in Boston, politics is an *interpersonal politics*— a politics that blends personal relationships into political relationships. By weaving politics into the fabric of daily life, Josefina Ortega illustrates how connectedness and mutual relationships increase Latino political participation. She also illustrates how electoral politics are not in a hierarchical relationship with participatory politics but form an inseparable thread, perhaps a continuum, one dependent on the interpersonal relationships of everyday life.

27

Portrait of Josefina Ortega: Connection and Mutual Relationships

Doña Fina,[18] as she is often referred to, was born in a "humble family" in Puerto Rico. Now in her sixties, she came to New York when she was twenty-three years old and became a professional singer of Puerto Rican folklore. She moved to Boston in 1966 and has spent much of her time here organizing and conducting dance classes for children in a studio in the basement of her modest home.

When I introduced myself on the phone, she made comments like *"Pues, yo no tengo mucho que ver con eso de la política"* ("I'm not very involved in things like politics"). But with little encouragement, she revealed that she does know many people who are politicians and that they have called and said, "Fina, we need a hundred people at this meeting." They count on her ability to bring people to political events—an ability based on her connections to people in the community, to *la gente del pueblo*.

Josefina Ortega has numerous plaques and awards on her dining-room wall honoring her community contributions, but she has not used her political connections to distract her from her community connections. Her major focus continues to be on dance and on helping Latino children maintain their folklore, culture, and artistic heritage. Her dream is to develop a truly community-oriented cultural center. She does not use her political connections for personal gain; she has never moved into any official position, and she continues to relate to the community as a dance instructor, as an organizer of cultural events, and as a volunteer at a program for *los ancianos* (the elderly) at a local community center. By serving traditional Latin meals and joining them in traditional Latin songs, she encourages *los ancianos* to come out of their isolation. Because she knows so many people and is trusted by them, when she calls and urges them to join her to work on community problems, they respond.

Doña Fina and her daughter, who was present at the interview, also participate in electoral politics. Both attended the Democratic Party caucuses in February 1990. Ortega votes consistently and sees the vote as a crucial tool for community betterment. She also works on getting people registered and urging them to vote. She is one of the women who put a megaphone on the top of her car to publicize election day, as described previously by Marta Correa. This portrait suggests several important lessons for political analysts and mobilizers: connections must exist within a relationship built on mutuality and reciprocity. Because Josefina Ortega *gives* of her time and energy to the children, when she calls on the parents for a political rally they respond. She donates much of her time, often charging no money for the dance classes in her basement, and perceives herself as not being in it for herself. She does not use her connections for personal gain but instead because of a belief that something needs to be done to help people.

Her more conservative or "old-fashioned" view of solutions to social problems creates somewhat of a generation gap with younger activists, but this probably endears her to the common folk, who may have more conservative leanings than are desired by the more liberal or radical leaders in the community. For example, one of the important issues in the community is teenage pregnancy, and there are few social service programs for pregnant Latina girls. She had the idea of bringing the girls into peoples' homes and teaching them something (her idea was embroidery—a somewhat passé occupation, but one that many Latina mothers probably remember from their youth). The program later implemented by other Latina activists did not incorporate Ortega's ideas; instead, it stressed counseling and education.

For Ortega, a political life consists of intertwining cultural activism, everyday relationships, dance instruction, and electoral politics. Latina women, in fact, often mobilize around issues related to their daily lives. Women's roles in the family may stimulate rather than inhibit political activism, a point discussed at length in Chapter 5. And this may not be unique to Latina women in Boston. Aviel (1981) suggests that "patterns of female political participation across Latin America reveal that women's roles in the family, although typically perceived as obstacles to participation, also serve as rationalizations for leadership roles as well as catalysts for mobilization" (quoted in Boneparth 1981, 3–4).

Doña Fina also dispels the notion that alternative forms of politics suppress electoral politics; she is intimately involved with voting and elections. In many ways, she reflects women's way of combining everyday relationships and political activism. Her life as a political mobilizer clearly challenges the distinction between private and public spheres of politics and suggests that this distinction is a social construct rather than a reflection of a universal political reality. Her success in increasing Latino participation, even in electoral politics, is due precisely to her personal relationships.

Political participation is thus woven into the fabric of daily life. The boundary between public and private becomes blurred.[19] People in poor communities, like the Latino community in Boston, may not respond to mobilization efforts that focus solely on the electoral and formal realms of politics. In addition, the social construction of poli-

29

tics as public, of politics as elections, diminishes the politics of every-day struggles in minority and working-class communities. As Morgen and Bookman (1988) indicate, "Until we broaden our definition of politics to include the everyday struggle to survive and to change power relations in our society, working-class [and Latina] women's political action will remain obscured" (8).

It is the feminist literature, also, that at least touches on the Latina woman's political contribution. Compared to the dearth of attention to women in the Latino politics literature written by men (as discussed earlier in this chapter), the feminist analysis of Chicana women's community organization focuses not on elections but on political development, not on voting rates but on ways of enhancing broader community participation. Pardo (1990), for example, writes: "The relatively few studies of Chicana political activism show a bias in the way political activism is conceptualized by social scientists, who often use a narrow definition confined to electoral politics" (1). Instead, she focuses on the *process* of what she calls "transformation" to describe how nonparticipators develop political consciousness and political skills.

Gender, Politics, and Power

The meaning of power is central to any theory of politics and political participation. The question whether gender differences exist in how power is defined, however, is another issue facing us in reconceptualizing politics in terms less biased by male experiences. As I will discuss at greater length in the next chapter, for women, politics appears to mean the power to effect change rather than the power over others. For example, Rosa López describes what politics is for her: "It's promoting change. And if you're promoting change, then you need to go about being there and identifying problems and knocking on doors and telling people, 'We're here, this is what we need, and we want to do it for ourselves.' That's political, that's what I mean by politics, that's what politics means to me."

Male concepts of power, in the feminist critique of theories of power and politics, seem to be defined as "the ability to augment one's own force, authority, or influence and also to control and limit others—that is, to exercise dominion or to dominate" (Miller 1983, 3–4; see also, Flammang 1983; Deutchman 1991). Male concepts of power do not acknowledge the view of power implicit in López's definition of politics: "promoting change." For women, power is linked to empowerment, "the ability to act with others to do together what one could not have done alone" (Ferguson 1987, 221). It is a process that stresses cooperation and collectivity. In other words, politics is the forum for achieving change; women have concepts of power and styles of exerting it that achieve change without exercising dominion and control over others.

Thus, the feminist contribution to participatory politics suggests that political participation is not defined by voting or joining formal organizations. Instead, interactions and relationships are what both create a need and respond to a need to work with others. In participatory—and feminist—theory, formal, especially hierarchical, organizations stifle participation.[20] Male-orchestrated public forums, with their panels of experts, speeches, and rules of order, limit the free exchange of ideas, inhibit tentative explorations of new ways of thinking about community problems, and prevent the development of the personal relationships that lead to political activity (Warren and Bourque 1985).[21] Women's skills at personal relationships set up looser affiliative groupings that are "nonhierarchical and decentralized," that "encourage individual initiative and, at the same time, . . . respect interdependence and cooperation" (Hamilton 1989, 131). Latina feminists stress consciousness raising; collective, nonhierarchical political organization; and less formally defined leadership.[22]

Empowering Latinos is the goal of most community activists in Latino communities. But, I suggest, mobilization strategies based on male visions of politics and power cannot work. I contend that the way public discourse, in general, is structured suppresses Latino political participation for both men and women.

Culture and Political Participation

Thus far I have focused on how gender informs our understanding of politics and political participation—but what of culture? Analyzing the impact of culture on political participation poses numerous problems: how to decide what counts as political participation, how to avoid an ethnocentric bias, and how to prevent an exclusive emphasis on the behavior of individuals from obscuring structural influences on political participation.

If political participation for Latinos in the United States is measured individually in traditional terms—voting in elections—then many Latino groups, especially Puerto Ricans and Mexican Americans, *do* evidence apparently low levels of political participation. In the 1988 presidential election, for example, the percentage of Latinos who voted was only 28.8 percent, compared to 59.1 percent of whites and 51.5 percent of blacks (U.S. Bureau of the Census 1989, 2).[23] Of course, when adjusted for lack of citizenship, the gap is not quite so large. In 1980, for example, 44.1 percent of *eligible* Latinos voted in the presidential election, compared to 50.5 percent of blacks (Pachon and DeSipio 1988, 4). On the other hand, Puerto Ricans are citizens, but their voting rates in mainland U.S. elections are among the lowest of all groups. Jennings states that, in New York City, "some important elections have experienced less than 20 percent turn out" by Puerto Ricans (Jennings 1988b, 72). Padilla describes heavily Puerto Rican wards in Chicago that failed to elect Latino aldermanic candidates because the Puerto Rican registration never rose above 25 to 33 percent (Padilla 1987, 196).

Measures of Latino voter participation in Boston are less reliable. A 1971 survey found that 36.3 percent of Latinos in the South End were registered to vote and that 49.4 percent of those registered turned out to vote (Camayd-Freixas and Lopez 1983, 73–74). Camayd-Freixas and Lopez (1983) estimated that 38.6 percent of eligible Latinos would turn out to vote in the 1983 Boston city elections.[24] They also estimated that, at that time, Latino voter registration rates in Boston were between 10 and 30 percent lower than those of blacks (Camayd-Freixas and Lopez 1983, 74). The influential Latinos in my sample indicated that they were all registered to vote and voted in the 1988 presidential election. Only 27 percent of the *gente del pueblo* I interviewed, however, were registered to vote in the same election.

Lower levels of Latino protest politics and organizational development also seem to indicate that Latino communities, especially Puerto Rican and Mexican-American communities, in the mainland United States are generally less political than black or Anglo communities.[25] The reasons given for such low levels of political participation, when measured by voting, range from cultural traits such as fatalism and "native mistrust" of leaders, to a lack of a sense of personal efficacy and to political apathy (Watson and Samora 1954, Kernstock 1972, Nelson 1979). Latinos in the United States have been called apathetic and apolitical throughout much of the literature.[26]

A problem arises, however, when politics is equated with voting and when the causes of apparently low political participation are attributed to supposed cultural deficiencies: culture becomes a "problem"—a constraint on participation. Cultural theories explain apparently low levels of political participation as failures of socialization in individuals. Most of the political-culture research (e.g., Almond and Verba 1963, Verba and Nie 1972) fails to consider the possibility that one of its basic assumptions, that causality goes from the individual's cultural upbringing to his or her input into the political system, represents only half of the political equation. In other words, the researchers see a variety of culture-based personal traits as the *causes* of low voter participation when it is just as likely that one's political responsiveness and behaviors are the *result* of interactions with political structures that block electoral participation for some groups.

What the cultural model ignores is the fact that the political structure for Puerto Ricans, Mexican Americans, and many other Latino groups is very different from that which received the European immigrants. For example, urban political machines did not encourage the participation of Puerto Ricans. "In cities such as New York and Chicago, the Democratic party did not welcome Puerto Rican potential voters, and the Republican party refused to woo them in their battles with the Democrats" (Jennings 1984b, 7). Pachon (1985, 249–250) points out that Mexican Americans live in areas where the political structures are extremely different from those that faced European immigrants at the turn of the century.

In addition, the Eurocentric bias inherent in the cultural model fails to take into account the historical tradition in American society of labeling immigrant groups as apathetic. The social science literature is replete with examples of how the ignorance, apathy, and deficient cultural traits of European immigrants at the turn of the century supposedly caused the deplorable socioeconomic conditions under which they lived.[27] The "deficient" cultural characteristics of these early Irish, Polish, Italian, and German immigrants sound remarkably similar to those cited in current depictions of Latinos. Yet these earlier immigrant groups are now held up as models for black and Latino communities; by following the European immigrant path of political participation, assimilation, organization, and membership in political parties, Latinos should be able to reap the benefits of American society.

Blacks, too, have suffered from the Eurocentric bias in the social science literature. Following the passage of the Voting Rights Act of 1965, political scientists were dismayed at the less-than-expected voter turnout by blacks in the South. The political scientists initially attributed this lower participation to black apathy. Salamon and Evera (1973), however, found that fear, not apathy, caused the low participation of blacks during that era. Discrimination, structural obstacles, and fear of physical harm or economic retribution were more highly correlated with participation levels than was disinterest in politics.

The suppressant effect of economic vulnerability and fear on black political participation is not limited to the South but has been found to operate in Boston as well (Jennings 1986, 62–63). Jennings

(1986, 62) adds: "Fear was described as one of [Mayor] White's most important political resources by every black elected official in Boston—one stated that fear of political and economic reprisals is what helped to maintain the paternalistic relationship between some black leaders and city hall." And fear, not apathy or cultural deficiencies, contributes to lower political participation in Latino communities. Guzmán (1976), for example, discounts the effects of language deficiencies and apathy; of more importance is "fear of the society that holds him (or her) in economic bondage" (62).

Just as a focus on traditional measures of political participation obscures the political life of women, however, an emphasis on traditional measures such as voting rates distorts the role of culture in understanding Latino politics. Where does the exclusive emphasis on electoral participation and representation come from, and why have non-Anglo groups, such as Latinos and blacks, seemed to suffer from cultural limitations? I suggest that "cultural apathy" is socially constructed to reflect the goals of the dominant group.

Pateman (1970) describes how, because of fears of totalitarianism originating during World War II, American political theorists turned from a vision of participatory democracy to a preference for representative democracy.[28] Prior to that time, there was a belief in the benefits of the participation by all members of society, and participation was defined broadly. In the shift to an emphasis on representative democracy, promoted initially by men such as Schumpeter (1943), Schattschneider (1975), Dahl (1961), and Sartori (1962), the institutional structures of politics and stability of government became more important than citizen participation. In fact, Pateman (1970) suggests, these contemporary theorists saw the lower classes as leaning toward authoritarianism; the increased participation of the lower classes would lead to the much dreaded totalitarianism and instability that seemed to be taking over countries in Eastern Europe. Their political theories stressed participation in the election of *representatives*, not in governing: " 'Participation', so far as the majority is concerned, is participation in the choice of decision makers" (Pateman 1970, 14).

Theories of representative democracy, in essence, require an "apathetic" populace. In the interest of stability, certain groups of people would do better not to participate directly in governing the country—by implication the less educated and the poor are discouraged from participating. According to Morone (1990), the irony of the progressive movement is that its goal was to bring democracy "back to the people"—to eliminate the intermediaries, the political bosses. The people who were empowered, however, were not the less educated, working-class, and immigrant populations but the conservative, business-oriented Anglo-Saxon Protestants. The welcome mat to American politics was removed for later generations of immigrants. Rather than achieving greater participation by all the people, American politics became representative of the elite.

The social construction of cultural (or racial) apathy to explain lower rates of Latino (or black) political participation helps maintain Anglo dominance of the institutions of representative government and obscures the suppressive impact of restrictive regulations, discrimination, or other structural causes.[29] What happens when the political structure and the economic and international contexts facing Latino immigrants are considered equally important in determining participation? Under these broader circumstances, the individual's culture can no longer be considered in isolation. Cultural values and cultural expectations of what politics means to different groups must be reexamined.

Culture, for Latinos, may indeed be reexamined as an asset. Cubans in America, for example, are well known for their active participation and successes in influencing politics in Florida. And Puerto Ricans in Boston unanimously voiced amazement at the proposition that Puerto Ricans—as a people—are politically apathetic. In contrast to Dahl's pronouncement that "*Homo civicus* is not, by nature, a political animal,"[30] Armando Meléndez, a Puerto Rican man active in a wide range of community and media groups, enthusiastically declares, "We're political animals! We love politics!" Juanita Fonseca insists: "It's not like somehow there's a genetic missing link here that somehow Puerto Ricans just can't seem to get it together; they just come from such a culturally deprived area that they're just not capable of mentally getting involved in the voting process. *Bullshit!* In Puerto Rico everybody votes, and politics is a big issue!" And Beatriz Bustillo exclaims: "*En Puerto Rico—pues, la política es completamente diferente. En Puerto Rico, si no eres político—si no votas, pues no eres ¡nadie!*" ("In Puerto Rico—well, politics is completely different. In Puerto Rico—if you're not into politics—if you don't vote, well you're *nobody!*")

Puerto Ricans vote at extremely high rates on the island; typically at least 80 percent of the eligible population votes (Jennings 1988b, 72). I propose that the dilemma of apparent political apathy of Latinos in the United States may be resolved by examining how gender and culture interact within the existing political structure. If the political experiences of Latinos are participatory in their homelands due to a political structure that enhances participation (as I will show in Chapter 6), then they will participate; if the experiences discourage participation—in the full range of community, work, and political institutions—then they will not participate (as happens here). While apathetic feelings may exist in some Latino individuals, however, cultural apathy should no longer bear the full weight of explaining low participation.

In conclusion, the meaning of political participation is challenged by feminist theories that suggest women and men differ in how they perceive politics and how they act politically. In the next chapter I begin to address the question, How do the politics of Latina women differ from those of Latino men? I demonstrate that Latina women in Boston, besides being political actors in the traditional sense of politics, and besides their activism at the grassroots level, conceive of politics in ways that differ widely from those of Latino men. For Latina women, politics is an interactive process, built on *making connections*. Politics for Latina women is *interpersonal* politics. The gender differences in how politics is defined by Latina women and Latino men in Boston cluster around four key elements of participatory theory—*connectedness* versus positions and status, *collectivity* versus hierarchy, *community* versus formal structures, and *consciousness* of the link between personal self-development and political activism versus a limited image of public action. In the next chapters, I demonstrate how Latina women and Latino men differ on these elements—the "4 C's" of political participation— how these differences inform their political-mobilizing methods and styles, and how the participatory vision of Latina women is more effective in mobilizing Latinos.

If one of the goals of political activists is to discover ways to increase political participation of Latinos who are *la gente del pueblo*, Latina women may be the missing link in the process.[31] In addition, I suggest that Latina women—more than Latino men—work politically in ways that meet cultural expectations about how politics should be; thus, Latina women have more potential to mobilize Latino communities than do Latino men. Latina women—in their role of *connectors*—are the mobilizers in the Latino community in Boston.

TWO

Making Connections

Politics is making connections.

—Julia Santiago

In developing a sense of connection with others, subordinated people often overcome the sense of powerlessness that can inhibit social change.
—Martha A. Ackelsberg, Free Women of Spain

Connection may mean many things: intellectual connections between seemingly different ideas, the concept of "having connections" (i.e., being able to wield influence by knowing powerful people), and connection as interpersonal connectedness—developing and maintaining personal relationships and networks.

Julia Santiago voices what many Latina women see as politics—people connecting personal problems with public issues—when she says: "Politics is making connections. How you relate your personal problem to other people's problems and then to a community or to a class and you see the contradictions and then you have to decide, 'Okay, this is what is happening, this is reality. This is the process of the problem, the root of the problem.'" Santiago is a forty-eight-year-old Puerto Rican who has been poor much of her life, who doesn't vote, but who is otherwise extremely political. She is aware of, and uses as her mobilization strategy, the connection between daily life and social change. Santiago defines as political the changes poor women make at the personal level. For example, she leads group discussions at the Latina women's center Mujeres Unidas en Acción. There, she and the staff challenge Latina women from many

37

different countries to question their assumptions, including those about the nature of work.

Muchas de las mujeres están siempre lavando y planchando en su casa y hasta que no llegan aquí, nadie les había dicho que eso era trabajo; así que para ellas es la primera vez que alguien está reconociendo que, sí, son personas que están trabajando, y que es según se defina *lo que es trabajo.*

Many of these women are always in their houses doing the laundry and ironing and, until they come here, no one tells them that that's work; so that for them it's the first time someone is acknowledging that, *yes*, they are people who work, that it's all according to how you *define* work.

Reflexionando (reflecting upon—in other words, making connections), according to women like Santiago, develops political awareness and, as a result, a more participatory community. At Mujeres Unidas en Acción, making connections between women's work and public policies about day care, welfare, and other so-called family issues obviously has the potential for increasing political mobilization.

Mujeres Unidas en Acción is an organization where Latina women learn English and learn to read and write in Spanish and English; on-site day care is also provided. Staff members at this agency routinely take groups of women to such events as the International Women's Day march and to rallies such as those formed to protest cuts in human services funding. The staff and women thus link their personal and family problems of low income, domestic violence, insufficient day care, and unemployment to political efforts for change. Young and Padilla (1990) explain: "We like to think of Mujeres Unidas en Acción as a 'social incubator' through which Latina women have the opportunity and access to develop their skills in community organization, development, and leadership" (2).

Making connections between foreign policy and Latino politics in the United States also stimulates the political involvement of Latinos in this country. U.S. actions toward Cuba, for example, have typically maintained a high degree of politicization in Cuban communities in the United States. U.S. intervention in Central America and U.S. policies on the status of Puerto Rico also have an impact on Latino political participation. For Puerto Ricans, the connection between the colonial—and ambiguous—status of Puerto Rico and the poor standard of living for Puerto Ricans both on the island and in the mainland United States has been a major mobilizing tool of the Puerto Rican Left. Using this method, the Puerto Rican Socialist

Party in Boston during the early 1970s, for example, invested tremendous effort developing political awareness among Latinos. Naturally, this kind of intellectual connection between foreign policy and U.S. politics is not unique to women or to Latinos as a group: witness how Jewish politics in the United States pivot on U.S. support of Israel. Nevertheless, Latina women such as those at Mujeres Unidas consciously devote time during group discussions to the task of "making connections" between the current standard of living for Latina women in Boston and U.S. foreign policy as well as U.S. domestic policy at the federal, state, and local levels.

"Having connections" (especially political connections)—the ability to gain benefits, prestige, or influence by knowing the "right person"—is another familiar meaning of the term *connection*. Both men and women in the Latino community refer to "having connections" as a political tool. Marisa Robles, for example, likes to use her influence with government officials to extract benefits for Latinos in the area of welfare and child care. Juan Maldonado works to make connections between government officials and the private sector to develop services for the community. Edwin Colina, a Puerto Rican in the mayor's office, has organized monthly meetings of a group of officials, community-based organization leaders, and prominent Latino people in the business world. This group, Networking for Latino Professionals, has as its goal promoting the utilization of Latinos in city-generated business and building a stronger professional and business infrastructure for Latinos in Massachusetts. Colina stresses the need for networks and connections; however, these connections are essentially limited by class and do not directly affect the participation or everyday life of *la gente del pueblo*.

"Staying in touch," another meaning of *connection*, has a more obvious impact on the political participation of Latinos in the community. Connection in this sense means that "leaders" need to stay connected with the people of the community. Latinos of both sexes reason that Latino political participation is constrained by feelings that Latino (and Anglo) leaders have moved into (mostly government) positions and have lost touch *con el pueblo*, with the people. Over and over again, Latinos expressed such sentiments as: "Once they get a position in government, they forget all about who got them there," "They don't give back to the community," and "They're in it for themselves." There is a sense that in their efforts to move up in the political world leaders use the people who support them and then abandon the supporters. Of course, it is hardly necessary to point out that dissatisfaction with leaders is not unique to Latino communities. A general sense of dissatisfaction seems to pervade today's politics regardless of ethnic or racial group: politicians are distant, manipulate or are manipulated by the media and their "handlers," and rarely come into the neighborhoods. Thus, Latino political sentiment lies squarely in the center of American political trends when so many people of the community refer to "need to stay connected" when discussing political participation.

Leaders also need to stay in touch with their constituents to bridge the gap between the activist and *la gente*, between people of different class and country of origin, and between officials and the common folk. Julio Rojas blames the current lack of connection between leaders and community members for the retreat from participation by *la gente de pueblo* since the mass participation of the 1970s. He describes what he told a Latino elected official: "I told him to go back to your own district, that's where you were elected, because you're doing like most of us do—we come from the community and we forget to go back to that community. We forget to go to the grocery store, to the barbershop. We lose touch with that community."

Armando Meléndez believes in staying in touch. He is very specific about how he stays in touch with individual people in the Latino neighborhood where he operates his business: "It's that personal touch; it's walking the streets and being stopped by twenty people and taking time to talk to each one of them. I do that at least two days a week. I just walk the streets. . . . People come and talk; they want to talk about problems. We listen to them. It might not be something that you can do anything about, but you can always say, 'Well, let me see who can take care of that.'" Because his constituents know him to be so responsive, Meléndez can make a personal phone call to get people to come to a meeting "as a favor to me."

Latino men and Latina women agree, then, that staying in touch is critical in the drive to mobilize the community. But they differ in two important ways: (1) Latina women discuss the need for connection much more frequently than men, and (2) Latina women are more effective at political mobilization than men because a politics based on interpersonal connectedness fulfills Latino cultural expectations of a personal style of politics.

Connectedness Versus Position and Status

Connectedness means a special type of making connections. Connectedness is connecting people to each other, developing and building upon personal relationships, and blending personal ties with political purposes. Contrary to the view that these "strong ties"—the more intimate bonds between family members, close friends, neighbors, and co-workers—are limited in their ability to generate political participation (Granovetter 1973, 1982), Latinos in Boston clearly hold the view that these personal ties create bridges to politics.[1]

María Ramírez, a Puerto Rican who works as a legislative aide, identifies personal relationships as the key to Latino political participation: "I think politics in the Hispanic community is very different from politics in other communities. I think Hispanic people prefer one-to-one relationships." The personal connection between people was also stressed at a workshop on how to organize the Latino community, where a Dominican mother said, *"El contacto directo es mucho más efectivo que el contacto indirecto"* ("Direct contact is much more effective than indirect contact") because when someone is approached indirectly, he or she says, *"Que vaya otro"* ("Let somebody else go").

Aracelis Guzmán echoes this sentiment and ties successful organizing to everyday relationships between neighbors: *"El contacto personal va a ser muy importante porque muchas veces uno le cree más al vecino que a la persona profesional ¿verdad? Porque uno tiene esa identificación inmediata"* ("Personal contact will be very important because people usually believe more in what a neighbor says than in the professional person, right? Because you have that immediate rapport with your neighbor").[2] Catalina Torres, a Mexican American who is a longtime activist in Boston, describes the importance of time-consuming, personal, "intimate" contacts for successful electoral mobilizing: "It means hard work—hard, hard work—of getting back, rolling up your sleeves, and doing some of the community activist type of things—some organizing—*having very, very personal, intimate sessions with people* about the importance of voting and registering" (emphasis added). Latina women *and* Latino men expressed a need for this personally connected type of political mobilization strategy. However, *Latina women in Boston talked about connectedness in relation to political participation twice as often as men did.*[3]

Tamara González focuses much of her interview on the need for interpersonal politics and describes women who epitomize deep personal connections with Latinos in the community. These women, the *alcadesas del barrio* (female "mayors of the neighborhood"), are intimately connected to the community, and they also connect people to information and services. González explains:

Where we come to the community level is what we call the *alcadesas del barrio, o cacicas*[4]—these are women that within their own little

41

geographical area know everything that goes on—*las portavoces.* They're the ones that go to the community health centers and say, "Well, you know, *la Señora 'Fulana de Tal'* [Mrs. 'So-and-So'] is having a problem." They're the ones that sort of mediate or tell the woman, "Go to this place and talk to someone there." We don't know a lot of those women; they do exist and they have an incredible role of empowerment to play within the community.[5]

Another potential political resource is found in the staff of Latino community agencies—most of whom are Latina women. Rosa López stresses that it is the personal connections these women have with people in the community that make them so effective: "The staff of the agencies are *very* grassroots people for the most part. They live in the community, they deal with their neighbors who could even sometimes be their clients during the working hours, but they deal with them at church, and they deal with them in the post office, at the drug store." These women—the *alcadesas del barrio* and the staff at community agencies—have direct personal connections to the community residents who are the targets of the mobilizers.

Personal relationships facilitate participation, even in the electoral arena, because they overcome the gap that exists between the political elite—*los profesionales,* as they are called by the common folk— and *la gente del pueblo.* Marisa Robles explains: "I don't think that they [*la gente*] respond so much to people who are in suits and ties and looking down at their noses and saying, 'We're the leaders; we are the professionals'—when the people who vote are the grassroots people—and if they don't vote, it's because they don't trust those professionals with those ties and those suits." In other words, Latino political resources lie not so much with the members of the professional elite (often men) but with the *alcadesas del barrio* and with the staff of the community agencies (most of whom are Latina women). Women, more often than men, stress the need for connectedness in politics and act as connectors within the community. These connectors are too often ignored when examining Latino political resources, yet they are able to pull Latinos into political participation precisely because of their personal, informal, and daily relationships. María Luisa Soto is one of these connectors.

Portrait of María Luisa Soto: Staying Connected

María Luisa Soto is a fifty-four-year-old Puerto Rican woman. After arriving in New York from Puerto Rico as a young adult, she lived what she recalls as a very homebound life. Her only political involvement was, as she describes it, occasionally voting when she was "led by the hand of her husband" to the voting place. Her personal and political life changed dramatically, however, when she came to Boston. Soto traveled to Boston in the early 1970s to seek better medical care for one of her children; she left her husband behind in New York. As she began to experience problems finding housing for her family, and as she began seeing other Latinos having the same problems, she realized that "no one was doing anything about it." She noticed many public-housing units whose plywood over the windows signaled that they were vacant but unavailable. Soto gradually became involved in joining neighbor to neighbor, gathering a group of women together. She recalls working throughout the years 1974 to 1978 to reclaim abandoned public-housing units.

Todos esos años fueron de lucha para lograr mejores viviendas porque estaban decaídas—lo que había era—de 1003 unidades, habían ocupados en el año 1974 unas 250 unidades. Y las demás estaban destruídas, vandalizadas, y llenas de basura. En fin, yo organicé un grupo de mujeres y limpiamos un promedio de 275 apartamentos para probarle a la autoridad de hogares que, sí, se podía hacer. Cada vez que dábamos una queja, ellos decían que no se podía—que había demasiada basura—bueno, veinte mil excusas. Yo, pues, un día, me cogí mi carro y empecé con unos autoparlantes por toda la calle, y por todos lados, y empecé a llamar gente.

All those years were a struggle to achieve better housing, because [the housing units] had fallen into disrepair—what there were—out of 1003 units, all that were occupied in 1974 were 250 units. The rest had been destroyed, vandalized, and were filled with trash. Finally, I organized a group of women and we cleaned approximately 275 apartments to prove to the Housing Authority that, *yes*, it could be done. Every time we had complained, they had said that it couldn't be done—that there was too much trash—well, they gave twenty thousand excuses. One day, well, I took my car and went out with some loudspeakers all through the streets, all over the place, and I began to call people.

At first, the response was small; Soto remembers: *"Me dieron ganas de llorar, y lloré de frustración"* ("It made me feel like crying, and I did cry in frustration"). Nevertheless, she persevered, and little by little women and youth joined her in her effort. She sent letters to the city and was given mops and buckets, rubber gloves, and cleaning supplies.

María Luisa Soto's story is one of Latina women challenging the political system in very direct ways. By cleaning up the apartments themselves, these women cut through bureaucratic excuses and reclaimed the apartments. Humor threads its way through her story as she recounts how she and the women confronted institutional obstacles:

Los empleados de mantenimiento que medían seis pies y más de estatura y pesaban como 250 libras de peso no podían ir a limpiar un apartamentito porque "tenía mucha basura." Pero un grupo de mujeres empezamos—y en ese tiempo yo no pasaba de 135 libras—nos metimos y lo hicimos. ¡Bien interesante!

The maintenance workers, who were six feet tall, and more, and who weighed like 250 pounds, couldn't go and clean a little apartment because "it was too filled with trash." But a group of us women started —and at that time I didn't weigh any more than 135 pounds—we went in and did it. Very interesting!

After months of work, and *"miles de llamadas"* ("thousands of phone calls"), the Housing Authority conceded. A program of reclamation was begun; prospective tenants would do the cleaning, and the Housing Authority would do the electrical, plumbing, and other construction repairs. The first units were assigned to the women who had participated in the cleanup demonstration project. By Christmas Day, about twenty-five women were able to sign a lease *"para regalos de Navidad"* ("as a Christmas present").

Soto continued to live in the same project for two decades. She put her children through school, and as an adult got a college degree. In addition to her efforts in the area of neighborhood housing, she has been active in voter registration and ward politics. Her politics has been the politics of everyday survival—access to the basic need of adequate shelter—and her methods have been to connect neighbor to neighbor.

Julio Rojas ties the mobilization success of Soto to the fact that she stays connected to the people. He provides the following tribute:

In Mission Hill you have María Luisa Soto, who spent a lot of time in the Mission Hill project; you know that she bought a house now about six months ago. She left the projects, but she spent most of her life in the projects. Her children grew up in the projects, and she was always fighting for the people in the projects. And she went to college, not as a teenager, but as an older person. . . . Now she's working a good job, but *she still comes back to the community every day* [emphasis added].

Personal connections—not in the sense of "having connections" but in the sense of connectedness within the community—lead to political participation because the strong ties of personal relationships bridge the gap between the known world of family, friends, and neighborhood and the unknown, and often hostile, world of government and other institutions. In addition, connectedness is directly tied to the other meaning of connections—"making connections"—when shared experiences with the problems of everyday life motivate the drive for social change—in other words, for political participation.

Gender and the Politics of Everyday Life. Latina women in Boston consider individual struggles with government and local institutions as political behavior and generally include more of a focus on "survival politics" than do the men. Recall Julia Santiago's belief that "taking a stand" against an abusive husband was her first political act, and Ivelisse Rodríguez's inclusion in a discussion of politics her fight with Traveler's Aid not to be sent back to Puerto Rico. One of the clearest gender differences I found in Boston was the frequency with which women talked about "survival politics."

Carla Gardner and Paul Henry, for example, were co-managers of a Latino election campaign. The early part of an interview with them focused on electoral politics, and Henry was much more talkative. At the end, however, Gardner changed the focus of the interview as she contemplated the question, "What is political?"

> *Survival is politics.* Struggling with DSS [Department of Social Services] to keep your kids, the landlord about your rent, keeping your kids safe from drugs, dealing with the trash and abandoned cars—it's everyday politics—trying to get control. Even if you look at the campaign, for all the men who worked on the scene there were women who made it possible. You saw women who pooled the kids, took care of each other's kids so someone could vote or work on the campaign. . . . How just surviving is political, to support your family, get support from each other, where do you get the energy to keep going? [emphasis added]

Henry was comfortable focusing exclusively on the intricacies of campaign politics: who made what decisions; how election strategies developed; and who managed the media, the voter registration drives, and the campaign staff. Gardner, on the other hand, was quiet through much of this part of the interview. Her vision of "everyday politics"—of people working together "to gain control," to struggle with government and local institutions—is a vision of interpersonal connectedness. In this interview segment, she illustrated the gender difference in how politics is defined when she changed from a focus on elections to "survival politics"—the politics of everyday life—and to women working together to promote political participation.

Gardner was only one of many women who viewed political participation in this way. Indeed, in my sample of Latinos in Boston, women were seven times more likely than men to identify socioeconomic survival and "survival politics" as crucial issues affecting political participation.[6]

What is survival politics? Survival politics, subsistence politics,[7] everyday politics, resistance politics,[8] grassroots politics,[9] these phrases are often used as alternatives to "traditional" politics. If traditional politics involves voting, running for office, joining formal organizations (especially political organizations), contributing to campaigns, and so on, then "survival politics" implies something different from these behaviors. But survival politics needs theoretical specificity so it can be useful for understanding the differences between Latina women's politics and Latino men's politics.

Survival politics, first of all, is a class-linked concept. We are not talking about the survival of Boston's upper-class Brahmin population—we are talking about working-class people, poor people, oppressed people. Second, as Gardner's quote reveals, survival politics includes struggles outside of political institutions: struggles with landlords, gangs, bosses. Third, survival politics includes individual, private efforts that go on behind the scenes: women who took care of each other's children so someone could vote. Fourth, survival politics is informal, private, and individualistic. It is less concerned with formal titles and organization structure and more concerned with process and results. Survival politics ebbs and flows, responds to a crisis, subsides, and resurfaces. As Scott (1985) says, these forms of struggle "have certain features in common. They require little or no coordination or planning; they make use of implicit understandings and informal networks; [and] they often represent a form of individual self-help" (xvi).

Latinos certainly participate in traditional political behaviors, as the stories of Josefina Ortega, María Luisa Soto, Marta Correa, and other activists make clear. When they explicitly or implicitly question the nature of politics, however, Latina women are much more likely to reveal as their alternative vision connecting people around issues of survival.

The Politics of Latino Men: Access to Positions and Status. Men, on the other hand, are much more likely to discuss politics in terms of gaining positions in government. As I have already shown, politics for men means elections. Latino men are also more likely to discuss political participation as if it *meant* being appointed or elected to a position in City Hall or the State House. Juan Maldonado, a well-educated Puerto Rican, spent almost the entire interview equating participation with Latinos becoming appointed (or elected) to city or state government. He did mention very briefly the push for bilingual education, the Latino fight against urban renewal in the 1970s, and the effect Latino voter participation had on Mayor Flynn's and Governor Dukakis's administrations, forcing them to appoint more Latinos. However, his interview was for the most part a chronological recounting of Latinos moving in and out of a greater or lesser number of politically determined positions in government.

> We're talking—first, the beginning of 1983. [Mayor] Flynn quickly incorporates and starts looking for some of the supporters of [rival mayoral candidate Mel] King and at the same time starts recruiting Latinos from state government, because it was not only Dukakis, it was [Secretary of State] Michael Connolly, who decided to do the same thing and it was Lieutenant Governor Kerry who decides to do the same thing so that for the first time ever when you walk into the State House and you go to the lieutenant governor's office, there's at least one or two Latinos. You go to the governor's office, you go to state government, you go to Michael Connolly's office, and you start seeing Latinos. Then the mayor starts doing the same thing, but he has to recruit some from state government and then he recruits some from [Governor] King's administration. So then you start seeing Latinos coming into Mayor Flynn's administration, of which there are a number. Edwin Colina—he used to be at the secretary of state's office—moves over to Flynn's administration. Russ Lopez used to be at the lieutenant governor's office; he moves over to the Flynn administration. Let me think, some of the folks—Juanita Fonseca, who used to be at MCAD, not MCAD, the MDC, moves over to the Flynn administration. Phyllis Barajas, who used to be at DSS moves over to the Flynn administration. Juan Vázquez, who used to be at DYS[10] moves over to the Flynn administration. Now some of these people moved on, like Vázquez is no longer there, but this just gives you examples of people who move into the Flynn administration.

The striking feature of this interview is that Maldonado maintains this focus on positions throughout the entire interview and, in essence, defines participation as achieving and operating in political positions when he continues the above discussion, saying, "So now you start seeing Latinos both in city government and in state government, *actively participating* and actively moving—at least putting together—an agenda" [emphasis added].

Recall from the Introduction Jesús Carrillo, who handed me a computer printout of his accomplishments when asked to discuss what he did politically. One might object and say that, after all, I had asked what he did and that my question invited a description of his activities. His equating political life with organizational positions and status accomplishments, however, was qualitatively different from that of the Latina women. With their emphasis on survival politics and the ways they tried to connect people with each other, Latina women simply did not respond with a list of their accomplishments, awards, and titles.

The difference in the number of times Latino men talked about positions and status compared to the number of times women talked about these aspects is as striking as the differences between the two sexes in discussing survival politics. *Latino men were* five *times more likely to define politics in terms of positions and status than were the women.*[11] Latina women, on the other hand, talked about connection twice as much as the men did and about survival politics—connecting politics to the problems of everyday life—seven times as much.

I am not saying that for all Latina women connectedness involves personal networks and that for all Latino men connectedness involves professional networks. I am saying, however, that the women I interviewed were *more likely* than the men to talk about politics as connection and to act as connectors in their political relationships, in contrast to men, who were *more likely* to focus on positions and status as politics. I also suggest that it is the personal network type of connectedness that is necessary to increase political participation in Latino communities.

Latina Politics, Latino Politics: Different Voices

An objection to my conclusion that Latina women and Latino men see politics differently might be: How much of this difference can be explained by gender differences in the style of communication? If it is simply that, as Tannen (1990) suggests, men and women "talk differently," what is the significance of the fact that Latina women and Latino men in Boston focus on connectedness and political positions to different degrees? Do the different ways of talking about politics reflect different perceptions, which translate into different political behaviors? Or is it simply a matter of women being more willing to share their introspective analysis of their political lives in the same way that women are apparently more open about their personal feelings? Did I simply find that Latina women and Latino men *present* their political experiences differently?

It is certainly possible that the emphasis on positions, status, and hierarchy I heard in the men's discussions of Latino politics reflects a way of talking. It might even be argued that the information they imparted to me was a typically male way of maintaining status within the research relationship. In other words, to attain status with me, the interviewer, the men may have wanted to show their knowledge about politics in Boston, especially about electoral politics— "real politics," in their view. Tannen (1990) suggests that men seek status within a hierarchical society "by exhibiting knowledge and skill, and by holding center stage through verbal performance such as story-telling, joking, or *imparting information*" (77; emphasis added). In other words, the more formal information imparted by men (as opposed to the stories of connecting people with one another told by the women) could be a male reaction to the interview relationship.

Although it is certainly possible that the gender differences I found simply reflect different styles of communication, I believe that the way Latina women and Latino men *talk* about politics reflects a very real difference in how they *envision* politics. Tannen (1990) suggests that women's ways of talking are linked to their orientation toward intimacy, connection, community, and closeness. Women's strivings for intimacy, interdependence, and relationship "dovetail with connection" (28). Men, on the other hand, are concerned with status. According to Tannen, the way girls and women talk show them "working hard to create a *community of connection*. . . . The boys and men are working hard to preserve their *independence in a hierarchical world*" (277; emphasis added). In addition, these gender differences in how Latinos talk about politics manifest themselves in how Latinos act politically. There are two sources of support for this belief.

First, other research suggests that "men's social orientation is positional while women's is personal."[12] A positional orientation encourages competition and the striving for personal success. Personal success becomes defined as "moving up" a social and occupational ladder. Meléndez, the businessman who, earlier in this chapter, acknowledged the need to "stay in touch," confirms the existence of this political ladder. He espouses the view that the person who is climbing up should always climb reaching a hand down to pull others up with him. However, he says that, unfortunately, the reality is that as someone climbs he kicks back to keep others from coming up after him. Meléndez, among other men, uses variations on the phrase *"quítate tu para ponerme yo"* ("move you out to get me in") to reflect this careful husbanding of political influence and power within the community. He also says, "Everyone wants to be a chief, not an Indian." Meléndez talks about politics as moving up a ladder of success.

In contrast, for women, connection to others and personal relationships infuse the political process with a desire not to limit what others can achieve but rather to enhance what many can accomplish together—in other words, to empower.[13] In the field of politics specifically, many researchers have claimed that women's politics is distinctly different from men's politics. The emphasis of Latino men on gaining positions as the meaning of political participation may not be related to their being Latino as much as to gender differences in how men and women think about social (and political) relationships.[14] Women, according to Flammang (1984b), view the world less in terms of competition and conflict and more in terms of the "politics of connectedness" (12). And even Kelly and Burgess (1989, 81), who challenge this notion of an essential difference between male and female politics, suggest that men and women do differ on the nature and types of connectedness. Kathlene (1989, 416) finds that male state legislators in Colorado think in terms of their own careers, and she concludes that men's and women's discourse—the way each sex communicates—does indeed reflect different perceptions and different political styles.

Second, the interview material itself and my observations in the community strongly suggest that, in addition to whatever gender differences exist in communication styles, the way Latina women talk about politics does in fact inform their political relationships, their political behavior, and their political-mobilizing skills within the Latino community in ways men's perceptions of politics do not. While men who *do* stay in touch with people in the community are able to successfully mobilize community residents—they do it differently. (This point will be discussed in the portrait of Tito Morales later in this chapter.) My point remains, however—Latina women tend to be more connected than Latino men, while men tend to focus on positions and status. My findings seem to support the idea of a "bimodal distribution" by gender discussed by Flanagan and Jackson (1990, 39).[15] In addition, as will be discussed later in this chapter, Latina women's focus on interpersonal relations and connecting people to each other for political purposes is more in tune with both men's and women's cultural expectations of a more interpersonal, connected, political-mobilization style.

Latina Women and Latino Men: Different Images of Power

I suggest that Latina women are able to create a more participatory model of political mobilization precisely because of their different perceptions of the nature of politics. Their emphasis on connectedness, everyday needs, and the *interpersonal process* of political mobilization rather than on political positions and personal status strengthens their ties to the community and builds political networks. Gender differences that affect political participation also surface in how Latina women and Latino men conceive of power.

Latina women in Boston talked more about participation and less about power. Latino men, in contrast, were much more likely to talk about power and control. In fact, they were more than twice as likely to talk about power than were Latina women. Almost all the influential men described incidents in which politics meant maneuvering for power and control, whereas less than half of the influential women discussed politics in those terms.[16]

Cuban-born and well-educated, Jesús Carrillo has been instrumental in many areas of Latino community service and politics: he led a drive to create Latino mental health services, challenged educational policies for Latino students, and succeeded in creating (with others) formal political structures to increase Latino political influence. His success in helping create a district in which a Latino candidate could win a seat in the state legislature is a major political achievement, and his contribution to Latino politics deserves high praise. At the same time, his vision of politics conforms to, and confirms, gender differences in politics as connectedness versus politics as positions and status. In addition, his spontaneous description of his own political efforts highlights the difference in how men and women conceptualize the relationship between politics and power: "You pretty well know, I think, the politics of human services—they're pretty vicious. I remember when I used to be in Dorchester doing my thing with the Boston Latino Counseling Center—they used to call me the 'Guru of Hispanic Mental Health.' I mean, I had enough power to control who came in and who didn't come into what area—who was hired and who wasn't hired, and that's politics."

Carrillo's self-description reflects commonly held images of power as "the ability to augment one's own force, authority, or influence

51

and also to control and limit others" (Miller 1983, 3). He seems to confirm Lane's earlier thesis that autonomy and power are driving motivators for political involvement: "The political man [sic] is primarily interested in *power*" (Lane 1969, 20). In this context, the key word may be *man*. While power certainly constitutes an important part of political reality, its centrality in theories of political motivation may originate in the gender of the research informants. For example, Lane draws his conclusions from interviews with white males (1962) and from young, white college men (1969). In addition, the whole concept of power may change depending on the sex of the researcher. For example, Dahl—a man—is famous for his statement: "A has power over B to the extent that he can get B to do something that B would not otherwise do" (quoted in Lukes 1974, 11–12). On the other hand, Miller—a woman—challenges the equation of power with "power over": power is "*the capacity to produce a change*" (1991, 198; emphasis in original).

The women in Boston do not discuss the nature of politics as the power to make someone do what "he would not otherwise do." Some, like Marisa Robles, talk about using influence and "political connections" to get services for Latinos, and Juanita Fonseca says she likes the negotiating and maneuvering involved in politics. However, Latina women put the greatest emphasis on participatory processes— the personal side, the relationships of political life within the community, and the way personal issues are intertwined with political struggles. Power, for Latina women in Boston, is the ability to work with others to achieve change.

María Ramírez, for example, was raised in a very traditional Puerto Rican family in New York City in the 1970s. One of her first jobs as a young adult was that of a housing worker. At that time, as now, racial tensions between community members of color and the Hasidic residents were running high. She connected with one of the young Latino men to develop a trusting relationship; together they worked to diffuse tensions between Hasidic and Latino residents by teaching Latino youth about Jewish customs. She recalled: "It was a real learning experience for me; it was a learning experience for everybody there, and the fighting stopped, the swastika writing on the walls stopped." She goes on to provide a vision of politics as promoting change: "Part of the *changing* of politics is to teach. It's not to say, 'Well, vote for this guy or that guy.' . . . It worked."

This emphasis on promoting change, working with people, and focusing on needs permeates the women's stories of being political, whereas maneuvering for power within formal structures and electoral politics is highlighted in the stories of Latino men.

Connection, Culture, and Political Mobilization

In the feminist political literature, interpersonal relationships are as political as institutional relationships. In addition, the feminist perspective adds depth to the study of Latino politics by suggesting that women maintain and nurture personal relationships in ways that make them better political mobilizers than men. For Latinos, men and women alike, these personal relationships are even more important because of the strong cultural value of *personalismo*.

Personalismo has two related meanings. The first acknowledges that personal relationships are as important in business, government, educational, and religious institutions as they are in private situations such as family and friendships. In the United States, there is a doctrine, only sporadically upheld in practice, that there should be a separation between personal and corporate or government relationships. Congressional ethics, for example, require politicians to file conflict of interest statements. Civil service rules require bureaucrats to treat all supplicants impersonally, according to written rules and guidelines: "Take a number and please be seated." Applications for public services are treated in the order received; personal friends are not supposed to receive preferential treatment.

This doctrine of separation is an Anglo cultural value; it strives for impartial (i.e., impersonal) legal, government, and corporate practices. Of course, reality conflicts dramatically with the ideal. The reality is: Who you know gets you more. Everyone in America uses, whenever possible, the connection with someone he or she knows to receive preferential treatment. Contracts in business are given to people "like us." Knowing someone in the legal system personally (or at least coming from the same background) may expedite or defer judicial proceedings. Major policies are decided in the locker room—not in the board room. Catalina Torres explains: "The decisions that are being publicly disguised—uhh, discussed [laughter at the 'freudian slip']—disguised in the committee have really already been discussed at the urinal, literally at the urinal. Or they were discussed at the athletic club at six o'clock in the morning when I was getting my son ready to go to school."

Anglo-Americans are uncomfortable acknowledging the extent to which personal connections (in the "political influence" sense of connection) affect public decisions. Many Latinos, however, are more open when they acknowledge that knowing someone personally gets you farther and gets you more than going through bureaucratic channels. In Puerto Rico, the Dominican Republic, and Central and South America, a sense of mutual responsibility is supposed to guard against rampant self-interest or abuse of privilege within these personal–public relationships.[17]

The second meaning of *personalismo* dictates how to treat someone within such relationships, whether the relationships are "purely" personal (e.g., friendships, family), or business, official, and the like. Within relationships that cross class, there must be respectful politeness, dignity, and friendliness that does not require obsequiousness on one level or become patronizing on the other.

Personalismo and Electoral Politics. *Personalismo* in Latino electoral politics means face-to-face, personal contact rather than impersonal, quick messages of "Register!" "Vote for . . .!" These face-to-face contacts must not be manipulative; the person in the more active, more powerful, more assertive position must not be trying to achieve change for him- or herself.[18] There must be a joining together, a reciprocal interest in the person he or she is trying to mobilize. Nelson Merced explains: "We have to do politics of organizing house to house which, to a great extent, is much more effective, because of *personalismo*. You end up *talking* to the people directly— it's more time consuming, more difficult, but much more effective over the long run."

María Ramírez describes how she urged the Anglo legislator she works for to take on a more personal approach with his Latino constituents. By personally going door to door, the representative becomes

> a real person to them. . . . Joe does door knocking, I really admire him because of his efforts—that he really puts himself out. He tries to be very *real* to people, he goes to meetings—so do we, but at least people know him, he's there, you can touch him, you can talk to this person, it's not a newspaper person, or a publicity person, it's a very *real* person. That needs to happen in the Hispanic community. People need to be very *real* to these people. You know, you're not just a name, or "the leader," and it's not just all professionals.

The personal touch also increases Latino likelihood of voting. Two Latinos ran for office while I was conducting the research for this book: Nelson Merced and Marta Rosa. Both personify Latino candidates who developed personal, door-to-door contacts to a high degree and achieved electoral success. Both are very conscious of how personal contacts and lengthy interactions contributed to their successes. Everyone I talked to who was at all familiar with these two candidates attributed their elections to strategies that stressed personal contacts.

Over and over again Merced knocked on doors throughout his district. His methods convinced some neighbors to register and vote.

> As we were walking down the street, I said to this gentleman who was coming out with his wife and kid, I said, "Have you registered to vote?" He gave me the classic, "Oh, I'm not registered; I'm not interested—I'll never get anything out of it," so I took an opportunity just to stop and say . . . , "Look, I'm an elected official, and we have people just like you, with similar attitudes, and if that were to prevail, I wouldn't have been successful." . . . I knew that, after a while, he went and registered to vote. . . . I think that's the kind of effort that you have to do. You really have to go out and talk to people individually, and you really have to say, "Look, this is why it's important."

Rosa combined this door-knocking strategy that goes beyond "Vote for me!" with the women's emphasis on personal connections—her "strong ties" to the community. She said that many people remembered her as a person who grew up in Chelsea and as a day care organizer and administrator: "I came across a lot of people—grandparents—who didn't recognize 'Marta Rosa' from the flyer, but once I came to their door, 'Oh! You're from the day care center. I remember you! Of course I'll vote for you!'"

Personal contact was crucial in overcoming the barriers to Latino voter registration. For example, many Latinos in Chelsea did not understand the ballot, know who was running, or differentiate between primaries and general elections; meeting people personally cleared up many of these misunderstandings. Personal contact also set in motion an educational process. Marta Rosa recalls: "This couple said to the voter registration person, 'But I was waiting for the card to come to my house,' because, I guess, where they come from you get a card in the mail and you vote. That's how you vote. There's a *lot* of education that needs to happen—people don't know how to vote, or it's different in this country, or they don't understand."

A final note on voter registration and personal relationships in Latino political mobilization: mass registration techniques, such as the Puerto Rican Festival, have only varying degrees of success. They may work for those who are already inclined to vote and who just need access to the tools. For the most part, however, registration drives preclude lengthy explanations of ballots, candidates, and issues. They also preclude the discussions necessary to overcome the hesitance of people who have never voted before. Marta Torrijos, a thirty-year-old Puerto Rican, for example, said she registered at the festival because of peer pressure and to avoid being hassled by the workers or her friends. However, she states that there was no discussion or personal interaction at the time of registration or afterward that would make her inclined to exercise her franchise.

I do not mean to downplay the contribution of the registration booth at the festival; thousands of Latinos have registered at that booth over the years. Nevertheless, without personal exchanges of information and ideas, mass registration may not reach Latinos who have few personal ties to electoral politics in the United States. Simply registering *la gente del pueblo* will not overcome other barriers to voting (such as understanding the process and procedures).

"It's That Personal Request". *Personalismo* plays a salient role in other types of political activity besides elections. Personal contacts determine whether attendance at community action groups, political education, and civic education efforts achieve or fail to achieve their desired results. For example, several people remarked on the failure to attract many Latinos to a meeting at which a school dropout prevention plan was to be presented to the community. This plan was intended to address a problem of great concern to many Latinos in Boston—a 53 percent dropout rate for Latino students in the public schools—and represented the culmination of a lot of hard work by a dedicated group of community activists. This group, the Comité de Familias Latinas de Boston, sent out thousands of flyers inviting Latino parents to a social and informative event at a nearby Latino community center.

Many Latino activists were extremely disappointed at the paltry attendance. Aracelis Guzmán remembers: *"Fue triste ver ese auditorio vacío ahí"* ("It was sad seeing that empty auditorium"). Her explanation for the poor attendance is the impersonal nature of mass mailings. She advocates more personal contact.

> *Creo que lo organizamos mal, creo que lo organizamos mal. Creo que perdimos mucho tiempo mandando once mil invitaciones, ¿verdad? Creo que el contacto debe ser pequeñito y personal.*
>
> I think we organized it wrong; I think we organized it wrong. I think that we wasted a lot of time sending out eleven thousand invitations, right? I think the contact should be *small and personal* [emphasis added].

Two men agree with Guzmán's assessment of the reasons for the failure of this endeavor. Edwin Colina, for example, reiterates Guzmán's explanation and adds that the organizers should not be people connected with government positions. Nelson Merced states simply: "It's that personal request—people will honor that more than anything else."

Latino men and women agree that personal contact is particularly successful in overcoming barriers of language, social isolation, fear, and a sense of vulnerability. María Ramírez, in particular, describes many examples of how direct contacts mobilized non-English-speaking Latino residents, many of whom were here illegally. By both responding to a personal contact from a community resident and then by connecting neighbor to neighbor, she was able to develop these Latino community members into a viable protest group that was successful in achieving better police protection. She recalls how these contacts created a protest march by Latinos typically portrayed as unlikely candidates for political action:

> There was a group of residents who spoke *very* little English, and they had complaints about the community and they didn't know who to talk to, so they finally got ahold of me, and it was a drug situation. . . . It was the community that really did it. They became very active, we held a march, we marched through the streets, and it was the first time that kind of grassroots non-English-speaking people got together and then we invited the rest of the community and it went very well.

Teresa Andrade also uses personal contacts and the personal request as a way of getting people involved. She spent her weekends for many years distributing the Puerto Rican Socialist newspaper, having political discussions, and holding political *charlas* (chats) in people's homes. In her experience, personal conversations in informal settings decrease social isolation, increase political consciousness, and extend political networks.

Another example is a social service worker named Marina Acebedo; she is staff member at a Latino agency who takes an entourage of clients to a variety of community and political events. They socialize, provide entertainment—and give testimony at public hearings. These mixed events, in the company of a group of friends, enhance their knowledge of the workings of political and government institutions in Boston and the state of Massachusetts. Even Marta Torrijos, who considers herself "apathetic" about politics, has responded to people she knows and trusts when they ask her for support and political participation. She has also attended political events as part of a group. And Juana Oviedo, an older, apparently "passive," Puerto Rican woman, when asked by a woman staff member of a Latino agency for help in protesting budget cuts, joined a group to make a videotape to lobby state legislators. She could name four different people she knows personally who would be successful at drawing her into a political event.

At the same Comité de Familias Latinas workshop just mentioned, José Pareño, a Cuban, said that they should each go home and call ten people for the next meeting. Isabel Domínguez responded that if they each brought just *one* person, the number of participants would be doubled. Julia Santiago feels that in groups people overcome their fear of facing new people and participating in new situations. As Pateman (1970) and Barber (1984) conclude, participatory experiences generate participation in politics. The consensus of people I interviewed and of group participants at a workshop sponsored by the Comité de Familias Latinas de Boston is that participation could be increased by a "simple" method of having each active person invite one, two, or maybe three or four individuals to the various events. It is probably true, of course, that most people, regardless of national origin, respond best to a request from a friend or neighbor, a point I will discuss at greater length shortly. This is especially true in an era of excessive solicitations by mail and phone.

Venir y Averigüar: Personal Politics and Cultural Expectations.
Latinos expect politicians to keep a finger on the pulse of the community and to stay connected. The common folk I interviewed spent hours sharing their expectations of a personal style of politics. Many Puerto Ricans recalled how in Puerto Rico, politicians would circulate through the *pueblos* and talk personally with *la gente del pueblo.*

Luis Hernández, for example, has lived in Boston for over twenty years. He is active in local elections and tries to get other Latinos to vote. Despite his slight attachment to the island, Hernández still wants politicians to act as they do in Puerto Rico: to *"venir y averigüar"*[19] ("come and find out") what is going on in the community by talking directly to the people. Hernández describes the process:

> *Cuando una persona corre para gobernador, para alcalde [en Puerto Rico], como le digo, va barrio por barrio, sitio por sitio. Conoce la gente, la gente lo conoce, saben si es una persona buena, qué puede prometer, que puede hacer algo por el barrio, por el país o por el pueblo donde está viviendo y la gente le da ánimo.*

> When someone is running for governor, for mayor [in Puerto Rico], like I say, he goes neighborhood by neighborhood, place to place, meeting the people. The people meet him; they get to know if he is a good person, what he is promising, if he can do anything for the neigh-

borhood, for the country, for the town where the people live; and the people cheer him on.

I probe whether it is the rallies (cheering on the politician) or the personal contact that is the key to an effective political relationship. Hernández responds by identifying cultural expectations of a personal political relationship.

Personalmente—pueden comunicarle, decirle los problemas que tienen en el barrio. . . las quejas y lo que está pasando. Lo que quieren que cambie. . . . El latino es como—es la parte del latino—que al latino le gusta no solamente hablar, sino que le hablen, y que a lo que está hablando se le ponga atención.

They can—personally—communicate with him—tell him the problems they have in the neighborhood . . . their complaints and what's going on. What they want changed. . . . The Latino person is like—it's part of being a Latino—that the Latino likes to not only talk but be talked to and to have what he's saying be paid attention to.

Personal connectedness between politicians, campaign workers, and the people in the communities is a hallmark of politics in many Latino countries—countries like Puerto Rico and the Dominican Republic. Puerto Ricans in Boston typically complain about the lack of personal connectedness in mainland American politics. They relate stories of candidates in Puerto Rico personally going to each *pueblo* shaking hands, and, as Ivelisse Rodríguez succinctly said, *"escuchando"* ("listening"). Juana Oviedo recalls her father telling how Governor Muñoz Marín would go into the *pueblos* to eat with the countryfolk. Politicians listened to the grievances and heard what a community felt it needed to improve conditions of life in the different villages.

I found Dominican women to be particularly political. Because I interviewed such a small number of individuals from Santo Domingo, I cannot speak with authority about gender differences and Dominican politics.[20] However, there is some support in the literature for the view that, compared with Anglo or other Latina women, Dominican women have a special relationship to politics. Mota (1976), for example, describes the feminism (albeit elitist, conservative, and regime-supportive) and political activism of Dominican women in the 1930s and 1960s. Mota (1976) and Aviel (1981) also describe the efforts of ex-president Trujillo and current president Balaguer to woo women's votes. Balaguer, in particular, assured the loyalty of many women by appointing women to all twenty-six provincial governorships. Dominican women also obtained the franchise relatively early compared to other Latin countries (Mota 1976, 269). In addition, the president's sister, Emma Balaguer, increased the participation of Dominican women through her policy initiatives to improve conditions for poor families. Her appeal to women to participate in survival politics was evidently successful.[21] In the United States, specifically Los Angeles and New York, Dominican women recount a history of membership in political organizations in their home country to a greater degree than other Latina women (Infante 1977, 37–42).

Personalismo: A Universal or Class-based Need? The expectation of personal connectedness in political life and the role of informal networks in generating political participation raise several thorny questions. First, do Latinos in Boston need personal contact in order to participate because of cultural characteristics? Second, does the more personal style of Latino politics reflect a class-based need? Finally, would everybody join organizations, attend meetings, and feel inclined to vote in greater numbers if politics were more integrated into daily life?

These three questions are all interrelated: how do culture, class, and universal needs intersect in political participation? Banfield (1958) and the political-culture school of Almond, Verba, and Nie imply that people of lower socioeconomic class have certain inbred attitudes, cultural predispositions, or national characteristics that limit them to what Almond, Verba, Nie, and others consider to be parochial types of participation. Parochial participation focuses exclusively on the benefits that accrue to the individual, his or her immediate family, or the clan. The need for concrete results, the need for personal contact, and the desire for small-group interaction as prerequisites of political participation are, according to the political-culture school, class and culture based. Parochial politics is perceived to be of a lesser quality in the ranking of political behaviors and attitudes—less democratic, if you will.

Even though the lower voter participation rates of the lower socioeconomic classes seem to indicate a class-based need for concrete benefits and personal politics, the American electorate *in general* suffers from electoral disaffection. Morone (1990, 125) observes that "voter participation plunged" after the reforms instituted by the progressive movement at the turn of the century. Perhaps the decline in American voting rates could be reversed if Latino-style political mobilization strategies (which include the contribution of Latina women) were to replace the current impersonal, mass-media approach.

In contrast to the "rugged individualism" touted as the American ideal, Latinos, as a cultural entity, value being part of a group. The political scene in Puerto Rico and the Dominican Republic, for example, involves "old-time" rallies, stronger group and party affiliation, and voting as a social event. Doing politics in a small social group increases participation among the general populace. Politics, for Latinos, is not a private, individualistic affair.

In the United States, political-mobilization efforts that respond to cultural expectations are more successful than those that inform or exhort but that leave the participatory behaviors up to the individual. Over and over again I heard people say that doing things together gets the less involved to participate in social *and* political events. Jaime Romero, for example, told me the story of how he registered to vote in Puerto Rico. His uncle asked him one day how old he was. He said he was seventeen,[22] so the uncle took him to the local school where Jaime registered and voted. He has been in the United States for six months, and no one has acted in that personal way to encourage him to register here.

Is there evidence that personal relationships are the path to political participation for groups other than Latinos in the Northeast? Remarkably little attention has been paid to the interpersonal aspect of voter registration or other types of political activity. It is as if people decide on their individual initiative to go register or to participate in politics. Studies on Mexican-American registration drives, for example, focus on organizational dynamics, not on what goes on between individual members of a given community.[23] I contend that people do not join organizations only because of what the organization does and that they do not attend political meetings solely on their own initiative. People often join organizations, and register to vote, because someone says, "Hey, come with me. This looks interesting."

The literature on political socialization typically presents demographic and family characteristics as the main politicizing agents.[24] Some consideration is given as well to the mobilizing impact of social movements: the civil rights movement for black Americans and the women's movement for women.[25] Little attention, however, is given to the interpersonal and interactive processes involved in becoming more politically active.

Gerlach and Hine (1970), Evans (1980), and Hertz (1981) are a few exceptions to the tradition of ignoring interpersonal interactions as a source of political behavior. Evans's discussion of white women in the civil rights movement and Hertz's analysis of the welfare mothers movement demonstrate that people join organizations because of other people. "People do not join an amorphous movement per se, but are recruited through face-to-face contact with a committed member of a specific group within the total movement network" (Hertz 1981, 119).

This contact, according to Gerlach and Hine (1970), "almost always involved a significant, pre-existing relationship—a relative, a close friend, a neighbor, an influential associate of some sort—with whom the new convert had had a meaningful interaction prior to recruitment" (79). The freedom schools in the South during the early civil rights movement generated political behavior (and voter registration) by tying politics to personal relationships. The literacy campaigns in Central America likewise provided a precedent for Latinos to blend personal relationships and political development. Friendship and citizenship have been linked since the time of Aristotle (Barber 1984, 70–71).

Personalismo: The Interplay of Culture and Gender

Personalismo is a cultural value, but even so, gender differences create a different emphasis on the value of interpersonal politics and transform personalismo into different political styles. All the examples given in the preceding pages show both men and women stressing the need for personal contact in political participation. All of them say Latinos expect an interpersonal style of political mobilization. Nevertheless, just as Latina women place a greater emphasis on connectedness and making connections than do Latino men, *Latina women refer to personal, face-to-face, contacts during political mobilization much more often than do Latino men—in fact, almost three times as often as men.*[26] In addition, the women went into much more depth (their transcripts included longer segments with more examples of *how* they interacted personally) than did the men. Latino men, in other words, might *state* that personal contact is important but for the most part do not describe their own efforts in using this mobilizing strategy.

In community group meetings, I also noticed that Latino men were more responsive than women to formal organizations and formal membership drives. For example, at a Comité de Familias Latinas meeting, José Pareño said that a *compromiso formal* (a formal agreement) was needed, and men talked more about setting up organizations rather than connecting through personal relationships.

Women seem to retain the cultural model of politics that is preferred in countries such as Puerto Rico, using an intimate and pervasive exchange of grievances, promises, and efforts to solve community problems. I contend that, with their emphasis on connectedness, it is Latina women in general who have kept the cultural flame alive and who are the untapped resource for generating Latino political participation in the United States. These women make Latino voices

62

audible to the institutional power centers; the key ingredient, however, is the attentive listening, communicating, and dialogue between *la gente* and the women.

Luis Hernández, who in the Introduction stressed elections as politics, nonetheless beseeched politicians: *"Hay que escuchar"* ("It's important to listen"). And Ivelisse Rodríguez made a plea for *"un intercambio de ideas"* ("an exchange of ideas"); she said, *"Hace falta un diálogo"* ("What is needed is a dialogue"). In Boston, it is often Latina women legislative aides who respond to this expressed need for a dialogue—for leaders, officials, and politicians to listen. Barber (1984) suggests that the exchange of ideas and listening promotes participation by creating feelings of mutuality and affiliation.[27]

Latina women also serve as the personal connection between officialdom and the community and function as the ears of the politicians. Legislative aides and women in nonofficial capacities provide important constituent work and act as personal intermediaries in Latino politics. Of course, Latino men also act as intermediaries. In the next section, for example, I discuss Tito Morales, who demonstrates a male style of *personalismo* in serving as a direct link between community needs and City Hall officials. For the most part, however, Latina women play this role within the community. For example, Angel Pérez, a South American man who directs a Latino social service program, describes a typical situation in which an official wishes to reach the common folk: "I contacted two or three key people in the community . . . to use their names and their influence to get these people to come here, because it's not easy. People, when they are approached . . . they always have something in the back of their minds, 'Can we trust this?' And the best way to do it is to go with leaders or well-known people in the community to be able to gain their confidence." And who are these "leaders and well-known people"? They are not men from City Hall but rather connectors like Fina Ortega and María Luisa Soto, the influential *women* who are of *la gente del pueblo*. Many Latinos turn to these women for advice and political direction—Latina women from the neighborhoods, women who serve as legislative aides, staff at community agencies, and the *alcadesas del barrio*.

Women add another layer to the cultural expectation of *personalismo*. María Ramírez stresses the need for the personal commitment: "I think you have to personalize everything that goes on in the community if you really want to see a change. . . . I think it needs that kind of personal commitment." She also shares the pain of the people she visits and feels torn between the political purpose and her personal ties and concern: "I mean, I have had cups of coffee like nobody else, and you go to people's homes and it sometimes puts you in a predicament. It's difficult; sometimes you can't help but feel the anger and the suppression—people who are on welfare or people who have kids on drugs and you don't know how to help them."

There are some Latino men whose political style is similar to that of Latina women—they too keep ties within the community and relate to the everyday survival needs of the people. Some Latinos I spoke with connected this everyday focus—for Puerto Ricans in this case—to what they called "rice and beans politics."

Rice and beans politics (like the Anglo metaphor of bread and butter issues) touches the everyday concerns of *la gente del pueblo*. Tamara González urges other Latino activists to explain to *la gente del pueblo* how political decisions will "cut their rice and beans"—in other words, affect them at a very elemental level. Julio Rojas says, "We may be in the State House, but we don't control the village," suggesting that all the efforts to achieve political appointments do little to nurture ties within the Latino community. Juan Vázquez, a Puerto Rican who aspires to political office, describes how Rojas, himself, understands what people in *el pueblo* need: "People that have to work on a daily basis, people that have to worry about—Can they afford to live where they live? People that have to be concerned about the school's education, kids' education. Julio really touches those people." I asked Vázquez to describe what is different about Julio Rojas. He replied: "Because he goes in there, he talks to people. . . . In the streets, meetings in his house, and he tries to—he projects an image of inclusiveness, and he really wants to deal with those issues and there's a sense also that he's not in it for himself. He's not in it to get a job in city government. He really is an *habichuela* [the 'beans' of 'rice and beans'] kind of guy." In addition to personifying this down-to-earth, inclusive, personal style, Rojas addresses the poverty and other problems facing the common folk in the Latino community in their own terms, by capturing the image of the *jíbaro*. For Puerto Ricans a *jíbaro* is a countryperson, a peasant, perhaps even a "hick." The *jíbaro* has become a folk hero, however—a Puerto Rican national symbol that recalls the simplicity of the rural past. Through this image Rojas touches the cultural longings of a displaced people.[28] Vázquez explains: "Julio has this persona of a *jíbaro*. . . . This guy was poor, I know. . . . I think that's what it is, I think in every Puerto Rican who was either born here or born on the island, there is that association with the *jíbaro*—and of course, the *jíbaro* has become a mythical hero." When asked, "Does that connect him better with *la gente del pueblo*?" Vázquez replies simply, "I think it does, because then there's an automatic trust."

Rojas illustrates that there are Latino men, as well as women, who are able to resist the pull to government jobs and who maintain personal relationships within the community. When Rojas invites people to a meeting, he is communicating a desire to include people rather than communicating a need to meet the requirements of his job.

Another man who deserves attention as a political mobilizer and who illustrates the more typically male form of *personalismo* is Tito Morales. For Morales, in contrast to Latina women and men like Julio Rojas, connection means "political connections" to those with high status—to those in power. And what are his goals? To gain for Latinos access to positions in government.

Portrait of Tito Morales:
The Personal Connection to City Hall

Tito Morales is a seventy-eight-year-old Puerto Rican with an almost mythical reputation as a great organizer. He is a true pioneer of Latino politics in Boston. Morales attended school only to the eighth grade and moved here from Puerto Rico at the age of thirty. He first directed his attentions to the defense of Puerto Rican rights in Boston, accompanying Latinos to court and fighting to assure that their lack of English did not deprive them of their legal rights. He, along with others, picketed City Hall to increase the representation of Latinos in administrative and official positions. In other words, his goal was to achieve access for Puerto Ricans to the high-paying jobs in city government. Most Latinos who have been in Boston for a while know his name, and he is still, despite his age, a presence to be recognized in the South End. I base my analysis of Morales's political style of my lengthy interview with him and on interview material from other Latinos.

Morales epitomizes the male style of *personalismo*. For him, *connection* means having connections at the highest levels of city government. Morales believes in going to the top. Rather than going through Latino liaisons at City Hall, he has cultivated a personal relationship with a specific assistant to the mayor of Boston. He first developed this connection during the Mayor White administration. Following a successful picketing at City Hall to demand more public housing for Latinos in Boston, Morales gained the ear of the mayor. He would not call the mayor directly but, as he said, *"Yo me veía con Kevin White en actividades de la comunidad y me—me preguntaba, 'Tito, ¿cómo está la situación de los hispanos?' y yo le decía, 'Bueno—'ya que ese era el momento de conseguir algo"* ("I'd find myself in community activities with Kevin White and he would ask

me, 'Tito, how are things with the Hispanics?' and I'd say, 'Well—'
since that would be the moment to get something"). He proceeded to
describe his access to the office of Mayor White and later Mayor
Flynn.

*Cuando yo siempre he ido a la alcaldía, nunca me han puesto ob-
stáculos para ver a White y, actualmente, ahora, Flynn nos está ayu-
dando mucho también, sobretodo su asistente, Fletcher—que yo tengo
la costumbre que, cuando necesito algo, entiende, no me gusta brincar
por encima, entiende. Yo voy a ver a Fletcher y, gracias a Dios,
Fletcher es el hombre de la mano derecha de Flynn, y cada vez que le
pido ayuda, me ayuda.*

Whenever I have gone to City Hall, they've never put obstacles in my
way to see White, and now Flynn is helping a lot too, especially his
assistant, Fletcher—I always, whenever I need something, you understand, I don't like to go over anybody's head, you understand. I go to
see Fletcher and, thanks be to God, Fletcher is Flynn's right-hand man,
and whenever I ask him for help, he helps.

Morales maintains a humble demeanor in the community, lives
modestly, and is proud of the plaques and awards he has received
from agencies, mayors, and Governor Dukakis for his years of community service. At the same time, he has held a position in an office
of city government and was on the board of a local hospital serving
many Latinos. Through these positions as well as through his access
to the mayor's office, he has pushed his agenda of increased positions
for Latinos in Boston and greater services to the community. He
claims that the mayor seeks his opinions because the mayor knows
he won't whitewash the truth.

*Cada vez que hay una actividad, pues, me llama y a veces me pre-
gunta, "¿cómo va la comunidad?" porque la verdad del caso es que
mucha gente que trabaja en las oficinas del gobierno, distintas oficinas,
le dicen a el alcalde lo bueno. El alcalde no quiere saber lo bueno que
hay en la comunidad, el alcalde quiere saber cual es el problema de la
comunidad. . . . yo soy un hombre franco.*

Whenever there's an activity, well, he calls me aside and on occasion
he asks me, "How's the community doing?" because the truth of the
matter is that lots of people who work in the government offices, different offices, tell only good things to the mayor. The mayor doesn't
want to hear what's good in the community, the mayor wants to know
what the problem is in the community. . . . I'm a frank man.

Morales is very active in electoral politics as well; candidates, hoping for Latino votes, seek out his endorsement. He goes on the radio

to announce his support for his candidates. He influences the voting decisions of Latinos in the community in two ways. First, he believes in using his personal relationships within the community not only to get people to vote but also to suggest whom to vote for. He says, *"Mucha gente me dice a mí, 'Tito, ¿por quién voto?'. . . Digo, 'Bueno, vota por éste, y por éste, por estas razones,' entiendes"* ("Many people ask me, 'Tito, whom should I vote for?' . . . I say, 'Well, vote for this one, and this one, for these reasons,' you understand"). He also gives testimony at public meetings and still serves as a watchdog *"para defender a los míos por la injusticia"* ("to defend my people against injustice").

Tito Morales is a rice and beans politician; he works indefatigably for the community rather than for personal gain. He is also "one of the people"—his demeanor, speech, and place of residence still locate him as one of *la gente del pueblo*, not one of *los profesionales*. He does not speak just *for* the Latino community; he speaks as one of the people. Thus, Morales is able to draw *la gente del pueblo* into the political process in ways professional activists or designated leaders cannot.

Protest got Tito Morales a direct connection to the mayor's office, a connection that still persists today. Having connections is a key aspect of the cultural value of *personalismo* (although, as I said before, it is a strategy used not just by Latinos). Nevertheless, this focus on attaining personal connections with City Hall reflects a gender difference in how the cultural value is acted upon.

The term *personal connections* acquires different meanings for Latino men and Latina women; these differences then inform different mobilizing strategies. Latino men, such as Tito Morales, use connections (meaning influence) with the mayor's "right-hand man" to wrest benefits for the community. In addition, careful scrutiny of his transcript reveals that women are the unsung heroes of his campaigns for justice as well as his campaigns for candidates. He remembers the picket at City Hall that gave him access to the mayor's office. Morales does not say explicitly that women were co-organizers, but he does point to a woman, Doña Petra, who was right there with him. Doña Petra is a "pioneer" from the late 1960s and early 1970s and a key player in the fight against urban renewal. She is renowned for her ability to engage large groups of Latinos in mass political activities. Morales says,

Me reuní con Doña Petra—nos reunimos y cuando fuimos a la oficina de Boston Housing nos dijeron que no podíamos entrar porque estaba

67

muy ocupado el director y dije—"¡Ah! que ¿está ocupado?" Y a la brava nos metimos.

I met with Doña Petra—we met and when we went to the office of the Boston Housing [Authority] they told us that we couldn't come in because the director was very busy and I said—"So! He's busy? [Good!]" And we forced our way in.

So Morales did not achieve access to the mayor's office alone, but with Doña Petra "right there with him." In addition, the mass of Latinos who actually picketed City Hall were women. Morales explains: *"Nos metimos—habían como cincuenta mujeres, entiende, con Doña Petra, y nos metimos a la brava, y nos tuvieron que recibir y apareció un apartamento para todo el mundo"* ("We forced our way in—there were like *fifty women*, you understand, with Doña Petra, and we forced our way in, and they had to receive us and an apartment turned up for everybody."

Connectedness, Feminist Theory, and Machine Politics: So What's the Difference?

Latina women emphasize connectedness as an essential ingredient of political mobilization; they stress personal connectedness when they talk about politics and when they act politically. A few of the men I interviewed also talk about and act in ways that reveal personal connections to people in the Latino community. However, *as a group*, Latino men evidence less connectedness than Latina women do.

But is what Latina women do any different from what other women— white women, black women—do? A feminist debate continues to rage about whether there are essential differences between women's politics and men's politics. Feminist politics emphasizes grassroots, personal politics—a politics tied to individual, family, friendship networks, and community relationships. Ackelsberg (1984) and Fowlkes (1984) discuss how women's views of politics are connected to home, family, friends, and community. Sapiro (1983) also finds that women, in general, link private experiences to public politics.

Research on black women in politics leads to similar conclusions. Dill (1988), for example, presents the personal relationships of black women domestic servants as evidence of resistance politics. In general, private actions and informal personal networks have provided support for lower-class black women to achieve major social changes (Dill 1988, Garland 1988, Sacks 1988). Latina women certainly seem to provide evidence for key elements in the feminist position that gender differences in the nature of politics do exist—that politics for women is more personal; stresses interpersonal relationships; and is an interactive process. Everyday concerns and relationships based on day-to-day networks form the basis of political mobilization for women. The gender differences suggested by previous research in psychology, morality, and social relations (Chodorow 1974, Gilligan 1982, Tannen 1990, Miller 1991, and Surrey 1991). Latina women, like non-Latina women, *do* see the world more in terms of relationships than do men. In addition, Latina women in Boston extend women's emphasis on interpersonal relationships beyond the arenas of psychology, morality, and social relations—and into politics and political participation.

Latina women's emphasis on connectedness raises two thorny questions, however. First, *why* should Latina women view politics in terms of connectedness and Latino men in terms of positions and status? Second, since old-time machine politics also stressed personal ties between constituents and politicians, is there any essential difference between the politics of Latina women in Boston and machine-style politics?

Connection and Latino Politics: Explaining the Gender Difference. The question why gender differences in Latino political styles exist is difficult to answer. The Latina women I met and talked with did not explicitly address this question, and I suspect different reasons exist for different individuals. Certain themes do emerge, however. First, avenues for women's advancement are blocked in what is described by women and men alike as a sexist environment for Latina women. "It's a men's club," explained Edwin Colina as he discussed the predominance of men in government offices. The constraints on women due to sexism will be discussed in Chapter 6.

Second, social subordination—the assumption that men have capabilities, drives, or qualities that make them more suited to public positions than women—may also explain why Latina women focus on community-based politics rather than on government positions or elected office. Social conditioning may prevent some women from considering positions and status as appropriate goals for women. María Ramírez even suggests that the fragility of the socioeconomic position of Latino men requires that they be ceded political positions. She feels that, despite Latina women's strengths in politics, the offices should go to men because of their otherwise reduced roles in the community. She explains: "I think my own personal opinion is that I would prefer to see a man in office . . . because of our kids. Because of the condition that our kids are in, because they need that positive role model." Tate (1992) suggests that a similar process may operate with black women as well. Black women's support for Clarence Thomas over Anita Hill during the Thomas Supreme Court confirmation hearings, according to Tate, revealed that "the urgent plight of black men" created a situation in which "the focus on race and racism overwhelmed and diminished the black gender issues" (80).

A third possibility exists: choice.[29] I suggest that many Latina women choose the politics of connectedness over the politics of positions and status because they are aware of the implications inherent in the two models. The politics of positions is a hierarchically based politics in which a certain degree of co-optation is inevitable. The problem is not simply that Latino men—men in general—are co-opted by moving into the Anglo political system. The problem may be that a political system based on representation and hierarchical power relations creates distances between the people and their supposed "representatives."

Latino men in Boston were less likely than women to express discomfort with the distance created by being a "role model" rather than a person directly connected to the community. The Latina women who *were* in some kind of official position were more likely to express pain at the distance. Tamara González, for example, was troubled by the fact that she no longer "shares their own needs on a day-to-day basis" with *la gente del pueblo* and firmly concludes: "That's definitely a limitation of mine." And Catalina Torres, who had risen from poverty to prominence had to stop the interview in tears when, in feeling the gap between her current achievement and "the common man," she heard herself say, sadly, "I want to *be* the common man."

Finally, the question must be raised whether women sense the limits of office holding for systemic change. Ackelsberg (1991, 172–173) suggests that most mainstream institutions, be they political organizations, unions, or government offices, fail to accommodate the forms of activism preferred by women. Thus, although Latina women did not explicitly state that they chose the politics of connectedness over the politics of positions, feminist theory certainly supports the possibility that women recognize the limits posed on activists, appointed or elected, once they move into public office. I raise these questions less to provide an answer and more to locate the gender differences between Latina women and Latino men within the larger debates of feminist political theory.

Latina Women's Politics as Machine Politics? Concluding that Latina women may resemble non-Latina women in integrating personal connectedness and political-mobilization methods is not particularly controversial, although such comparisons may detract from the unique experiences of Latinas in politics.[30] The question whether Latina women's mobilizing style, with its emphasis on personal connectedness, resembles white, male, machine-type politics at the turn of the century is much more likely to stimulate a lively debate.

Stylistically, there are indeed similarities between the personal connectedness of Latina women's politics with the methods urban machines used to stimulate participation among earlier groups of immigrants. There are, however, behavioral, structural, and motivational differences that cannot, should not, be ignored. I begin with the similarities.

Latinos in Boston stress the need to develop and maintain personal connectedness to stimulate political participation. Machine politics achieved party loyalty, voter turnout, and immigrant participation using what appear to be similar methods: "The machine wields its link with ordinary men and women by elaborate networks of personal relations. Politics is transformed into personal ties" (Merton 1957, 74). Machine bosses and their ward heelers knew the early immigrant communities intimately. The source of strength of the political machine was "its roots in the local community and the neighborhood" (74).

Machine politics responded to the needs of the community by providing concrete, tangible—what Dahl referred to as "divisible"[31]— benefits. Informality and particularism represented the hallmark of service provision by the urban machine. Serrano, the Puerto Rican boss in Rogler's study of New Haven, was adept at responding to the people of the community. For Serrano, "no problem was too big for him to handle or too trivial for his immediate personal attention at any hour of the day or night. He got them jobs and housing, served as their interpreter, counseled them about personal problems, lent them money, and reprimanded or commended them according to what he felt was appropriate to behavior in the new setting" (Rogler 1974, 59).

Machine politics also operated on the principle of the exchange of favors; loyalty to the boss, to the party, and to the vote determined the receipt of benefits. During the heyday of the political machine, voter turnout was stimulated by membership in organized groups; various social and even cash incentives were provided for voting. Ward workers expected, and were expected, to pass the time in social exchange—holding babies, drinking coffee (and stronger refreshments), and attending local cultural events. Politics blended culture, sociability, and entertainment.

Finally, good jobs were bestowed upon the most loyal of the machine participants. Patronage was criticized by reformers during the Progressive Era, but for earlier immigrants, one function of the machine was "that of providing alternative channels of social mobility for those otherwise excluded from the more conventional avenues for personal 'advancement'" (Merton 1957, 76).

Obviously, women like Josefina Ortega, Marta Correa, and María Luisa Soto display a connectedness that resembles aspects of the urban machine. Soto stayed in the community, was a member of her neighborhood, and struggled side by side with her neighbors for "divisible" benefits. She didn't fight abstractly for improved housing *policies*; she joined women in cleaning up abandoned public-housing units and then watched women move into the new apartments at Christmastime. Marta Correa used her personal connectedness with *la gente del pueblo* to rally voters and acknowledged asking for personal favors in return. The blending of social, cultural, and political events so crucial to Latino mobilization resembles, at least in retrospect, the social–political affairs of an earlier era.

There are even a few structural similarities: most of the abovementioned individuals are strong supporters of the Democratic Party in Massachusetts. Ortega and Soto, along with their male counterparts, have received awards for their contributions to the community. They have worked to increase voter turnout by using megaphones on car roofs, a method typically used by male political workers.

"So what's the difference?" one might ask. Despite all the stylistic and structural similarities, there are tremendous differences between the machine politics in the era of the European immigrants and the politics of connectedness employed by Latino immigrants in Boston today. Some of the behavioral and stylistic differences are subtle; the motivational and structural differences are more clearcut.

While women like Ortega, Soto, and Correa do deliver voters and supporters for public events, often at the behest of party leaders, they do not take jobs in exchange. In fact, the most effective mobilizers build their reputations on refusing to be "bought." Getting something for the community played a role in early machine politics, but the linchpin of the urban machine was concrete benefits for the ward leaders themselves. The good jobs some of the male Latinos interviewed have received may reflect a remnant of patronage: spokespersons then and now receive awards, public recognition, and jobs. However, Latina women in particular are unlikely to maneuver for, or receive, a patronage job, despite their mobilizing effectiveness.[32]

Gender differences are even greater when the principle of the exchange of favors is examined. Latina women explicitly and implicitly adhere to the rule: *"Los favores no se cobran"* ("Don't ask to be repaid for a favor"). There is no "currency of exchange" (an important feature of machine politics); "favors" are not extracted for party loyalty or the vote. There is a subtle difference between Correa feeling she can turn to a City Hall liaison for a favor after helping him out and a ward boss keeping track of who owes what to whom.

Motivational differences also exist between the connectedness and group-oriented politics of Latina women and white, male, machine politics. I found that Latina women were less concerned with power and control.[33] For them, politics is not deals and manipulation. In fact, the theme of "I'm not political"—especially when expressed by very politically active women—was a direct rejection of that side of politics. For Latina women, politics is a process (interactions, interpersonal relations); the connections themselves are as important as the product (the vote, political rewards). Self-interest is subsumed under community interest. Even more important, a great number of Latina women, for example, Julia Santiago, Aracelis Guzmán, and Inez Martínez, do not operate like Ortega, Soto, and Correa. Their methods bear even less resemblance to those of machine politics.

Santiago, Guzmán, and Martínez are *gente* who work politically—they build on informal networks to educate, engage, and cooperate with others for social change. They do not, however, work for a party at all; they do not focus on the vote or campaigns. They have none of the "political connections" that make up part of the connectedness of women like Ortega, Soto, and Correa. For Santiago, Guzmán, and Martínez, politics *is* connectedness; politics is change within the individual that leads to change by working with others. In addition, there are other women, both professional and *gente*, who see politics as an interactive process of social change, cooperation within informal networks, and as personal change and growth.[34]

The differences discussed thus far are subtle qualitative differences—differences in degree, perhaps. The structural differences are much clearer: there is no machine. Machine politics includes a hierarchical chain of command, well-oiled gears, cadres of workers at the beck and call of the higher-ups. While certain male community leaders like Julio Herrera[35] and Tito Morales might claim to have the ear of City Hall and be able to get workers out on election eve to rally the Latino voters, Latina women like Josefina Ortega, María Luisa Soto, and Marta Correa neither follow the orders of a higher-level ward boss nor command a league of underlings to do their bidding. They do not have the resources of the male-dominated machine, and they do not use power and control as it did.[36] The women are *connectors*, not underlings or bosses; they speak individually and collectively, but as equals.

Latina women use connectedness, not for personal advancement, but to respond to need, to engender participation. Latina women weave the personal and political development of Latinos into their mobilizing work. In sum, Latina women do use some of the methods of machine politics. There is no urban machine, however, nor are there Latina ward bosses in the Latino community in Boston. The lack of a hierarchical chain of command is an important structural difference between the connectedness of the Latina women and the male-dominated machine politics of old. And, as I show in the next chapter, collectivity, rather than the hierarchical organization of machine politics, is the cornerstone of Latina women's vision of participatory politics.

THREE

Collectivity Versus Hierarchy

Nosotras participamos como grupo—participamos todas.
(We participate as a group—we all participate.)

—*Dalia Ruiz*

Communities—and even political movements—succeed not because of hierarchical lines of command, but because groups of people build the day-to-day connections that sustain them.

—*Martha A. Ackelsberg,* Free Women of Spain

Dalia Ruiz has been a student at the Mujeres Unidas en Acción women's center for three years. She is forty-two years old and came to the mainland United States from the island of Puerto Rico almost twenty years ago. An outreach worker from Mujeres[1] invited her to sign up for the ESL (English as a second language) program. At the center, she receives advice about her son, learns English, and develops personal skills *"en cuanto a como relacionarme con las demás personas, porque yo antes ¡no hablaba con nadie!"* ("insofar as how to relate to other people, because, before, I didn't talk to anybody!"). Although Ruiz had been interested in politics in Puerto Rico, reads the newspaper, and follows some of the issues here, she always felt "too shy" to participate in anything more than mere voting until she arrived at Mujeres Unidas.

As a member of groups from Mujeres Unidas, Ruiz has supported legislation submitted by the Latino state legislator to combat the English as the Official Language movement. While she has not decided her personal position regarding abortion, she also participated in the march to show solidarity with pro-choice women on International Women's Day. As a member of the public relations committee at Mujeres Unidas, she was chosen by the committee to contact State Representative Nelson Merced to ask him to use his influence so that Mujeres could move to larger quarters. She also went on *una caminata*—a march—to protest the increasing violence in Latino neighborhoods in Boston. (A young Latino boy had been shot to death in her neighborhood.)

Ruiz attributes her expanded political participation to the group-oriented activities and collective organization of Mujeres Unidas en Acción. She spontaneously connected her increased participation to "doing things together": *"Yo voy a todas las protestas que han habido . . . porque de aquí mismo nos llevan; forman un grupo y nos llevan a todas las protestas que se dan. Nosotras participamos como grupo—participamos todas"* ("I go to all the protests that there have been . . . because they take us right from here; they form a group and they take us to all the protests that are held. *We participate as a group—we all participate"* [emphasis added].

Collective Methods, Collective Organization, and Latino Politics

Much of liberal democratic theory views politics as an individualistic set of actions, and most political organizations are organized hierarchically. According to this theory, the "truly political is the formally structured" (Ackelsberg 1991, 172). An examination of political participation in the Latino community in Boston reveals that (1) the most successful mobilizing experiences in the Latino community are those that involve "doing things together," not those that rely on isolated, individual initiative; (2) collective methods and collective organizational structures promote a more participatory model of politics; and (3) Latina women stress collective methods and collective organization to a much greater extent than do Latino men.

For many Latinos, and new immigrants in general, migration causes a disruption of communal and social ties. Social integration is a critical prerequisite for participation in explicitly political activities. Familiarity with where to go for personal and community problem-solving, who is receptive to Latino issues, and which government institutions offer useful services contributes to a sense of political efficacy. Group-oriented, collective methods provide democratic experiences and social integration, thus leading the way for participation in politics. In fact, communal participation—the participation in community institutions, groups in the workplace, and informal groups—is an essential component of participatory politics.[2] Through this larger view of politics, many of the barriers to political participation can be overcome.

Cuban communities in parts of the United States like Miami demonstrate that the creation of communal ties within an ethnic enclave, and the use of collective action, can result in considerable political clout for Latino communities. On the more personal level, collective methods overcome fears, insecurities, and self-doubts. Doing things together with friends, neighbors, and trusted colleagues provides information about new situations, new people, new issues. At the most basic level, doing politics together decreases the chance of getting lost on the way to a political event. Doing things together fulfills social needs while new political skills are forged. Political socialization theory has long held that emotional ties within peer groups play a major role in stimulating political participation and providing experiences in political education.[3]

Virtually all the Latino participants I observed at community events held outside of Latino organizations came as part of a group. Recall the group of *ancianos* (old folks) described in the previous chapter that sings Puerto Rican songs at many social events. The members of this group were active participants in the workshop on organizing the community around Latino educational problems at a conference sponsored by the Comité de Familias Latinas de Boston in April 1990. Members of this group also gave testimony about proposed budget cuts at a Hispanic town meeting held at Boston City Hall in October 1989. It is unlikely that, alone, these individuals would have participated at these meetings. Simply negotiating the dark, rough, concrete-walled corridors of Boston City Hall or the imposing marble labyrinths of the Massachusetts State House is an intimidating task for most people unfamiliar with such public buildings.

Developing political activism from personal relationships within existing groups may also be more effective than formal organizational membership drives. There is time and opportunity within existing groups to explore the reasons for political actions to a greater extent than during contacts between strangers. Having to relate to strangers inhibits questions, contrary opinions, and the expression of doubts.

Juana Oviedo, for example, describes herself as very unpolitical. Nevertheless, she was part of a group effort that made a videotape for the state legislature. In this videotape, clients from a Latino community agency, the Comunidad Boricua en Acción (Boricuan [Puerto Rican] Community in Action), described how useful they found

77

agency services; the group then went to the State House and pro-tested the budget cuts. What caused this "apolitical" woman to par-ticipate in a relatively sophisticated political effort? She participated because Angelina, the leader of Oviedo's support group, explained the cuts and organized the group of clients to join the protest.

Participation in political lobbying is thus generated via collective methods. Oviedo speaks out on the videotape and advocates her con-victions with a certain passion. She recalls what she said:

> *Quieren quitar esa ayuda y ¡es imposible que quiten eso! Porque ima-gínese tanta gente pobre y los viejitos—como ahora misma yo—que no tengo a nadie, y yo voy y me oriento con ellas. . . . Si quitan eso, los pobres viejitos que no tienen quien les ayude. . . . Yo le digo, yo voy a todo. Yo no sé hablar bien, pero yo digo, "¡No!"*

> They want to take that help away, and it's impossible that they would take it away! Because, imagine how many poor people —and the little old people—look at me, even—I who don't have anyone, and I go [to the support group] and they help me.[4] . . . If they take that away, those poor old people who don't have anyone to help them. . . . I tell you, I go to everything. I don't know how to speak well, but I say, *"No!"*

What was the appeal of the collective approach for Juana Oviedo? Part of it was a combination of self-interest and collective concern.

> *Porque él que no ha vivido la pobreza—y él que no ha pasado—no puede dar opinión ninguna, pero los que hemos vivido en carne propia lo que nos ha pasado, tenemos que ayudar a los otros hermanos.[5]*

> He who has not lived in poverty and he who has not gone through it— has no right to give an opinion, but those of us who have been through it ourselves, we have to help our brothers and sisters.

Throughout our interviews, Oviedo makes it clear that, as an individ-ual, it would never have occurred to her to join a protest, let alone speak on a videotape destined for public officials. The combination of social connectedness and collectively sponsored activities pulled Oviedo into political participation, translated her message into the language of the politicians and government officials, and involved her in influencing public policy through political action.

Oviedo would score low on traditional measures of participation if interviewed by someone from the school of "civic culture." She would list no formal organizational memberships because these par-ticipatory events took place in the context of her daily life—with a group of friends and a woman who *leads* but who is not a designated leader within the Latino community. Political activities such as those she participates in are likely to be missed if only formally structured political organizations "count" as political. Guzmán (1976, 129–131), for example, suggests that part of the reason Mexican Americans are called apolitical is because a listing of ethnic mixed-purpose groups misses the political intent of what are perceived to be merely social groups.

Why does the collective method work better than methods rooted in individualistic initiative? The women from Mujeres Unidas en Acción as well as many others of *la gente del pueblo* feel the group method pulls them into political participation because it meets social needs and breaks down the barrier of social isolation. Thus, Dalia Ruiz explains why she joins the groups at Mujeres Unidas:

Porque a mí me gusta participar en todo lo que ellos hacen . . . porque la verdad es que, cuando una está sola en la casa una se pone a pensar, a pensar, y se puede volver loca. Y yo lo mejor que hago es distraerme. Salgo acá, y me distraigo.

Because I like to participate in everything they do here . . . because, the truth of the matter is that, when you're alone in your house, you sit there and think, and think, and you can go crazy. And I—it's better to enjoy myself. I come here, and I enjoy myself.[6]

Gender and Organizational Structure

It is the Latina women—not the Latino men—who stress group-oriented, collective methods to stimulate political participation in the Latino community in Boston. In thirty-four separate segments of the interviews, Latina women discussed the need for "doing things as a group," "doing politics together," "*participando como grupo,*" and "a more collective way." Latino men, on the other hand, consistently ignored the role of group ties in political-mobilization methods, and they generally operate within hierarchically structured organizations. With their focus on the politics of elections, positions, and power, *Latino men did not discuss collective methods or collective organizational structures at all.* In addition, their political methods often displayed a hierarchical structure.

Latina Women and Collective Organizational Structures. Andrea del Valle uses the term *collective* to describe the organizing efforts of Latina women. She was active in a group formed to protest police inaction in a domestic violence case that resulted in the death of a Puerto Rican woman. Del Valle says, "We were very persistent, and that's very important. You show people that process, *that you have collective decisions.* We met every day. We'd get out of work, have

79

dinner, talk about different things, get new information" [emphasis added].

In addition, this group had an explicitly collective, not hierarchical, structure. Legal, political, informational, and relational needs of the group were shared: "So there were three, four, different levels, and everybody was in charge of some area." For Latina women, collective political methods are linked to collective organizational structures—structures that deemphasize the role of the leader. Del Valle resists any efforts to designate a "leader"—either of this group or of another organization she had been instrumental in forming. Aracelis Guzmán, a Mexican-American woman who became active in Latino educational struggles, likewise identifies as a problem in community mobilization the overemphasis on "leaders." She prefers a more collective approach:

> *Te ven así como un rayo de luz y entonces esta persona se convierte en* ¡LA LÍDER! *Y aunque es cierto que hay personas que tienen una visión, ¿verdad? que tienen una serie de destrezas que les permite conmover más allá—decir, "Miren, lo que tenemos que hacer es esto y esto y esto," yo creo que debe ser más colectivo—de que debe haber màs de una cabeza.*

> They see you like a ray of light and then this person becomes THE LEADER! And even though there are clearly people who have a vision, right, who have a set of skills that enable them to stir people up later on—to say, "Look, what we have to do is this and this and this," I believe that it should be more collective—that there should be more than one head.

The predominance of hierarchically structured organizations is often taken for granted by those who work in traditional settings. Del Valle recalls how hard the police, individuals from City Hall, the newspapers, and various officials found it to work with a group organized collectively. She echoes Pateman (1989) and Ackelsberg (1991), who contend that the more collective politics of women is often devalued and considered "disorderly" rather than political. Del Valle recalls: "We were in the newspapers, in the news—so, in the beginning they'd call us a group of 'angry Hispanic women,' because we didn't have a name." Del Valle, in a move consistent with participatory models of democracy, also resisted the efforts of officials to designate a "leader." She seems to concur with Barber: leaders that facilitate the founding of participatory groups should simply fade away. Barber (1984, 239) also advocates revolving leadership, and the selection of leaders by lot.

The emphasis on collective methods and collective organizational

80

structures is not limited to *feminist* Latina women like Andrea del Valle and Aracelis Guzmán, or to influential Latina activists. Latina women who are not influential also stress the need for group-oriented political activities; they are also more likely to participate in politics when organizations are structured collectively, not hierarchically.

Latino Men and Hierarchical Organizational Structures. Latino men, in contrast, develop hierarchical, "chain of command," organizations. The portrait of Tito Morales in the previous chapter, for example, is of an effective political organizer who developed personal connections to City Hall. His election campaign work reveals a hierarchically organized group of campaign workers. A group of friends operate, to some extent, as his precinct workers. For example, when asked if he distributed flyers or went door to door during election campaigns, he replied firmly:

> No, no. Me daban hojas sueltas para que yo hiciera campaña. Yo se los daba aquí a los amigos para que ellos lo hicieran. Yo no tengo que—yo tengo gente aquí que trabaja para mí.

> No, no. They gave me flyers to use in campaign work. I would give them to my friends here for them to hand out. I don't have to—I have people here who work for me.

Morales's role is not to distribute flyers; that job belongs to his "people." Morales's role is to circulate through the neighborhood: *"Voy chequeando por todos lados"* ("I check around") to identify who needs help with the voting process and to explain the ballot and the voting machine. Julio Herrera was another man who operated within a "chain-of-command"—hierarchically organized—political structure.

Portrait of Julio Herrera:
Hierarchy and the Chain of Command

Julio Herrera was a Puerto Rican who moved to Boston in the early 1970s. He was not of *la gente del pueblo*, but was well to do and he attended an Ivy League school. Herrera was hired to be the director of Comunidad Boricua en Acción, the Latino agency that grew out of an urban renewal struggle in the South End. This struggle, which resulted in the development of a Latino residential and commercial complex known as Villa Victoria, will be described in detail in the next chapter.

During his tenure as director of the Comunidad Boricua en Acción, Herrera worked tirelessly to support the agency and the Latino residents in the South End neighborhood. He represented Latino interests "downtown" (i.e., at the mayor's office and the State House) and became a spokesperson for the Latino community. Juan Maldonado remembers Herrera very well: "He understood that his role was to be the bridge between the community and downtown. . . . He also understood that the only results he could come back with every time he went downtown were *good* results. And he had to demonstrate to the community, 'Look, what I'm doing is going to get us something.' And he did that." Julio Herrera, in other words, delivered. He was instrumental in the development of the garden apartments that make up part of the Villa Victoria complex. He also had a vision—and was able to articulate that vision to the community; according to Maldonado, Herrera would say, "This is the vision I have of Plaza Betances [the plaza at the heart of Villa Victoria]. I have a vision where we're going to have retail stores down here. I have a vision of where we're going to move the post office down here. One of these days, we'll be able to eat at a restaurant around here. . . . And one of these days we'll have a cultural center."

Julio Herrera "got results." Concrete benefits, tangible goods, and the articulation of a vision enhanced Herrera's reputation as a "mover and a shaker" in the Latino community. He also had a side that was even more explicitly political: in many ways, he functioned like a Latino ward boss. Herrera held candidate nights; he "would fill up the Epiphany Church with all the residents; he would do it upstairs in the elderly housing projects," recalls Juan Maldonado. Latinos turned out to these political events because Herrera asked them to personally. He would also campaign for candidates he supported. Maldonado says that Herrera could get out the Latino vote because he tapped into the culture: "How do they move? Puerto Rico and Latin America are influenced very much by—your pattern of voting, your pattern of doing things, is influenced by—spokespersons. Not just Puerto Rico—if you go and you look at the work of Councilman Alatorre in California, the late Willie Velázquez in Texas, and so on, folks move by their spokesperson." Herrera would walk through Villa Victoria with a candidate and say, "Look, here's somebody I'm going to give my vote to," and they would go for it. He also had access to political machinery of sorts. As director of a major Latino agency, Herrera transformed agency staff into a cadre of campaign workers. Maldonado explains, "He would have his social workers, he would have his housing advocates, he would have his youth counselors, he would have all his 'machinery' actively move

[Latino residents of Villa Victoria] to participate in the electoral process."

Julio Herrera "got things" for the community. He extracted concessions from City Hall; he helped develop the later stages of Villa Victoria. He had connections to the mayor of Boston and used these connections well. He also cared deeply about the community. As one woman reflected on Julio Herrera, she said, "He was a brilliant and complex man; he was not into self-promotion." To the shock of the Latino community—especially to his friends and fellow activists—Herrera died suddenly in 1986.

Julio Herrera used Latino agency staff as a cadre of campaign workers. He galvanized his staff on election day and turned them into ward workers. Herrera's politics, in contrast to those of Latina women, were a "chain-of-command" method of politics. Herrera was not a community mobilizer. In addition, like Tito Morales, Herrera relied heavily on Latina women to bring people to the rallies, candidate nights, and voting booths. He had agency staff get out the vote, but the community mobilizations that led to the development of Comundad Boricua en Acción and Villa Victoria were masterminded by a Latina woman, Luz Cuadrado.[7] And, like Morales, Herrera was comfortable following a tradition of telling people whom to vote for, unlike certain women, who had battles over the issue of coercing Latinos into voting as a bloc.

Clearly, Latina women and Latino men differ substantially in their emphasis on collective methods and collective versus hierarchical organizational structures. What is less clear at this point is whether there are, in fact, any negative implications of hierarchical structures for participatory politics. Why are collective methods and structures preferable? Do hierarchical structures indeed stifle political participation?

Hierarchy and the Suppression of Participation

The organization of public forums suppresses participation through the elite (and typically male) control of the agenda and by the hierarchical structure of most meetings. Public meetings frequently begin with formal presentations and speeches by "experts." Those in the audience are structured into the role of listeners. (The word *audience* in fact derives from the verb *to listen* or *to hear*.) Instead of an exchange of ideas among equals, interactions at public forums are shaped and constrained by rules of order. Rarely is interaction in these forums not hierarchically organized; in other words, the pattern of interaction goes from the speaker to the audience and from a recognized member of the audience to the speaker. Time allotted to audience participation is typically limited, and since speakers often exceed their time, participation is reduced even more to a few questions at the very end of a meeting.

The "Hispanic Town Meeting" held at Boston City Hall is a case in point. Organized by a number of men deeply concerned with the current socioeconomic plight of Latinos in Boston, the meeting nevertheless created a structure that stifled community participation. Visualize a formal room with the Boston City Council members aligned at the front of the room and elevated on a dais behind a long table. In front of, and facing, the dais is a lone chair and a microphone. Behind this single chair are many rows of seating for the members of the Latino community and other interested parties. For over two hours, agency directors, for the most part, singled their way to sit in the lone chair. One by one they sat, with their backs to the audience—and they spoke for the community. They spoke eloquently, with passion, but they merely *represented*—both physically and verbally—the community. For the most part, community members did not speak.

It might be argued that the Latino agency directors, in their role of spokespersons, were speaking for the community. For several hours, however, there was no invitation or permission for the people of the community to speak. Andrea del Valle criticizes those people who dominate the public forums: "Sometimes there are so many opportunists in our community that they don't allow—don't allow the community to speak, and they want to speak for the community, and who the hell knows what the hell they say when they go to different places?"

On two occasions during this meeting, isolated individuals did not remain passive, instead challenging the hierarchical physical and symbolic structure of the "town meeting"—and interrupted the proceedings. Tito Morales, for example, strode to the front of the room, declined to sit in the chair, and spoke. Another person challenged the proceedings by asking, "And when will the people have their turn to speak?" These attempts to change the organizational structure were listened to politely, but the structure did not change. For the most part, the time available for genuine participation was very limited, and the people did not speak until the very end; they were structured into silence.

"Political muting"—structured silence—occurs when people are rendered unable to speak, either because of intimidation, a sense of inadequacy, or organizational structures (Warren and Bourque 1985). The experiences of the Comité de Familias Latinas de Boston demonstrate how control of the agenda (Bachrach and Baratz 1962; Lukes 1974) and hierarchically organized structures stifle political participation. The Comité de Familias Latinas de Boston is a grassroots organization founded to confront the superintendent of schools in Boston with a new agenda. While many Latino children attend bilingual education programs, an equally large number attend classes in "mainstream" schools. The dropout rate of Latino children not in bilingual programs is the highest of any group in Boston. Parents feel that the problem is due to a lack of support within the schools. The children attend schools where the principal and virtually all the staff are Anglos who cannot communicate with the parents (many of whom do not speak English). The schools convey to the parents the message, "If you cared you would learn English." The lack of bilingual secretarial and office staff means non-English-speaking parents cannot initiate contact with the school; non-Spanish-speaking office staff serve as gatekeepers.

The Boston public schools have been unwilling or unable to address the impact on Latino families of issues such as teacher and staff seniority: seniority rules prevent the hiring of bilingual staff to replace non-Spanish-speaking staff. Latino parents withdraw—are *literally* muted—when they are unable to discuss their children's education with school staff. The parents are then described as apathetic and lazy.

In addition, the structure of organizations (e.g., Robert's Rules of Order, and the tradition of presentations by experts), when imported into the Latino community,[8] stifles the ability of Latinos to participate fully at meetings and presses them into essentially passive roles. Organizational structure often explains sparse attendance at community meetings; it stifles discourse on the perceived needs of the community and does not build on the Latino style of joining and conversing, which is more fluid, gregarious, and interactive. Whenever I found an "expert" expounding on a given topic—whether domestic violence, school problems, or politics—I found a passive Latino audience. When meetings were organized less hierarchically (i.e., more collectively), many more people joined in the discussion.

The depoliticizing effect of hierarchically organized public meetings was nowhere more evident than at a long-awaited meeting between the Comité de Familias Latinas de Boston and the Boston school superintendent. A large number of Latino parents (eighty to one hundred) attended this meeting. Irrespective of any substantive issues that were resolved at the meeting, the parents' participation was stifled—muted—by the very nature of the process. Formal presentations and rebuttal between the panel and the superintendent took up one-and-one-half of the two hours allotted to the meeting. Parents, many of whom came after work, brought small children, or left children at home, were essentially structured into *listener* roles rather than active, participatory, roles. There was very little time for participation by the very people whose interests were the focus of the meeting. From the people who did have time to speak, however, the extent of their political awareness and passion came through loud and clear.

One woman from Central America, for example, made her grievances known, and despite her limited education she was also able to make complex connections between educational processes in the city of Boston and international politics. She began by demanding to know why, every time there was a new plan for improving the Boston schools, it began with school closings. Last year the school committee closed her child's school, and her daughter had to get used to a new school. Now the new school in the Brighton neighborhood is slated to be closed. She began,

> *En la Brighton—la Brighton ahora ha mejorado aunque hay muchas deficiencias en el programa bilingüe—pero ha mejorado porque yo, hace como cinco años iba a ese lugar, me sentaba, y no había nadie quien me tradujera lo que estaba pasando. . . . Ahora que hay una persona que me* oye, *que me* entiende, *ahora que ya hay un traductor, ahora resulta que lo quieren quitar—una escuela que tiene muchos muchachos, que está en una área* buena, *no entiendo por qué lo van a quitar. . . . Porque eso es lo que pasa en nuestros paises—las universidades se están cerrando—las escuelas—porque no quieren gente estudiada, porque no quieren gente que los pueda, seguramente,* juzgar. [Loud applause] *Y eso es lo que va a pasar en este país.*

In the Brighton school—the Brighton has improved although there are many deficiencies in the bilingual program—but it has improved—because I used to go there, some five years ago, I'd sit myself down, and there would be no one who could translate what was going on. . . . Now that there is a person who *listens* to me, who can *understand* me, now that there is a translator, now of course, they want to take it away—a school where there are many children, that's in a *good* area, I don't understand *why* they're going to take it away. . . . Because this is what goes on in our countries—they're closing the universities—the schools—because they don't want an educated people, because they don't want people who can, surely, *judge* them. [Loud applause] And *that* is what is going to happen in this country.

Apathy? Hardly. Was this woman muted by the structure of the meeting? At this point in time, clearly not. But the message that was communicated to all the other people who spent so much of their time in forced silence was that it was not *their* participation that was valued. The end result was that, at subsequent meetings of the Comité de Familias Latinas, the attendance by *la gente del pueblo* was considerably less than that of professionals and agency staff.[9]

Latino Leadership and Political Participation

When asked why some Latinos do not participate in politics, virtually everyone I met mentioned Latino leadership as a constraint on participation.[10] Interview after interview, complaints emerged about leaders "not doing enough." Aracelis Guzmán faults those who promoted their own aspirations—who were thus "false leaders." Armando Meléndez and Julio Rojas see leaders who "don't give back" to the community. Catalina Torres mentions "unfulfilled dreams"; *caciquismo*[11]—everyone wanting to be in charge—troubles Tamara González.

The use and abuse of power by persons appointed to positions at City Hall, the State House, or to directorships of community agencies were identified as sources of mistrust and resistance to community organization efforts. Rosa López explains:

> I think there's a lack of trust; there's a huge amount of suspicion among the groups within the community. There's a huge amount of suspicion based on facts and reality that certain people—leaders— have surfaced and grabbed ahold of an issue or a certain amount of authority or power and kept others out. Those are *facts!*—people know that has happened—and/or have used politics in the larger sense—American political avenues—to promote themselves—and that's clear and obvious to everyone as well. And I think people *resist* becoming a part of or supporting that unless they're going to also get something out of it.

Julio Rojas says, "In the Spanish community you have a leader at every corner, everywhere. But none of them work as a team; none of them work with priorities. Too many of them want to pursue their private agendas, and too many are looking for a job in government."

On the other hand, there was a simultaneous acknowledgment of the tremendous effort the activists and "leaders" were expending working within the community. Few interviewees were willing to "name names" or expose specific wrongdoings. For the most part, as Rojas says, "99.9 percent of the Hispanic leadership are good people, honest people, people who want to do good for the community."

A dilemma emerges: how to reconcile contrasting pictures of a dedicated, hard-working core of people who spend their professional and private time on community affairs and yet are criticized for their failures? What are some explanations for the apparently self-serving nature of some of the leadership in the Latino community in Boston?

Dilemmas in Latino Leadership. The first explanation of why Latino leadership bears the brunt of community criticism stems from the very definition of the term *Latino leader.* There is a difference between a person who can influence others—achieve a following— and a person who has been *designated* a "leader" by Anglo institutions. The path to Latino political "leadership" in Boston has been, for the most part, through Anglo appointments to positions at City Hall and the State House or through directorships of community agencies.

Antonio Rojas ran for public office and achieved a high-level position in Boston government. He explains that most of the leadership in Boston is concentrated in the social service agencies and that the Anglo institutions, in essence, create the leadership opportunities. He explains: "We're given money and then we hire our Latino leaders. The agency directors become our Latino leaders, because downtown needs a link." Rarely are these designated leaders able to maintain a link to downtown and to the community at the same time.

Julio Herrera was praised by several men as being able to bridge the gap between the "community and downtown." However, he was in fact hired to become a director, and his leadership derived from that position. Camayd-Freixas and Lopez (1983) conclude: "Lacking developed institutional structures, [the Latino] community political systems . . . consist largely of agency politics" (63).

According to Jennings (1984, 80), when asked to define a Latino leader, Puerto Rican activists in New York and Boston focus on people who can represent Latino interests; effectiveness in delivering benefits to the community is not stressed. These "City Hall-oriented" spokespersons then convey the needs and grievances of the Latino community to the appropriate government institutions but have less ability to rally the masses within the Latino community itself.

The second explanation for the criticism of Latino leadership in Boston is best understood in the broader context of the relations between minority leadership and Anglo institutions in general. There is little explicit analysis in political (or social) science literature of the internal politics within minority communities.[12] Black-American leaders have traditionally been pulled between accommodation and struggle (Marable 1983, 186; Travis 1990). The tension between these two poles is played out in the relationship between black leaders and City Hall. For example, "by the creation of an artificial leadership for the black community and the appearance of access and influence through the careful use of limited patronage, [Boston] city hall ensured that segments of the black community remained quiet and loyal" (Jennings 1986, 73). In essence, the small level of patronage (in the form of jobs for the leaders, or grants for agencies) inhibited "the effectiveness of independent black leaders" (73). Thus, within black communities, the apparent "deficiencies" of black leaders really reflect tensions in the structure of urban politics and the sociopolitical context (Walton 1985).

The problems of Latino leadership in Boston—limited community connections and restrictions on how much individuals can accomplish in official positions—are similar to those faced by black leaders. What Jennings (1986) considers "liaison leaders" in the black community, what I call "designated leaders," may represent the community to City Hall but do not actually have much influence to affect policy and do not necessarily have strong ties within their respective communities.

In addition, the vulnerability of designated leaders, whether black or Latino, also inhibits broad-based political participation in the community. The threat of job loss curtails independent political action by black and Latino appointees.[13] One Latino man told me that after participating in a protest at one of the government offices last year, an official threatened the job of one of his relatives. Prohibitions against explicitly political behavior by government employees also discourages political activism,[14] although these prohibitions were routinely waived by the Mayor Kevin White political machine when it served White's own interests.

For Latinos in the Southwest, Guzmán (1976) identifies the sources of criticisms of Mexican-American leaders: "(1) competition among ethnic leaders before Anglo audiences, [and the] (2) surrender of substantive social demands to offers of status and prestige" (195). Latinos—and Latino men in particular—may see progress in their increased visibility in government positions, or even elected office. Once connected to the Anglo power structure, however, the Anglo leadership is able to convince them to desist from any independent mobilization efforts.

The third explanation for the problems of Latino leadership is linked to gender. Three important dynamics emerged in the interviews and at Latino community events: (1) the path to political appointments and designated leadership status by the Anglo political institutions is through community-based agency directorships, (2) the agencies have developed essentially hierarchical organizational structures, and (3) the leaders identified as being "in it for themselves" (i.e., had gotten jobs in government and "abandoned" the community) are, for the most part, men.[15]

These leaders find it extremely difficult to maintain personal connections between both Anglo government institutions and *la gente del pueblo* in ways that facilitate mobilization. Because of resource limitations and hierarchical organizational structures, the Latino agencies involved are unable to support political-mobilization efforts, a point that is discussed in Chapter 6. The people who are independent leaders, in contrast, people who will be followed into political activism, are more likely to be *gente del pueblo* whose political-mobilizing style draws people into politics. These mobilizers are also more likely to be women. These women are the *connectors*—the people who reach out to their friends and neighbors, who issue rallying calls to join in community actions, and who spend the time connecting personal problems to community needs. These connectors gather small groups of people together to attend community functions, blend social and cultural events with political purposes, and make politics part of the daily lives of people in the community.

Gender, Leadership, and Hierarchy. Why has the literature on Latino politics never commented on the gender differences between designated leaders and independent community leaders? A possible reason is that Latina women in their role of political mobilizers have been ignored.[16] Seven of the ten broad-based Latino agencies in Boston are headed by men,[17] and most of the Latino government appointments are given to men. The connectors are, however, for the most part Latina women.[18] Latino agencies play a powerful role in the political life of Latino communities, and how they increase or suppress political participation is a critical question.

I do not claim any conclusive proof of how gender and the leadership of Latino agencies interact to affect political participation in the Latino community of Boston. One theme that emerged from my research, however, is that male directors of agencies tend to be concerned about protecting the power they accrue in their positions. A second, related theme is that concern over jobs and turf discourages participation by members of the community.

The extent to which agency directorships have been a path to government appointments is illustrated by this quote from Jesús Carrillo: "If you look at the leadership, every single person has been a director of agencies, OK? I don't think there are any exceptions around.

Why? Because those were the only institutional bases available to Latinos ten, fifteen years ago here, so the leadership . . . today . . . came through that bottleneck."

Edwin Colina, who has over twenty years experience as both a community organizer and as an appointed official, confirms the gender difference I observed in the designated leadership: Latino men end up at City Hall "because it's men making decisions on who gets hired. . . . The men's club. I think that's a reality—it's a sexist society." Other men, such as Julio Rojas, suggest that having a job within the Anglo structure creates a distance from Latino concerns: these are men who "want to be close to the master."[19]

At least six Latina women specifically discussed the gender of prominent leaders as a constraint on political participation. For example, when Andrea del Valle says, "We have poverty pimps in our community, nobody wants to talk about it, but that's true," she is referring to certain men who defend "their turf" but who don't connect to the community people or to others who are trying to achieve change. Rosa López tells how her voter registration efforts were hampered by leaders "concerned primarily with enhancing their reputation." Aracelis Guzmán describes how male concerns for dominance constrain participation. According to Guzmán, men,

> en cuanto se convierten en líderes [she slaps her hands together sharply], se van solos. Se montan en su caballo y no los puede bajar de ahí. Y eso es muy divisorio, muy dañino . . . porque todo el mundo está así—diciendo que "Sí, sí" [nods several times], aunque en realidad no están de acuerdo con él. Y es la mentalidad de que el hombre—el macho—tiene todas las respuestas.

> when they become leaders [she slaps her hands together sharply], they go off on their own. They get on their horse and you cannot get them down from there. And this is very divisive, very harmful . . . because everyone is there, like this—saying, "Yes, yes" [nods several times], when, in reality, they do not agree with him. And it's the mental set that the man—the macho—has all the answers.

Marta Rosa describes the men who obstructed her unexpected rise to electoral success as having "big egos." Blanca Schoolman criticizes the dominance by a Latino man of a key Latino community program: "People don't want to give up their power."

Catalina Torres describes her experience with male agency directors while she was working with a group to develop projects to benefit the Latino community. As part of the process, she contacted the agency directors for letters of support. The agency directors resisted and complained that she should have come to them first on any project development. She tried to explain to them, "You need this project to go forward, so your people, your constituencies, the people that come to your agencies for you to provide services—they need jobs, they need housing." She describes what happened: "They blew it off. It's like, 'I can't make this phone call now.' Why? I have this saying, 'La envidia mata' ['Envy kills']. La envidia—God!—played such a role in this. People saying, 'Who does she think she is? We were here first. Why is she doing it; why didn't you call on us?'" La envidia—concern about who is going to be first, competition over turf, desire to retain power—got in the way of an economic development project. Who were these people resisting support for the project? She says, "These are the guys."

Male directorship of Latino agencies may contribute to the hierarchical organizational structure of the agencies. In general, hierarchical structures dominate most organizations in the Western world, and the vast majority of these organizations are headed by men. Most of the Latino agencies, despite efforts to involve staff and community members on their boards, operate hierarchically. The physical layout and organizational arrangements serve gatekeeping functions as well. A receptionist greets clients, who must present their business, be screened, make or keep appointments, and function within fairly traditional rules. There are obvious benefits to hierarchical organizational structures: they are efficient and provide clear-cut chains of responsibility and accountability.

Despite any such benefits, in Boston's Latino community at least, different levels of participation exist between Latino organizations, agencies, and meetings organized collectively and those organized hierarchically. For example, at several meetings for women on a variety of topics such as depression, domestic violence, and child rearing, experts gave lengthy lectures or speeches; the audience was quiet until a designated question-and-answer session followed. Attendance at these meetings was sparse, and caseworkers sighed when they shared their frustrations about trying to increase participation. The agencies involved were organized hierarchically and in almost all the cases headed by men.

I anticipate three objections to my proposition that gender, agency leadership, and suppressed participation are linked. The first is that these characterizations may simply be complaints of a disgruntled group of women. My response is that men also identified gender as a problem for participation. When men such as Julio Rojas and Armando Meléndez lament the "private agendas" of agency directors and Latino appointed officials, they are not talking about the women.[20] Rojas attributes the difficulty of male "leaders" to connect with and lead *la gente del pueblo* to their desire to get a good job in government: "I don't believe that most of the people you call leaders have any support in the community. I believe that most of them are not known in the community. . . . Most of them respond to—respond to the power structure, not to the needs of the community. . . . Everybody wants to be close to the master." And Nelson Merced says, "Look at all these issues in the community. *I see all these women—all the leaders—and all the men who are like figureheads, and the men don't deal with the women*" [emphasis added].

A second objection may be that my findings about gender, agency leadership, and participation are unique to Boston. It is certainly possible that this theme does not hold true in other cities. Pantoja and Martell (1989–90) and Bonilla-Santiago (1990) suggest, however, that Latino male concerns over political turf also suppress community participation in New York City and New Jersey. For example, Bonilla-Santiago (1990) describes her efforts to pass legislation establishing three Hispanic women's centers in New Jersey. One stumbling block was the opposition by the directors of the Hispanic agencies, virtually all of whom were men. According to Bonilla-Santiago, the men felt threatened by her efforts to circumvent their power.

A third objection may be that the relationship between male directors/appointees, agency practices, and participation is ambiguous. It is true that I did not trace the historical process by which community organization efforts in the previous decade (with active participation of many Latina women) led to a male-dominated agency directorship. Pantoja and Martell (1989–90), however, describe the collective nature of Latina women's leadership patterns in New York during the early 1970s: "We would meet a lot in each other's homes and we'd eat together. . . . It was that type of environment. We arrived collectively at decisions and helped one another . . . , which is pretty much the way women go about things. You might have the baby in one hand and you're talking on the phone to some politician and then you put it [the phone] down and go tend to the baby" (49). Once Latinas began emerging as leaders, the men started questioning why so many women were in leadership positions; Pantoja and Martell (1989–90) remark, "Later on some of the women I talked to told me, 'I killed myself out there organizing and then when they hired a paid organizer it was a man'" (50). Pantoja and Martell (1989–90) highlight the differences between Latino male and female leadership styles once the men moved into directorships: "The coming of a male leadership made a difference in organizational objectives and philosophy. The main characteristic of functioning [in the male-led organizations] has been a *one-person, hierarchical and closed-system leadership style, concern[ed] with personal and career goals*" (50; emphasis added).

I cannot say with certainty that this takeover took place in Boston. As I discuss in the next chapter, however, women played a major role in the grassroots mobilization that created Latino community agencies designed to respond to the needs of Latinos in Boston. These are the very agencies now run, most often, by men. The earlier quotes about leaders who "are in it for themselves" and who are looking for good jobs do fit with the picture Pantoja and Martell describe. The path to leadership for Latina women and Latino men and the process by which community organizations become led by men is a subject for future research.

Political participation is constrained by perceptions in the community that Latino directors and appointed officials operate in their own self-interest or in the interests of the Anglo power structure, as opposed to the interests of the community. The consensus among the activists, however, is that the designated leaders, while certainly concerned about power and turf, do not operate for their own self-promotion alone. Regardless of their concern for position and job security, the men in high positions care about the community, struggle for the community, and use their positions (to the extent possible) to get benefits for the community.

The problem is that the agencies themselves, and their directors, are unable to play a larger role in political mobilization because of structural constraints. Jones (1972) and Jennings (1986, 73), for example, suggest that leaders in the black community are often selected for nominal positions *precisely* to defuse their mobilizing power and then are prevented from continuing the community efforts that brought them to the attention of the Anglo elites in the first place. A similar process may occur for Latinos in Boston. Jesús Carrillo says that the Latino community is too hard on its leaders. The men who have achieved access to supposedly "high" positions in government are actually only at the middle-management level; their actual influence on government policies and the benefits they can wrest from the public institutions they work for are extremely limited. In addition, competition for funds and the limited resources in a shrinking economy (to be discussed in Chapter 6) decrease the actual leverage of Latino leaders in determining public policy.

Latina Women and Collective Organizational Structures

Collective organizational structures are inherently more participatory because participation is built into all levels of organizational operation. Rather than a stratification of administrators, workers, and clients or receivers of service, all who are concerned with the goals of the organization join together in planning and running the organization. Budgetary decisions, service or product decisions, and procedural decisions are the responsibility of everyone concerned. Boards of directors in collective organizations do not, under ideal situations, include merely a few token clients or recipients of services who listen passively and object or advise occasionally. Members of the organization are valued as contributing on an equal level despite differences in class, education, and background.

Collectively structured organizations are more participatory, not only because of these structural differences, but because they generate new roles for individuals—and these new roles are essentially political. When clients and workers of agencies make decisions with others about hiring, budgeting, and policies, the distribution of power shifts and new skills develop. When community members move from passive audience roles to active participants in determining organizational procedures and practices, expectations rise and are asserted. Changes in beliefs about personal efficacy—about one's ability to achieve change—occur. Role changes translate into political action when organizations transfer new skills into political struggles.

The following portrait of Mujeres Unidas en Acción illustrates the way collective organization enhances political participation for Latina women, in contrast to the suppressive effects of hierarchical organizational structures. I suggest that, at least in Boston, Latina women's organizations are more likely to be organized collectively than are male-run organizations or meetings.

Portrait of Mujeres Unidas en Acción: Collective Organization and Political Participation

Mujeres Unidas en Acción is a nonprofit Latina women's organization in the Dorchester area of Boston. It was founded in 1979 as an offshoot of a weatherization program. At that time, the federal government responded to the energy crisis by funding programs to teach low-income homeowners and tenants how to weatherstrip their dwellings and install insulation. The goal of the programs was to curb consumption of home-heating oil. When lack of fluency in En-

95

glish was identified as a barrier to program participation for low-income Latina women, English as a second language (ESL) classes were added. Programs have grown to include a wide range of services: literacy in Spanish, literacy in English, support and counseling, and a variety of forums, *charlas* (chats, discussion groups), and minicourses. Funding comes from city and state government, foundations, and fund-raising efforts. Prior to the current round of state budget cuts, eighty to one hundred women participated in the programs, and child care was provided for about thirty-five children.

Over a period of months, I sat in the waiting room of Mujeres Unidas, joined Latina women at community protests, observed the women's forays into the legislative chambers at the Massachusetts State House, and participated in a *charla* on *La Política y la Mujer Latina* (Politics and the Latina Woman). I also formally interviewed five women from Mujeres Unidas en Acción.

The first thing one notices upon entering Mujeres is how different the ambiance is from most other agencies. Upon entering virtually all agencies, whether Latino or Anglo, you are confronted by a receptionist—a gatekeeper—and a more or less quiet waiting room. You state your purpose and whom you wish to see, and you are told to wait until you can be attended to. Climbing the stairs into the modest quarters that is home to Mujeres Unidas, in contrast, you hear the reverberation of multiple voices; you enter and see many women talking to each other in small groups. Staff and students are not clearly distinguishable; this is not surprising since some of the women begin as students and graduate into some type of work position. Children drift through the group while waiting for the day care program to begin. Latin American food is cooking on a hot plate; women gather together to eat and talk. It is clearly a place of comfort and camaraderie.

Mujeres Unidas offers many different kinds of services. It is also organized as a collective. All staff members, including the person designated as "director" (for outside funding purposes), receive the same salary. Decisions are reached collectively, with students and staff participating. Even the educational programs function collectively: curriculum for the ESL and Spanish literacy classes is developed interactively with students, who discuss what they need to know and how to learn it.

The organizational structure of Mujeres Unidas en Acción stimulates political development and participation through its collective orientation. Participation is institutionalized at all levels. Student members are encouraged to participate in running the organization by being members of the board of directors; 60 percent of the board is composed of low-income Latina women. They also rotate through all meetings of the collective and participate by choice and by lot in various committees: Evaluation, Planning, and Personnel; Fund-Raising and Special Events; Development, Maintenance, and Dissemination; and Public Relations. Latina women are selected or volunteer to serve as spokespersons for the organization. All members are expected to participate in the weekly *charlas* and to go out into the community as part of lobbying, protesting, and giving testimony at political events.

Collective, as opposed to hierarchical, organizational structures encourage political participation by exposing women to democratic, participatory experiences in a safe environment. The freedom to express themselves and to develop opinions and decisions is very different from the muting effects of formal presentations common in the hierarchical structures that typify male-dominated organizations.

In response to my question whether the women participate in the community affairs forums, Julia Santiago says, "*Sí, se conversan más. . . . De cierta manera es como si se sientieran más libres de hablar, como que 'Aquí no tengo que tener tabú' . . . que no la estamos criticando"* ("Yes, they talk more. . . . In a way it's like they feel freer to talk, as if 'Here there's no taboo' . . . that we are not criticizing them").

The Latina women at Mujeres Unidas en Acción participate actively in all aspects of the organization and turn their efforts outward into the larger political system. Within the collectively structured organization, Latina women learn new roles, join together, and overcome their fears and cultural expectations.

Collectivity is also connected to social change. The goal of the participatory experiences at Mujeres Unidas en Acción is to develop critical thinking. According to Paolo Freire's (1970) liberation pedagogical theory, which serves as the ideological underpinnings of Mujeres Unidas, critical thinking leads to action—"women united in action."[21] Young and Padilla (1990) write of the women at Mujeres Unidas: "When knowledge leads to action, social change is achieved, because 'one makes one's presence known'" (16).

Collectivity: A Prelude to Community

One of the lessons to be learned from the collective methods of Latina women and the collective organizational structures specifically illustrated by Mujeres Unidas en Acción is that participatory models of politics depend on people working together. Groups of individuals create supportive structures that generate, rather than suppress, political participation. In building on the interpersonal connections that exist within small groups, participatory experiences occur.

Collective methods and structures also contribute to participation in another way—by creating a sense of community. Collectively organized groups are intrinsically linked to the idea of community. The rejection of authority and hierarchy that marked the early civil rights movement in the United States is an example where the participants aimed for the ideal of the "beloved community" (Evans 1980, 41). Mujeres Unidas en Acción creates a community for its members—a community of support, encouragement, and empowerment. Through participatory experiences within the organization, individuals take on roles and develop skills that increase participation in the broader community as well.

FOUR

Community and Citizenship

At the grassroots—at the community level— Latina women have been the major force for change.

—*Julio Rojas, Puerto Rican community activist*

Citizenship is the "lost treasure" of American political life.[1]
—*Mary G. Dietz, "Context Is All: Feminism and Theories of Citizenship"*

In traditional, liberal democratic theory, the term *community* seems narrowly defined as a collection of individuals bound by geographical proximity, as in the "Jamaica Plain community" or the "South End community" in Boston; or by racial and ethnic characteristics, as in the "Latino community" or the "black community." *Community* also comes to mean a type of political entity through which individual interests—held in common—are asserted; Ackelsberg (1988, 298) suggests that, under liberalism, *community* comes to mean merely a group of individual interest maximizers. Within such a limited concept of community, diversity and dissension are suppressed in the pursuit of common goals and the general will.

Likewise, in liberal democratic theory, *citizenship* is narrowly defined to mean legal status bestowed upon the individual by the sovereign state and conferring certain rights within the legal/political system. Legal status is granted, for the most part, on the basis of national territorial boundaries, place of birth, and family relationships. Under the narrow definition of citizenship as a social contract between the individual and the state, the political expression of citizenship is reduced to a limited set of behaviors. According to Dietz

99

(1989), "Democracy is tied more to representative government and the right to vote than to the idea of the collective, participatory activity of citizens" (5).

In theories of participatory democracy, on the other hand, community becomes something more than a collection of individuals bound by geographical proximity or ethnic and racial characteristics, and citizenship becomes a "dynamic relationship among strangers who are transformed into neighbors, whose commonality derives from expanding consciousness rather than geographical proximity" (Barber 1984, 223). Community and citizenship, therefore, do not simply describe geographical or legal characteristics of individuals or groups of individuals but rather emerge from collective participation in the affairs of a group of people linked together interactively. Community, citizenship, and participation are thus in a dialectic relationship: "To participate *is* to create a community that governs itself, and to create a self-governing community *is* to participate. Indeed, . . . the two terms *participation* and *community* are aspects of one single mode of social being: citizenship" (Barber 1984, 155; emphasis in original). Thus, in any vision of a more democratic, a more participatory America, the concepts of community and citizenship are intricately intertwined.

Feminist theories of citizenship also question the way masculine experiences have often shaped the definition of citizenship and community (Jones 1990). According to feminist theeory, the emphasis on citizenship as legal rights reflects male concerns for legitimacy and individualism. The concern for legitimacy may also be tied to the "competitive norms of capitalist culture" (Jones 1990, 807), since property rights of inheritance traditionally belong to legitimate heirs alone. When male concerns for rights and legitimacy dominate the discourse about citizenship, the focus becomes less on maximizing citizen participation and more on deciding which groups should be recognized as citizens and which should be excluded. Gender, race, and class become subordinated (Jones 1990, Young 1990), politics becomes exclusionary, and participation is suppressed.

For feminists, a citizenship based on equality, mutuality, and consensual, face-to-face relationships has as its goal the desire to maintain community while it protects individuality (Jones 1990) and to develop collectivity while respecting diversity (Young 1990, Ackelsberg 1991). Community is built out of personal relationships, and citizenship is more than a set of interactions between individuals and state institutions. A feminist vision also calls for the inclusion of groups commonly excluded from citizenship, not only from legal citizenship, but also from the opportunity to contribute to and to shape the discourse about citizenship and community. Two such groups are women and those immigrants who come to the United States without legal documents—"illegal aliens."

Community, Citizenship, and the Latino Experience

A crucial question in any analysis of the Latino political experience is: How does one generate political participation in a community characterized by diversity and a large number of members who are not citizens (when citizenship is narrowly defined as legal status based on territorial borders)? In essence, Latinos in Boston, as in many other parts of the United States (and as is true for many other groups of people), do not so much *belong* to a "found" (or ascribed) community but seek to create a community (Friedman 1990, Weiss 1991). In such a community, diversity is not something to suppress in the interest of political unity but reflects a reality that must be built upon. Latinos in Boston also struggle with the task of developing participatory citizenship among people who have no legal status— who, in common parlance, are "illegal aliens" or, using a term preferred by many Latinos, "undocumented immigrants."

A second question, less often addressed, is: What role does gender play in the task of creating community and developing a more participatory model of citizenship? Observations of Latinos in Boston reveal that women and men promote the creation of community and the development of citizenship to substantially different degrees; this difference is similar to the way, as discussed in Chapter 2, gender determines the extent to which politics is defined in terms of connection versus positions and status. In this chapter, I discuss two ways in which gender and participatory models of community and citizenship interact.

First, Latina women in Boston emphasize creating community in their recounting of Latino political history, whereas most Latino men focus on more traditional elements of politics such as redistricting, the creation of formal structures, and electoral campaigns. Second, Latina women, through their mobilizing efforts, emerge as the force behind a more participatory model of citizenship—one that transcends legal status.

When political participation becomes reduced, in theory or practice, to measurable behaviors such as the vote, a great deal of political action that is more participatory becomes obscured. When Latina women and Latino men in Boston pondered the question, What efforts have you been involved in to increase the political participation of Latinos, especially *la gente del pueblo*? and were asked to talk about the successes and failures of efforts to mobilize Latinos, a wealth of political action was revealed. In answering these questions, Latina women and Latino men described the political history of Latinos in Boston. Within this history, a pattern emerges of Latina women emphasizing the creation of community. For Latina women, creating community means grassroots politics and the incorporation of large numbers of people into the political process. Latino men, in contrast, create organizational structures that, however important in generating Latino *representation* in government, depend on and generate considerably less participation within the community.

Latina Women Recounting Political History: Villa Victoria and Grassroots Politics

Marisa Robles immediately focuses on grassroots politics when asked for examples of political-organizing efforts by Latinos in Boston. She recalls the community fight against urban renewal in the early 1970s:

> The most successful effort that comes to mind is Villa Victoria. . . . You have the government, I guess it was, come in and build new housing and the Latino residents were going to be evicted, period. They weren't going to have a chance. They fought it, and it was a community grassroots movement and they won. That is, I think, the best model that we have in terms of the Hispanic community—it's really grassroots, and Villa Victoria was built.

In general, it was Latina women who recalled and described in detail the grassroots mobilization of *la gente del pueblo* that resulted in the success of Villa Victoria. In fact, only one male activist discussed Villa Victoria, whereas over half of the women gave historical accounts that *revolved* around Villa Victoria. In addition, *women were twice as likely to specifically use the term* grassroots *to describe historical events.*[2]

Latina women in Boston, through their spoken words in interviews and through their writing, emphasized the grassroots, community-building effort that resulted in the residential development, neighborhood plaza, and group of stores that is Villa Victoria. The history is worth recounting: in the mid 1960s, the Boston Redevelopment Authority (BRA) had developed plans for a parcel of land in the South End—Urban Renewal Parcel 19—that was the geographical heart of the Puerto Rican community at that time. The housing stock was old and dilapidated and merited replacement. The BRA plans,

102

however, required the displacement of virtually all the primarily Puerto Rican residents and the gutting of the community.

The potential loss of housing to gentrification stimulated the greatest degree of participation ever seen in the Latino community then or since. Early efforts included those of white seminarians and activists from the local Catholic church who worked to educate Puerto Rican residents about urban renewal and housing projects. Miren Uriarte (Uriarte-Gaston 1988) describes how these efforts branched out into "intense organizational activity . . . that was directed to the concrete needs of the community" (152).

Uriarte is a Cuban woman who has been a community activist for decades and who has written extensively on Latino community efforts such as Villa Victoria. She stresses throughout her account of Villa Victoria that a key factor in the success of this fight was the participation of the community members. She also points to how participating together in a fight against urban renewal created an ethnic identity—created a Latino community. In taking the place of professionals and organization leaders, the community itself took control of the process. The community meetings grew from small, informal gatherings to events attended by hundreds of Latinos. *¡es-pierta Boricua!* became the rallying call.[3] The role of church activists diminished as the community took over and the Emergency Tenants Council (ETC) was formed.

Ongoing political negotiations between the ETC, city officials, and the BRA resulted, late in 1969, in ETC being designated the developer of the parcel. An alternative plan was proposed to develop the area without displacing the Puerto Rican residents. Over the course of several years, Villa Victoria, an 844-unit housing complex with stores, townhouses, a residential tower, and public spaces, was built. The development of Villa Victoria represents a significant political achievement for the community. With its town square called Plaza Betances and street names like Aguadilla, which bring to mind the *pueblos* of Puerto Rico, Villa Victoria has left a permanent record of Latino community participation on the map of Boston.

Villa Victoria was a triumph of grassroots politics. Grassroots politics, as discussed in Chapter 2, is one of the ways women differ from men in their definition of politics. Grassroots politics, in that context, emphasizes the connection between everyday survival and political action; it also focuses on the connectedness between people at the local level as they struggle for social change. Grassroots politics, in the *present* context of Latino political history, adds another layer of meaning: a group of people struggling together to create a community.

103

Villa Victoria—the name translates to "Victory Village"—was a political victory for the emerging Latino community. The housing development preserved an existing community of Puerto Ricans and created a community center, a symbol of successful community action. This battle and success was also the turning point in the ethnic identification of the Latino community. Developing an ethnic identity was not limited to an emerging sense within an individual of "being Puerto Rican" or "being a Latino," however. The development of an ethnic identity also stimulated a pragmatic response to the lack of bilingual and culturally sensitive social services for Latinos in the city.

In this arena of political action for improved services—the arena of survival politics—the role of Latina women emerges as a salient factor in achieving political success. For example, although men had been hired to lead the ETC, Latina women like Luz Cuadrado led the way for its reorganization into Comunidad Boricua en Acción. The emphasis of Luz Cuadrado was to move beyond building housing to "building community."[4]

Uriarte (Uriarte-Gaston 1988) also recalls the welfare-rights activism of Latina women, in which "over 100 Puerto Rican women from the parcel demonstrated against welfare abuses" (165). Latino activists, many of them Latina women, challenged existing Anglo institutions and were successful in creating a large number of Latino organizations and agencies. Fourteen major organizations developed between 1968 and 1972. Frieda García, for example, was instrumental in creating a bilingual health clinic and another Latino social service organization; García is well known in the community and continues in her organizing efforts today.

Juanita Fonseca is a longtime activist who, despite her ties to Boston City Hall and membership in both the Democratic Party and the Latino Democratic Committee, considers grassroots organizing the key to Latino participation. She spent considerable time describing the grassroots nature of Villa Victoria. She also joined other women in their assertion of politics as community empowerment. She said, "We had a lot of fun; we did a lot of good stuff too. A lot of commotion of people taking control of their lives and empowering them. They stopped the BRA—they said, 'We shall not be moved.'" Fonseca echoes Ackelsberg's (1988) contention that politics is about community, not about individual interest maximization. The mutuality, pleasure, and fulfillment—the "fun" Fonseca refers to—that stimulate participation come from the personal relationships developed by working together. Empowering residents to take control develops, in a reciprocal fashion, the capacity for full citizenship through participating in community struggles.

Latino Men Recounting Political History: Electoral Politics and Redistricting

What did the Latino men present as the political history of Latinos in Boston? With only a few exceptions, Latino men recounted stories about elections, redistricting, and the development of formal organizational structures. *Latino men talked about campaigns and elections in their historical recollections more than twice as much as Latina women did.*[5] Latino men focused extensively on electoral politics as the meaning of politics. In addition, within this focus on elections, the strategizing and maneuvering of a select group of political individuals for power and influence at the upper echelons of the political system was a much stronger theme for them than for the women. Thus, men discussed electoral politics less as maximizing the participation of many people in choosing candidates and elected officials and more as the strategizing of a few leaders to gain Latino access to elected office.

When Armando Meléndez was asked about political participation in the Latino community, he framed his answer in terms of electoral representation: "Politics, per se—we have one state representative in the whole state where there are over 300,000 Hispanics. . . . So that shows me that there isn't very much Latino politics in the state." Men who represent the political elite, like Meléndez, Jesús Carrillo, Edwin Colina, Juan Maldonado, Nelson Merced, Antonio Rojas, and others, work toward the goal of increasing Latino representation in government, and, therefore, their recounting of politics as elections is understandable. But it was not only the male political elite—the leaders—who focused on elections. As indicated in the Introduction, men who hold no political position, who work as janitors, house painters, mechanics, human service workers—men like Luis Hernández, Octavio González, and Jaime Romero—also assumed politics was about elections.

Latino Electoral Politics in Boston. The first Latino from Boston to run for office was Alex Rodriguez, currently the director of the Massachusetts Commission Against Discrimination: he ran for state representative in the South End in 1967 but was defeated. The next effort was by Carmen Pola, who also ran for state representative, this time from the Jamaica Plain–Mission Hill area. Both the South End and Jamaica Plain–Mission Hill areas had relatively high concentrations of Latinos[6] but insufficient support to achieve the election of a Latino to office. Pola's campaign, though it did not result in her election, did, according to former candidate Felix Arroyo, force the winner, Kevin Fitzgerald, to "wake up" to the potential Latino vote; Fitzgerald became more responsive to the Latino constituency in his district and more solicitous of Latino support during his campaigns.

The campaigns of Felix Arroyo, Director of Personnel for the city of Boston, illustrate the problem of campaigning in citywide districts. Arroyo ran for the school committee in 1981 and 1983.[7] In 1981, he won in the primary but finished eighth in the final election with 27,000 votes. He estimates that 3,000 of those votes were Latino votes. In 1983, he ran again; Arroyo reported that his campaign increased the number of Latinos registered to 7,000, and although he lost, he garnered a total of 55,000 votes. Bruno and Gaston (1984) describe Arroyo's contribution to Latino election history: "In many respects, his campaign was the major event in the electoral efforts of Boston's Latinos; in the eyes of many it was more important than the mayoral election" (71). Arroyo was running in an at-large, citywide district; his Latino support was diluted substantially by being dispersed throughout the city.

In 1983, Grace Romero, originally from Panama, was elected to the Boston School Committee. Black voters in the city provided much of her election support, and she made fewer direct appeals to Latino voters. Nevertheless, she participated in Latino voter registration drives at the Puerto Rican Festival (Bruno and Gaston 1984, 71) and represents the first Latino person to be elected in Boston.

The election campaigns of non-Latino candidates have also generated increased Latino voter participation during the past two decades in Boston. As noted above, State Representative Kevin Fitzgerald enjoys Latino support in his district, and he, as well as State Representative John McDonough, has used his Latina legislative aides to provide constituent services to the Latino community.

Mayor Kevin White's relationship with the Latino community began, for the most part, following his close contest in 1967 with Louise Day Hicks. White used all the powers of his political machine to gain support in the black and Latino communities, especially employing patronage, fear, and manipulation of voter registration procedures. His patronage appointments of Latino spokespersons to government positions assured loyalty, or at least reduced Latino criticisms of his policies, and gave the illusion of Latino progress.

White's ability to manipulate voter registration procedures to his advantage affected Latino political participation. When White reconsidered his poor showing among black voters in his 1970 bid for the governor's office, he subsequently smoothed the way for easier voter registration procedures in the black and Latino communities. Frieda García, in her role as a leader of human service reform, also led the way for Latino voter registration during the White era. She documents "how easy it was to register blacks and Latinos to vote during this period. The mayor made it possible for potential voters to be registered in their homes! Workers were allowed to carry official registration rosters to various sectors in the black [and Latino] community" (quoted in Jennings 1986, 70–71).

The non-Latino campaigns that stimulated the most widespread Latino participation were the campaigns of Mel King, a black, progressive community activist and former state representative; he ran for the office of mayor against Kevin White in 1979 and against Ray Flynn in 1983. While some of the more traditional Latino Democrats supported White and Flynn in these elections, King appealed directly to *la gente del pueblo*; succeeded in generating substantial interest in his progressive agenda; and, through his Rainbow Coalition, promoted a model of citizenship in which diversity was welcomed, not suppressed.

Coalition Politics: The Appeal of a Rainbow Coalition. Latinos and blacks in Boston worked together for Mel King's progressive agenda. Coalition politics implies the more or less equal partnership of different groups working together toward a common goal. The Rainbow Coalition developed in the Mel King campaign has other implications as well for Latino politics. Young's (1990) conceptualization of what she calls "differentiated group citizenship" contends that, instead of requiring homogeneity in service of a unified purpose, diverse group interests can be allotted a voice within a given organization, social institution, or movement. Thus, Latinos in Boston did not subsume their diversity of origins or goals to see King elected but rather developed their own "Latinos for Mel King" to see their priorities receive attention as *Latino* issues.

Even more important for the present discussion is the way Latina women created their own arm of the Mel King campaign to push for sensitivity toward and the defense of issues facing Latina women (Cerullo and Erlien 1984). A concept of citizenship that recognizes and draws strength from rather than suppresses diversity is perhaps an even more important lesson to be drawn from the Mel King campaign than his ability to create a coalition between Latinos and blacks as ethnic and racial groups.

Elena Rivas was the Latina campaign coordinator for the Jamaica

Plain neighborhood. She explains her support for Mel King: "Mel's commitment to ensure all people's participation led many women to begin to see our ethnic and racial diversity as indeed a strength rather than a weakness, and helped Latinas to see themselves, often for the first time, as a group with a distinct and important contribution to make" (quoted in Cerullo and Erlien 1984, 55).

Julia Santiago's politics, as discussed in Chapter 2, is a politics of connection—connections between public and private issues and connections between people. When she talks about electoral politics she reveals that, although as a Puerto Rican she is a citizen, she generally does not vote. In her view, the vote rarely achieves significant social change; voting has little effect on policies affecting poor people. She recalls, however, that she once registered and voted for Mel King for mayor of Boston because he reflected her progressive ideology and because he made ties between different groups of people.

Por lo menos tu ves gente trabajando junta—gays, straights, black, white—y era diferente . . . en el sentido que él, pues, por la igualdad racial, trataba de bregar con eso.

At least you see people working together—gays, straights, black, white, and—he was different . . . in the sense that he, well, [was] for racial equality, he tried to struggle with that.

During the 1983 election, the candidacy of Felix Arroyo, a Latino, and the progressive agenda of Mel King brought out Latino voters. Real choices increased voter registration substantially: voter registration after the primary rose by 30 percent and "[Mel] King won 40 of the 48 precincts with significant Latino concentration" (Bruno and Gaston 1984, 71). Campaign activism built on community activism: "Most impressive for us was the kind of political energy mobilized for this period. Old activists who may have been involved in a housing struggle here [i.e., Villa Victoria] or a desegregation fight in the school there came out of the woodwork to get their neighbors out to vote. Best of all, young people knocked on doors, talked to strangers, passed out flyers, and defended their positions in the streets for the first time" (72). Both King and Arroyo lost their respective elections, and citywide electoral participation of Latinos again declined. In 1988, however, Nelson Merced made history by being the first Latino to be elected to statewide office.

The Nelson Merced Campaigns. Nelson Merced was elected state representative for the newly created Fifth Suffolk District, a district that includes parts of the Dudley area of Roxbury and North Dorchester and is one of the poorest areas of the city. It was created as a minority district following a redistricting battle that will be described shortly.

The Latino population makes up 20 percent to 25 percent of the Fifth Suffolk District. Many, however, are new immigrants who are not U.S. citizens. Also, according to campaign activists such as Paul Henry, Carla Gardner, and Felipe Aviles, and Merced himself, the lack of legal citizenship reduces the number of eligible Latino voters in this district to as little as 10 percent.

Merced's 1988 campaign, and his 1990 reelection campaign, were marked by an extensive outreach effort; he knocked on doors several times throughout his district and spoke to potential voters in groups and individually throughout the campaigns. He also developed a very effective campaign strategy in which he appealed to the interests of the diverse groups in his district: blacks, Latinos, gays, and poor white ethnics. These were not campaigns built on Latino participation, however. Merced certainly appealed to the Latino community and obtained financial and other support from Latinos throughout Boston (and from all over the state), but he did not derive winning support from Latinos in his district.

Within this context, Latino voter participation in Boston has not resulted in changes in the conditions of life within the community. Neither has the vote addressed the issue of citizenship and the Latino community; when politics is defined as voting, large numbers of Latinos who do not have legal status or have only legal residency are essentially marginalized from political participation. The potential political influence of increasing numbers of Latinos in Boston is thus diluted because of their legal status and inability to vote.

At the same time, Merced's influence at the city level is also limited, as he himself has recognized at many community forums. Merced is a state representative elected from Boston to the large body of the state legislature; he does not have direct influence on city politics. Despite his election, Latino influence on city government is still limited for the most part to appointed Latino officials. There are still no Latino representatives elected to the city council by the mass participation of Boston's Latino community members.

In addition, whether by coincidence or as a result of redirected efforts, community activism declined in the Latino community in Boston just as electoral efforts increased. The interaction of a decline in community activism and increased efforts by certain Latinos to be elected poses a dilemma for students of political mobilization. Community-building mass mobilizations demonstrate that Latinos, even in small communities of recent immigrants, *can* be mobilized to participate in political action and political protests. This period of mass participation in politics declined after the 1970s were over, however. Uriarte and Merced (1985) conclude that, as of 1985, "in great measure, the community has been demobilized, no longer organized at the levels of earlier years" (22). The withdrawal of federal support and changes in the way the community agencies operate contributed to the decline in community activism, as I will discuss in Chapter 6. Suffice it to say for now that community activism and mass participation declined in the Latino community after the mid 1970s.[8] Yet, just three years later, Nelson Merced became the first Latino to be elected to statewide office. The critical difference between the community activism of the 1970s and the electoral activism of the 1980s is that efforts by Latino individuals to be elected to political office did not depend on mass participation as much as did the grassroots activism of Villa Victoria. Merced's election served, nevertheless, to inspire and galvanize other Latino candidates throughout the state to run for office. Unfortunately, on September 16, 1992, as this book was going to press, Nelson Merced lost the primary election in his bid to retain his seat in the legislature. Some of the signatures on his filing papers were challenged on a technicality, and he was forced to run a sticker campaign. Merced's defeat, after a mere four years in office, demonstrates the tenuousness of relying on redistricting and electoral activism as the vehicles for Latino political empowerment.

Marta Rosa and Diana Lam: Breaking New Ground. The election of Marta Rosa to the school committee of neighboring Chelsea is included here for two reasons. First, her campaign, with its political-mobilization style based on interpersonal relationships as a political resource, surprised and energized the Latino community in Boston. Second, the Latino communities in Boston and Chelsea are closely connected; leaders of both communities consult with each other, the problems faced are not dissimilar, residential mobility assures a flow of community residents across the bridge that separates the two cities, and Boston politics influences, and often overshadows, those of Chelsea.[9]

Rosa is a young woman—thirty-three years old at the time of our interview. She has been active in day care and other areas of social service for many years. As a member of Latino community agency boards and as a woman who was educated in the Chelsea public schools, she ran for and was elected to the Chelsea School Committee in 1989. Latinos make up about 40 percent of that community, although the large number of undocumented Latinos cut the eligible Latino voting population to no more than 20 percent. (These percentages are estimates at best.) Throughout her campaign, Rosa, her

110

husband, her children, her extended family, and Latinos from all over Boston and the state worked endless hours toward her election. Her campaign also drew heavily on her direct personal appeals to large numbers of Latinos throughout Chelsea.

Rosa also made effective use of door-to-door canvassing to increase voter registration, and she and her workers would take interested Latinos directly to the registration center. Whole families made the trek to register in their company. Rosa recalls: "During the day we would knock on people's doors and people would say, 'Yes, I want to register but I don't know how,' and they [the campaign workers] would take them. 'Dress up the kids; we'll wait for you,' and they actually drove them."

Diana Lam is in her early forties and came to the United States from Peru as a college student. She began her work with the Latino community as a bilingual classroom teacher and over the years became influential in bilingual education in Boston. She eventually became a zone superintendent in the Boston school system until she was selected to become superintendent of schools in Chelsea. In the summer of 1991, Lam quit that position to run for mayor of Boston.

Lam's candidacy focused on forging a more progressive, inclusive vision of Boston city politics but was derailed by extensive media coverage of her failure to file the previous year's tax return. As the campaign faltered under this scrutiny, Lam withdrew from the race. Her candidacy marks, however, the first effort by a Latino person to run for the office of mayor of Boston.

Redistricting and Formal Structures: Latino Men and Politics. Electing Latinos and blacks to political office often requires concerted political struggles to redraw district lines that more accurately represent minority population distribution. Formal structures are often created to serve as the vehicles through which redistricting decisions are enacted. Latinos have participated in two such redistricting efforts in Boston.

Latino men and Latina women differ, however, in the degree to which they emphasize the politics of redistricting and formal structures. And the gender difference is considerable: *Latino men were fifteen times more likely to talk about redistricting than were Latina women.* Nine men discussed redistricting a total of fourteen times; only one woman mentioned redistricting as part of the political history.[10]

The transcripts of Jesús Carrillo and Juan Maldonado, for example, consist almost entirely of historical facts about redistricting and elections. Carrillo focuses throughout his interview on his own role

111

in creating an election district in Boston from which a Latino could get elected.

> There was a push to create another minority district defined as something like 70 to 80 percent minority where the majority of the district—over 50 percent—would be black. I then disagreed with that and I basically said that, . . . why this whole thing started . . . was that Hispanics were pushing for this and then other groups joined up. I reminded people of the ultimate purpose here—to create a Latino district.

Redistricting is not a political activity whose importance should be dismissed because of gender differences in how politics is defined. Racial segregation, and thus political dilution, is severe in Boston. In 1981, referendums were passed to allow district elections for city council and school committee. To press for Latino interests in the redistricting process, the Latino Political Action Committee (Latino PAC) was formed. This body, together with the Black Political Task Force, the Lawyers' Committee on Civil Rights, and several Boston residents,[11] brought suit against the city of Boston, the mayor, the city council, the school committee, the Board of Election Commissioners, and other official institutions.

The Latino PAC plan for redistricting city council and school committee seats to increase the potential influence of Latinos in the South End was rejected (Camayd-Freixas and Lopez 1983, 143–155). Jamaica Plain continues to be split into two districts, the Latino impact in the South End is reduced, and the Latino neighborhood in the North Dorchester–Dudley area is split into three sections. All these districting decisions reduce the impact of Latino electoral participation.[12]

Nelson Merced's election was the result of a second, more successful, redistricting effort that involved the state representative districts. The Latino PAC continued working and brought suit again. This time the same parties were successful in creating the Fifth Suffolk District in North Dorchester. An outgrowth of efforts such as the Latino PAC was the Latino Democratic Committee. Many of the same Latinos who were instrumental in the redistricting efforts wanted to create a presence within the Democratic Party that would push for a Latino agenda. The Latino Democratic Committee supports candidates, holds banquets, sponsors debates, participates in Democratic Party functions, and develops a Latino platform.

In general, the residential dispersion of Latinos precludes an easy solution to electoral representation through redistricting reform.

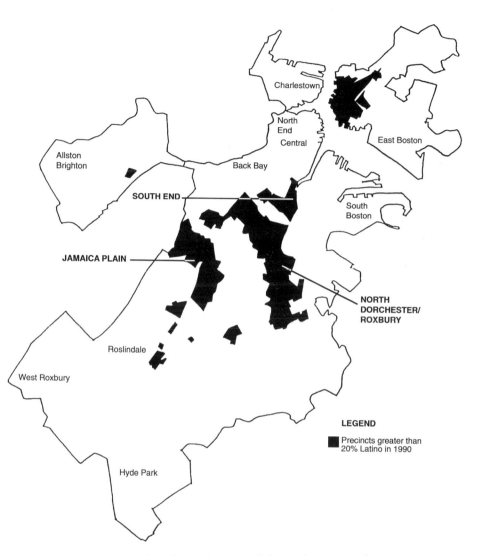

Map 2. Latino Residential Distribution and the Redistricting Dilemma, 1990. *Source:* 1990 Census; map courtesy of Rolf Goetze, Boston Redevelopment Authority Research Department.

Map 2 illustrates how the areas of greatest Latino population density in 1990 do not have contiguous borders; the geographical distance between these areas makes it difficult, if not impossible, to consolidate them into a Latino district. The increased dispersion documented by the 1990 Census discussed in the Introduction and the lack of contiguous borders between the current Latino neighborhoods as shown in Map 2 decrease the potential for district representation in the 1990s.

Gender and Electoral Politics: The Vote as Community Participation. Latina women in Boston, in their interviews, *did* discuss elections and campaigns. Many women included a discussion of elections as politics, but their emphasis was less on "getting elected" than on maximizing the participation of the community. Elections, for the women, were the means of increasing general participation, of empowering the community, and of creating citizens.

A female campaign worker in Nelson Merced's first campaign describes what the campaign meant to her:

> Pulling people into the political process; people who really wanted to vote for the first time because they had something to vote for. . . . It still pulled a lot of people into the process, and there is a place for people even if they weren't registered to vote. . . . But you're not going to organize lots more people, particularly in communities of color, unless you get people involved, and you can help them feel like change is happening. . . . Campaigns really are a place for people to be pulled in—to be a part of something, in this particular case, of a victory—and to stay involved.

Latina women actually discussed *voting* somewhat more frequently than did Latino men.[13] Even when women talked about formal structures like the Latino Democratic Committee, they did so in relation to maximizing participation. For example, Rosa López describes at some length the development of the Latino Democratic Committee and her work in the election of Nelson Merced for state representative. Rather than focusing on the behind-the-scenes maneuvering, however, her portrayal of the history of the organization and the campaign focuses on how she, along with other women in her district, worked on voter registration. She recalls: "We mobilized probably twenty to thirty volunteers. . . . We targeted the Latino neighborhood." The effort she led was the most successful of all those organized by the committee. Nevertheless, in the end, the group gave up: "We failed to mobilize many people beyond this core group of fifteen, twenty people—there were just certain basic organizational issues, lack of follow-through, lack of resources—some people, myself included, being unwilling to continue to do the largest share of the work." Her reason for not continuing to further the organizational efforts of the Latino Democratic Committee? "Our group felt that the larger organization was concerned primarily with enhancing their reputation with the then-leaders of the Democratic Party in Massachusetts." Concern for positions and status at the elite level overwhelmed her efforts to maximize participation at the community level.

Obviously, any discussion of community, citizenship, and gender, in which women emerge as more oriented toward participatory politics than do men, must not create the false perception that exceptions do not exist. Latina women did cluster around a participatory vision of political mobilizing that stressed community and grassroots activism, while Latino men were more inclined to focus on elections and the formal structures of political organization. There were, however, women who did talk about more than grassroots politics; some did not discuss Villa Victoria, and many talked about elections and formal organizations. In addition, some men promoted participatory politics. The current discussion of gender, community, and citizenship should not be taken to mean that all women emphasize creating community and grassroots participation and all men are concerned only with elections and formal structures.

There have been Latino men in Boston who have contributed to building community. Mauricio Gastón, for example, during his all-too-short lifetime, contributed a great deal to building a Latino community and making connections between people at all levels of society.[14] In addition, a few Latino men whom I interviewed recalled political history as grassroots, community-based politics in ways similar to the Latina women. Edwin Colina's story about grassroots community participation in the development of bilingual education, for example, contained the same community-based elements of political participation as did the stories of Latina women.

Bilingual Education and Community Activism: A Political Success Story. Prevailing theories suggest that language, specifically the lack of ability to speak English, impedes Latino political participation (Glazer 1985). Despite the practical obstacles posed by limited English-speaking ability, language has often been the starting point for political mobilization when Latino parents, concerned about their children's education, fight for bilingual programs in the public schools. The political struggle for bilingual education is particularly relevant in a study of Latino politics in Boston because Massachusetts was the first state in the country to pass bilingual education legislation as the result of Latino community pressure.

Edwin Colina grew up in New York City during the massive protests of the 1960s, when belonging to groups such as the Young

Lords was, as he phrased it, "almost a rite of passage." Colina tells
the story of the creation of the Comité de Padres Pro Defensa de la
Educación Bilingüe (The Parents' Committee in Defense of Bilingual
Education). El Comité began by challenging the racial categories instituted by Boston's court-ordered desegregation case. The original
plaintiffs in the case were the parents of black children, and school
assignments were made on the basis of black and white—a process
that threatened to divide the Latino family.

Latinos in Boston, as elsewhere, are a racially diverse group of
people. Even in the same family, Latinos may reflect skin color and
facial characteristics that combine black, white (Spanish), and native
Central and South American and Caribbean "Indian" characteristics.
In a society polarized by black and white, Latino diversity challenges
standard solutions to the problems of school segregation and employment discrimination. Bilingual education also challenges American assumptions that immigration requires complete cultural assimilation, including relinquishing one's native language.

Most immigrant groups, including Latinos in the United States,
value the acquisition of English and eagerly sign up for English
classes. At the same time, they may resist losing the ethnic and cultural identity upon which a sense of community is built. In addition,
as Jones (1990) explains, "language constructs experience" (783),
and the politics of bilingual education is one vehicle through which
Latinos strive to construct a positive experience in the United States.
Given contiguous geographical borders, bilingualism is an asset
rather than a liability for most Latinos in America. Children who do
not have access to bilingual education programs in the public schools
frequently become monolingual in English, even when Spanish is spoken at home.

Colina, now a City Hall official close to the mayor, recalls how
the Latino community effort for bilingual education began: "It was
started by one parent who has twin sons, one darker and one lighter.
As a result of the desegregation order one was sent to where they
needed lighter skin and the other one was sent to where they needed
darker skin. . . . As Puerto Ricans, we saw that as totally contrary to
what we are and what our characterization of race is. And from that
the Comité de Padres was organized." El Comité was a group of
Latino activists, professional educators, lawyers, and parents who developed both technical resources (legal representation, money, political support) and community resources (five local chapters at the
grassroots level). This group urged Judge Garrity—the judge responsible for the desegregation case—to establish bilingual classrooms
that would satisfy language and cultural needs, do so within reason-

able distances from Latino neighborhoods, and create a truly bilin-gual "magnet school."[15] Bilingual education expanded, over time, to include other language groups besides Latinos: Chinese, Cape Verdean, Haitian Creole, Vietnamese, and Portuguese, to name a few. The bilingual education program has become a permanent fixture within the Boston city structure.

Colina stresses the grassroots organizing strategy of El Comité. "We never accepted state, federal, city funds. We did everything that we did strictly on volunteer contributions and just a lot of energy, sweat, and blood." Apart from those participants who contributed technical skills, the bulk of the participants were "strictly grass-roots—mostly *padres* [parents]." Political participation took the form of protests and demonstrations, as Colina describes:

> We took 'em on. We took on the school department, the city, the state, the federal court—a lot of different places. We had demonstrations in our own community down Dudley Street, or along Tremont Street in the South End, or in front of the school committee, or in front of the Federal Court House. We had Judge Garrity's courtroom packed many a time. We demonstrated in front of the State House in the snow. We had, on a constant basis, in the early years of the organization, over two hundred fifty people, easy, that would come to a demonstration on a day's—two days'—notice.

Parent advisory councils were developed to assure parent participation in decision making, and a bureaucratic structure became institutionalized within the Boston School Department.

In his passionate description of the community-based, grassroots effort to promote bilingual education, Colina recalls political history in a way that echoes the image of politics held more typically by Latina women than by Latino men. Nevertheless, the fact that he was virtually the only man to frame political history in these terms,[16] supports my contention that an essential gender difference does exist in how politics is defined.

Of course, what Latino men *do* politically in terms of creating political structures such as the Latino PAC and the Latino Democratic Committee may have at least as much impact on improving socioeconomic conditions of life for Latinos in Boston as what the Latina women do. For example, as discussed earlier, the election of the first Latino (Nelson Merced) to hold state office was due to the behind-the-scenes "politicking" around redistricting—not to a substantial increase in Latino participation. I have no intention of diminishing the contribution of Latino men in achieving influence or success in other forums of politics. But if the goal is to increase political *participation*, especially by poor Latinos, it must be recognized that working on political structures requires a high level of education and skills but does not necessarily require mass mobilization. My focus on the factors that increase participation among the common folk, *la gente del pueblo*—the masses, if you will—reveals that it is at *this* level that Latina women are more successful than Latino men.

Citizenship and the Creation of Community

The lack of citizenship or legal status in the United States is a barrier to political participation often mentioned in the literature on Latinos and politics.[17] Pachon (1987), in fact, concludes: "Thus, in the 1980s U.S. citizenship is the single most important obstacle to political empowerment in the Hispanic community" (x).[18] The lack of U.S. citizenship obviously prevents voter participation by Latinos who are not citizens—those who are not Puerto Rican, those who have only legal residence, and those who are here illegally. In Boston, the percentage of Latinos who are not legal citizens is difficult to estimate. Puerto Ricans, who are automatically citizens, now make up only about 42 percent of the Boston Latino population; some estimates suggest that as many as 30 to 40 percent of Boston Latinos are not citizens.[19] What percentage of those are here without legal documents is impossible to determine.

The lack of citizenship or legal status represents a complex dynamic in the question of how to mobilize Latino communities. People who are here illegally may contribute to the economy and provide needed services. As one of the largest groups of undocumented immigrants in the history of the United States, however, Latinos may live on the fringe of politics for years or even decades.

Political analysts frequently discuss "the problem of illegal immigration" in terms of how to *exclude* more effectively certain groups of people from coming to this country illegally.[20] I do not plan to discuss how to "solve the problem of illegal immigration," because it is beyond the scope of this book. In addition, theories of citizenship based on exclusion obscure the debate about the nature of citizenship itself. A central problem in traditional theories of citizenship, and one that directly affects Latino politics in this country, is the way citizenship is limited to a set of legal rights conferred on specific categories of people. According to this theory, citizenship becomes a mechanism of exclusion and inclusion. Various groups are welcomed or banned from immigration and legal status in the United States depending on whether they are needed for economic production or geographical expansion.[21]

Walzer (1983), for example, while purporting to advocate a pluralistic government, states emphatically that protecting our borders from "illegal aliens" is one of the few absolute national requisites. A problem occurs, however. Exclusion, even if desirable, fails as a policy when it fails to take into account the international relations between developed and developing countries. The waves of illegal immigrants from Latin America and other countries affected by U.S. foreign policies strain our law enforcement institutions. Hostility toward immigrants of color increases.

An even more important issue is how, once Latinos are here, they can be incorporated into a participatory model of community life. There are several compelling reasons to expand our understanding of citizenship to incorporate the Latino experience.

First, the United States cannot afford to have within its borders a population made up of isolated, unwelcome, and marginalized Latinos. Latinos who are isolated and marginalized because of a lack of legal status are vulnerable to discrimination and economic exploitation. If they are not encouraged to participate in community political activities, they also become marginalized politically. Their children, many of whom are legal citizens by birth, then grow up in homes and communities where the drive for political participation is suppressed. The long-term negative consequences for Latino political empowerment are obvious, and severe.

Second, an understanding of citizenship based on rights, legitimacy, and the power to exclude eliminates noncitizen Latinos, and other noncitizens, from entering the discourse around both the foreign policies that stimulate the migration patterns in the first place and the laws and discriminatory practices that create their marginalized status after arrival in the United States. Feminist theories, in contrast to traditional definitions, suggest an idea of citizenship that builds on heterogeneity and diversity. Discourse about citizenship must include the ideas of groups like women and immigrants, so that "all experiences, needs, and perspectives on social events have a voice and are respected" (Young 1990, 129).

Third, given the large numbers of Latinos who are not legal citizens, if political-mobilizing efforts are restricted to Latinos who are citizens (efforts such as voter registration drives, for example), the political influence of Latinos is considerably diluted.

Citizenship is a hot political issue intimately tied to the Latino community, but it is an issue that has not been addressed by the Latino community in Boston thus far. In today's political climate, it is virtually impossible that the vote would ever be extended to noncitizens. As of now, lack of U.S. citizenship and illegal status are absolute barriers to participation when participation is confined to electoral politics. When citizenship is understood to mean more than a set of legal rights bestowed on certain groups of people, however, a more participatory vision of community may emerge for Latinos in this country.

Within a participatory model of citizenship, political education and political action occur irrespective of legal status. And legal status itself is reexamined from the perspective not only of the nation enforcing its territorial boundaries but from the perspective of those fleeing oppression within their home countries—a repression often supported by U.S. foreign policies.

Latina Women and the Political Mobilization of the Noncitizen or Undocumented Latino

The political mobilization of Latinos who are not legal citizens and the development of participatory citizenship—being active in determining the policies that affect life within the community—require two shifts in thinking about who it is that promotes citizenship and community. First, legal status is not a prerequisite for political activism; there are Latinos who are not citizens and who may not be in this country legally who contribute to political mobilization. Second, it is Latina women, not Latino men, who best illustrate effective strategies for the development of citizenship by providing participatory experiences in politics for Latinos who are not legal citizens.

There are numerous examples of Latinos who are not citizens but who nevertheless work to mobilize other Latinos for social change. Women like Inez Martínez and Carmen Gómez have lived here for decades and represent an important pool of community activists. Martínez is active in tenant organizing and group protests; she is from Mexico and has never become a U.S. citizen. Gómez, who was born in South America, is extremely active in politics and is a recognized leader in the community. She has consciously decided to maintain her native citizenship because of ties to family in her country of origin. Aracelis Guzmán, who is from Mexico, is very effective in drawing friends and neighbors into politics despite her own lack of citizenship.

Other examples of Latina women and Latino men who are passionately political but who are here illegally or who have chosen not to relinquish their original citizenship abound. Recall the people described in the previous chapter, for example, who went as a group to the State House for political lobbying efforts. These people were, for the most part, clients of Latino agencies. Staff at these agencies informed me that the clientele of the agencies is generally shifting from Puerto Rican citizens to Dominicans and other Latinos from Central and South America. Many, if not most, of these recent immigrants are here either as legal residents (noncitizens) or without legal status.

Marta Torrijos provides another example. In her work at a Latino agency, she met a man who was able to transform his fear of exposure into participation in political events. At first he said he was from Puerto Rico; after talking with her over time he acknowledged that he was actually from the Dominican Republic (he thought he had to lie about his illegal status to get the job training he needed). Through his connection to Torrijos, he later participated in another lobbying effort at the State House regarding budget cuts. In addition, at a protest march down Dudley Street against a referendum to cut human services, the group of marchers was made up of equal parts Dominican and Central American noncitizens and Puerto Rican citizens.

Noncitizen activists also stimulate political mobilization by leading social groups. Social groups within the Latino community directly affect naturalization rates. Participation in such groups provides opportunities to discuss the decision to acquire legal status or to become naturalized citizens. In the *charla* on politics at Mujeres Unidas en Acción, for example, noncitizen Latina women provided information and led discussions about how to acquire legal residence and about the naturalization process. Following that discussion, several women expressed interest in learning the regulations about becoming citizens and were encouraged by their friends to try again to pass the language test for citizenship. Virginia Alvarez, for example, said at the *charla* that she had voted in Nicaragua. However, she did not feel her vote made a difference there; here, in the company of others, she finds her opinions solicited, valued, and encouraged. The *charla* is a particularly effective blending of social, cultural, community, and political interaction and education for noncitizens and undocumented residents.

Men like Francisco Salamanca and Juan Betances, in contrast, seemed to have few ties to social or community groups and thus to have less opportunity to learn about citizenship. Organizations like Centro Presente provide individual and group support for undocumented immigrants. I hypothesize that those who are left in an isolated, marginalized, and fearful state are less likely to legalize their status than those who receive support.

The experiences of Latinos in Boston suggest, therefore, that noncitizens can be effective mobilizers and that many undocumented immigrants are ripe for inclusion in participatory democracy *if* their

fears and sense of vulnerability can be overcome and *if* appropriate
methods of inclusion are utilized. Latina women, as the next two
portraits illustrate, demonstrate how to promote inclusion of the
noncitizen and the undocumented immigrant Latino into the political
process.

Portrait of María Ramírez:
Mobilizing the "Illegal Alien"

María Ramírez is a Puerto Rican who is active in election campaigns,
hosts fund-raiser parties in her home, and values the vote. However,
she also sees a role for nonvoting, noncitizen Latinos in the political
process: "With those people who *can* vote, you need to get the vote
out because that's the only threat that we have to a politician . . . but
I think that the Latinos who cannot vote can work politically—you
know, there's different ways of doing things." She feels that her personal investment in her neighborhood creates change. Personal caring
is communicated to people, who then are more willing to get involved in the community. Ramírez works with Latinos in her neighborhood—Latinos who cannot vote, are not citizens, and are here
illegally—to solve community problems.

She first focuses on the need to connect neighbor to neighbor, to
build community in a way that encompasses diversity. Whether the
people involved are from Puerto Rico, Santo Domingo, or El Salvador, she appeals to common problems and urges common action
to achieve common solutions.

> I've called a couple of people and said, "Look, these are our kids; we
> either see them get their heads beat in, put away for life, get shot up,
> or we go out there and we help them." They're not my children *per-
> sonally*, but they are *our* kids and we all get labeled the same and the
> police don't care if the kids are Puerto Rican, if they're from Santo
> Domingo, if they're from El Salvador. The police don't care—they
> speak Spanish, they're Hispanic, that's all they know. So we either *do*
> something about it or we don't. We're trying to talk to the parents,
> and I have neighbors talking to neighbors, talking, saying, "Look, let's
> not have a riot this weekend, let's try to talk—what's the problem?"
> but that's the only way to do it.

Ramírez then describes how she succeeded in mobilizing undocumented immigrants in a Latino neighborhood to tackle the problem
of drugs.

> We had this drug house, and I told the people on Boylston Street—
> they could not vote, the majority of those people could not vote. And

they weren't Puerto Ricans either. I said, "You live on this street, you want it to be good, you take responsibility." [I ask: And what did they do?] They first thought I was *crazy*! They said, "What do you mean?!" I mean—some of these people were even—*illegal*, and I said, "I don't care if you're legal or not, you want responsibility, you do something about it." We have to decide what we want and go after it. [I ask: And so what did they do?] They did it. We put this march together, we had the New England Telephone Company donate the BAD shirts—Boston Against Drugs—we had buttons, we made banners, they cooked, we rallied in front of the drug houses with the cops and everything. We pointed the people out. *They* did that—I mean, I was there, but *they* did it. And every time there was an incident, they came out to the streets, and they said, "No more," and it took us a year, but the drug dealers aren't there anymore. The elected official was there, the police were there, and these are people who do not vote!

Working with neighbors helps overcome both the disinclination to get involved and the inhibitions imposed by illegal status. Here in this example, Latinos who are *illegal* residents worked side by side with the police in the city of Boston—and they were being led by a Latina woman.[22]

Latina women like María Ramírez thus play an important role in building community by encouraging the development of citizenship; this role often also develops in the context of Latino community agencies. Several reasons account for the connection between Latina women, community development, and the Latino agency. First, most of the front-line workers at Latino agencies are women who understand about the need for ongoing relationships. In addition, they know the individual members of the community most intimately and are leaders of existing client groups. Second, most Latinos—recent and longtime immigrants, legal and undocumented residents—turn to the Latino agency at one point or another. Latino agencies help them solve problems, direct them to appropriate government institutions, and provide a buffer in the process of adaptation to the United States. Finally, the women in agencies like Mujeres Unidas en Acción, Comunidad Boricua en Acción, and many others, develop and promote participatory political experiences that encourage community participation—by Latino citizens and noncitizens alike. The following portrait of a Latina woman working at a Latino agency illustrates a model of civic education that promotes citizenship and builds community for new Latino immigrants.

Creating Citizenship through Participation: A Portrait of Camila Alvarado

Camila Alvarado has worked for many years at the Concilio Latino. Although the agency's current emphasis is on quickly turning out trained workers through a jobs program, at the height of her influence several years ago, Camila Alvarado instituted many programs that created citizens.

When Manuel Sánchez became director of the Concilio Latino, Alvarado was already working at the agency. He recalls following her philosophy that there is a responsibility to educate for life, not just to teach English or to provide training for a job:

> There, at the agency, the politics became broader because the politics then involved working with adults and ensuring that they understood what their rights were under the law. We would have workshops— seminars—for incoming students to inform them about their rights. It was very much part of a curriculum. Understanding, making sure they knew what the laws were. . . . Part of teaching English is teaching the culture and the language, and teaching the values and teaching the importance of civic participation.

Civic education included having everyone take out a library card, encouraging voter registration, hosting candidate nights, and having students participate as board members. The students/clients participated in community events; an example of a community event that provided a service as well as an education was a survey of local Latino businesses. The rationale for participation in such events was as follows:

> We were providing more than education and training. We were really trying to help people become fuller citizens in the society. We wanted them to get involved in economic development issues. We wanted them to get involved in community organizations outside of Concilio Latino. We wanted them to get involved in neighborhood associations and business associations. We thought they needed to get involved with the rest of the community and not just simply think about themselves as "number one" and "I'm gonna get out of here and I'm gonna make it." I think that's the basic difference.

According to Sánchez, Alvarado consistently encouraged a broad range of participatory opportunities.

> We had a component that was community development, and Camila Alvarado was the one that did a lot of the community development—

like we helped organize a businessmen's association, where you'd say, "What does this have to do with adult education or training?" I'd say, "Well, if you're Hispanic—I mean, in every country that *I've* been in, there are very successful businesspeople, why not here?" Well, because they didn't know the rules, the regulations—so we created a business program that helped small businesses.

Camila Alvarado established a precedent of participation at this agency while at the same time clients learned about regulations, laws, and procedures in this country. Participation was enhanced as staff members also invited candidates and government officials to meet agency clients at open houses.

Latinos arriving at the agency then did not have a higher level of political knowledge or sense of "political efficacy" than do Latinos in Boston today: the program itself developed their political skills, which they then translated into effective political action. Participation in the running of the agency, participation in community institutions such as the library and a business association, and participation in election events hosted by the agency also led to participation in traditional, electoral forms of political life. Sánchez recalls their philosophy: "Politics needs to be part of the school curriculum—adult basic education training, literacy courses, ESL courses—elections or local elections must be part of those curriculums if you really want people to understand that *that* is a way to voice your concerns, by getting them elected."

This broad-based education taught Concilio clients/students to tackle community problems in an effective way. Sánchez describes, for example, how another Latina woman worked with agency clients to save a branch library from being closed and worked with elected officials on a plan to curb neighborhood violence.

Other women have used their agency-based resources to develop political participation by encouraging clients to take on the roles of citizens. Carmen Gómez, for example, used the stimulus of the state budget cuts to involve clients in planning how to lobby the legislature. She went to the clients and told them about the potential loss of funds. The clients, who in the past had been passive recipients of agency services, responded positively to her invitation to work on the problem with the staff. Gómez then describes how the supposedly passive clients rose to the occasion and became political participants: "Among the groups there are some people who have the capability to be more outspoken than others, and they choose among themselves who the presenter will be and that's how they do it."

The clients ended up meeting with several state representatives. Gómez explains why this effort was successful in getting the Latino clients to participate and how people felt about the experience:

> I think for the majority of them, it's a scary thing. I don't think that we can say that everybody was excited—that everybody felt good coming out of there because some of them don't even know what a state rep is . . . but I think it's just—we need to do more of that, just the initial step that we were able to take them. . . . We didn't have to bend their elbows. . . . And we even provided them with transportation—you know, as long as the transportation is there, there's no problem.

Transportation, child care, asking people to help the agency, not just receive help from the agency, all these factors provide an opportunity, in a sense, to *practice* political participation in the safety of a trusted group of people. Participation is a social event that takes place within existing personal relationships; fear is overcome through the support of friends, and participation is not left up to the individual alone. Politics is not an isolated behavior, a private act, but a social event embedded in the security of language, culture, and friendship ties. The true leaders are people you know, people you will follow, people who are like you and accompany you into the political world.

Encouraging Latinos to take on the roles of citizens—to be active in self-government by being members of their own agency boards as at Concilio Latino, by joining protest marches, and by lobbying, as well as by collectively creating a community like Mujeres Unidas—takes on another dimension when confronting the lack of legal status of many Latinos. Latina women, again, demonstrate their contribution to creating a sense of community out of ethnic diversity and to developing citizenship irrespective of legal status.

FIVE

Political Consciousness:
Being Political,
Becoming Political

Es como una chispa que prende ¿verdad? y, que el espíritu de la persona en ese momento está listo.

(It's like a spark that ignites, right? and the person's spirit, in that moment, is ready.)

—*Aracelis Guzmán*

For Latina women, political participation is inextricably linked with the development of the political self. At the same time, the political self evolves in conjunction with *personal* self-development. In reciprocal fashion, political consciousness—a sense of "being political"—contributes to, and emerges from, personal and political self-development.

Political consciousness and personal development are also closely connected to community empowerment. Aracelis Guzmán is a Mexican-American woman in her late forties. She has been in the United States for twenty years. Her concerns about her two daughters motivated her first tentative then enthusiastic participation in the struggle for better education for Latinos in the Boston schools. According to Guzmán, community empowerment derives from the development of the self and of political consciousness.

En general, pienso que si una persona aprende a desarrollar ciertos conocimientos, que desarrolla destrezas, pero más que nada creo que es el estar consciente *de que uno puede aprender y de que uno puede soñar y alcanzar ciertas metas y que va a haber vehículos. . . . Y de que*

127

pueda contribuir a su casa, a su familia, a su comunidad, ¿verdad? Y que ese conocimiento ayude a que se fortalezcan las comunidades.

In general, I think that if a person learns to develop a certain degree of knowledge—that one develops skills—but more than anything I believe that it is the *being conscious* that one can learn and that one can dream and can achieve certain goals and that there will be a way. . . . And that one could contribute something to your home, to your family, to your community, right? And that understanding helps to strengthen the community.

Tamara González, in essence, equates being political with political consciousness and community change: "Political is anyone who is aware of what the issues of your community are and who makes a decision that, somehow, you could be a catalyst to make things happen."

Virtually all the Latina women in Boston identify personal development with political consciousness and political change. In addition, just as Latina women talk about connection, collectivity, and community to a greater extent than do Latino men, they stress the need for expanded consciousness far more than do the men. In fact, *there were twenty-six separate discussions of political consciousness by the women, in contrast with only one discussion by one man.*

María Luisa Soto makes a connection between her personal development, her political consciousness, and her emergence into the arena of political activism. Her early life in Puerto Rico and New York City was within a very "traditional" Latina woman's role, restricted to the home under the watchful eye of first her father, then her husband. When asked about the roots of her community-based politics, Soto focuses on social and affiliative needs. Being a political person dates to her arrival in Boston. She recalls that after hearing about a meeting on the problem of housing, "I went and I said to myself, This seems interesting." Meeting people and expanding her horizons outside of the home brought up new ways of thinking and provided new opportunities for Soto. As she connected with other women, she began to see the vacuum in leadership and began to take action.

Soto is eager to point out that she did all this while raising her two children in the projects, going to school full time, and working full time—her pride in her personal development permeates her story. Listening to the story of María Luisa Soto also reveals that her politicization ran counter to her upbringing. Leaving her husband seems to have been the beginning of branching out into a broader lifestyle. While male researchers like Lane pay scant attention to the needs for affiliation in political development, the fulfillment of social, affiliative needs—meeting other people—contributed substantially to the politicization of María Luisa Soto.

Soto ended her interview by making a connection between her personal and political self-development. With great force and feeling she said it was *"parte de mi desarrollo como una mujer"* ("part of my development as a woman"). She is not unique in her belief that personal development and political development go hand in hand; the women at Mujeres Unidas en Acción combine the development of the self—as a woman—with political consciousness. Silvia Barajas, for example, expresses a deep desire to *desenvolverse*—to develop herself to the fullest. For Barajas, this self-development involved learning English, taking classes in sewing,[1] and attending discussions on AIDS and alcoholism. But, *desenvolverse* also involves a political component: the development and nurturance of her political self. At the march down Dudley Street to protest state budget cuts, Barajas explained why she was an eager participant: she wanted to understand decisions that would affect her.

While waiting for the march to begin, Barajas introduced me to a friend who had just moved to Boston from the Dominican Republic. She and her friend began arguing about which of the party leaders in their home country had done more for the people. Barajas exclaimed, "But look at the new roads! Look at the new buildings!" Her friend came back with, "But what good are buildings if the people are hungry?" They were still debating the point after the march had begun; they continued as they marched down the street and banged spoons on the bottoms of pots.

"Being political" for Silvia Barajas, Aracelis Guzmán, María Luisa Soto, and other Latina women is a complex process deeply rooted in the themes of connection, collectivity, and community. Understanding the development of political consciousness, the sense of "being political," requires a reexamination of this process and how self-perception and political participation are tied to the definition of "What is political?" For many women, changes in consciousness are associated with individual and collective empowerment.

"Being Political": Self-perception, Participation, and the Meaning of Politics

Some of the people I interviewed, typically women, opened their interviews with statements like "I'm not political" but then went on to describe a life full of "being political."[2] Here, for example, is Marta

129

Correa's response to my opening invitation to tell me political activities that she had been involved in:

¿De política?—[pause] ¿política?—En realidad, la política no me gusta mucho, digamos. . . . Por ejemplo, las actividades con la comunidad, sí, pero política, política—sinceramente no me gusta mucho en realidad. Yo le di mi voto—antes yo no podía votar porque yo no era ciudadana. Hace como seis años que yo soy ciudadana. Pero en realidad como la política—sinceramente de política no tendría nada que decir.

Politics?—[pause] politics?—Actually, I really don't like politics much, let's say. . . . For example, community activities, yes, but politics, politics—really I don't like it much. I vote—before I couldn't vote because I wasn't a citizen. It's been about six years that I've been a citizen. But really, about politics—honestly, about politics I wouldn't have much to say.[3]

What she enjoys and wants to talk about is community work—helping *los viejitos* (the old folks). For Correa, being political involves making connections—drawing people into politics. Nevertheless, look at what she does in terms of traditional political behaviors: she works on election campaigns, encourages Latinos to vote, and contacts public officials at the mayor's office. She has also organized and been involved in political education and protests.

Political education can be as simple as informing others about the location of their state representative's office. Correa describes how other Latinos in her neighborhood did not know about the neighborhood office of their representative, Maura Hennigan. The office was located in what previously had been a pharmacy, so she went about *"avisándoles que está ahí"* ("telling them it's there").

Correa also orchestrated a neighborhood protest when, after hearing many neighbors complain about exorbitant utility bill increases, *"Yo comenzaba llamando a las personas y les decía, 'Vengan—vamos a hacer una protesta porque las utilidades están muy altas y en el futuro van a estar más altas y más altas'"* ("I started calling people and I'd tell them, 'Come—let's form a protest because the utility bills are very high, and in the future they're going to get higher and higher'").

If Marta Correa says, "I wouldn't have anything to tell you about politics" and then goes on to describe a wealth of community and conventional political behavior, there must be a discrepancy between what the literature means by political and what the Latina women I spoke with mean. And Correa was not the only person to disavow being political while engaging in traditional political behaviors. Juana

Oviedo also said she did not know why I would want to talk to her since she does not have anything to do with politics. And yet she votes, she has gone to protests, and she has joined lobbying groups at the Massachusetts State Legislature. Even Josefina Ortega, who, as described in Chapter 1, combines cultural events with political activism, began her interview with a statement that she wasn't political.

Then we have Silvia Barajas from the Dominican Republic. Barajas works in a factory, has been in this country only three years, and, like Oviedo, has only a sixth-grade education. She gave me her phone number at a discussion group at Mujeres Unidas en Acción and volunteered to talk with me because she "*adores* politics"

Barajas was eager to tell me about her political involvement. With great enthusiasm she described being part of the Cruzada de Amor (Crusade of Love) in Santo Domingo. The Cruzada de Amor was started by Emma Balaguer, the sister of the current president of Santo Domingo; its purpose is to serve the needs of poor people in the country. A network of women like Barajas go through the countryside and to the villages to give out food and clothing to the poor.

Does this "count" as politics? Certainly in her mind it does. In tracing her feeling of "being political," Barajas sees herself as coordinating her efforts with those of other women, as responding to the needs of the people, and as following someone in government she admires, Doña Emma. She is also one of the women who would go house to house to inform fellow volunteers that Doña Emma was calling a meeting; Barajas is enthusiastic about her success: "*Y el salón estaría* lleno *de gente!*" ("And the room would be *full* of people!"). She is clear about the time-consuming quality of political life when she describes how she would have to retrace her steps if the meeting were canceled or rescheduled.

Is this volunteer work, social work—or politics? The implementation of government social policy? Or does the political nature of her work lie in her perception of the collective effort and the organizational method of making connections with others to fulfill a policy and to fill a socioeconomic need?

Religious or charity work is often not considered political (Aviel 1981, 161), even by the women participants themselves (although Barajas certainly considers it political). Nevertheless, the charitable work of the Cruzada de Amor in the Dominican Republic, according to Aviel (1981), "had important political implications in promoting support for parties of the right and center" (161). And Mota (1976) agrees with the political origins of La Cruzada de Amor in her article on women's politics in the Dominican Republic. According to Mota, President Trujillo in the 1930s and 1940s and President Balaguer in the 1960s developed programs like the Cruzada de Amor to assure party loyalty among Dominican women.[4]

What do people mean when they talk about being political? What "counts" as political? At the heart of this question is the debate about the public–private dimensions of politics.

Public Politics, Private Politics. Liberal theory makes clear distinctions between the supposedly public and private spheres of life. In addition, as Pateman (1989) says, "In mainstream political theory, the public sphere is assumed to be capable of being understood on its own, as if it existed *sui generis*, independently of private sexual relations and domestic life" (3). Within liberal political theory, politics is essentially a public enterprise. Even theorists like Barber (1984), who urge a more participatory vision of democracy and who struggle with the public–private dimension of politics, come down on the side of politics as an activity within an essentially public realm and concerning "public" issues. In so doing, they create a tension or dichotomy between an apparently public politics on the one hand and what has become accepted only of late as a vast arena of private politics. This tension may be related to the prevailing view that politics is about conflicts, competing self-interest, and power (Barber 1984, 128; Stone 1987). In this context, a perceived conflict exists between private concerns and the public good; the idea of community and cooperation rests uneasily next to this mistrust of the private sphere. Unfortunately, political activity that challenges the power distribution within the supposedly private sphere—interpersonal relationships, domestic life, and sexual relations, and that confronts the socioeconomic subjugation of women—is often dismissed as nonpolitical or "disorderly" (Pateman 1989; Ackelsberg 1991, 171).

One of the main contributions of feminism to political theory has been its challenge to this conception of politics. With the emergence of feminist political theory, the politics of this supposedly private sphere has begun to receive some attention. Feminists see less tension and contradiction between the private and public—there is no dichotomy between the two. It is not that there are two spheres that compete or that are evaluated as "real" in terms of their worth for political concern or action. For example, many issues of concern to women, from birth control, abortion, and domestic violence to poverty, illness, drunk driving, family relations, parent–child relations, and many others, are simultaneously private and public issues. What creates the (misnamed) public issue is not an intrinsic quality of the issue at hand but rather *political consciousness* and collective action. In other words, making a connection between one's personal situation and the situation of others (consciousness) and making connections between people to take action on the common problem (collectivity) is what shifts a personal (private) problem to the larger (public) domain.

Barber himself admits (1984) that the line between private and public "is often obscured or controversial" and suggests that "it is one primary function of political activity to provide a continuing forum for the discussion and definition of these terms" (123–124). The experiences of Latina women in Boston, however, suggest that there is no real line—no tension—between a public sphere and a private sphere of life, or between a public politics and a private politics.

Latina women often bring issues that have not been on the male agendas into the realm of politics. One of the major political organizing efforts for Latina women, for example, has been the issue of domestic violence. Andrea del Valle describes the emergence of a women's group that battled the Boston Police Department's handling of a 1987 domestic violence case. In this case, a Latina woman was murdered by her boyfriend despite having made multiple calls to the police. Del Valle describes the collective efforts to publicize a private case, to involve women who had previously been too timid to challenge the status quo, and to overcome the political obstacles facing Latina women in confronting male-controlled institutions. She also describes as political history a series of consciousness-raising workshops within a conference called Encuentro (Encounter) that the group developed to focus on "building bridges"—making connections—between the different classes, ethnicities, and sexual preferences of the Latina women in Boston. Changes in political consciousness thus occur in connection with other women, in the context of personal networks, and in social situations where women can explore new ideas and thoughts.

Political Consciousness and Political Education. Political consciousness is related to, but distinct from, political education. Consciousness raising is a process "which enable[s] the participants to locate their experiences in a social context and to build solidarity with others on the basis of shared perspectives" (Ackelsberg 1991, 164). Political education, on the other hand, often involves a more pedagogical style of information dissemination. Latino men and Latina women alike discussed the need for factual information and education;[5] the need for information about government, candidates, legal rights and rules, and political strategies was a particularly important theme for *la gente del pueblo.*[6]

For Latina women, however, being political involves the intense and far-ranging *exchange* of ideas. Activists like Blanca Schoolman and *gente* like Ivelisse Rodríguez envision a more intimate political mobilization effort. They and others, like Teresa Andrade and Luis Hernández, cross the barriers of class and ideology to insist on an "exchange of ideas"—*"un intercambio de ideas"*—and *"un diálogo."* Like Barber (1984, esp. 233–234), Latina women see formal political education less useful than involvement in participatory experiences that blend what might be called "private-sphere" social activities with political purposes.

In a community focused on "just surviving," abrupt, one-sided calls to political meetings or to go vote are relatively ineffectual mobilization tools. Latinos, like most people, resist being coerced into voting or going to endless meetings to serve someone else's agenda; a reciprocal relationship is crucial. And the development of political consciousness is part of this relationship.

Latina activists stress their role in consciousness raising. It must be remembered that, although some of the women interviewed were feminists (seven of the twenty-nine), the great majority were not. While the number of consciousness-raising groups so prominent during the early years of the women's liberation movement have decreased among white women, many Latina women feel that participation (among men and women) will not increase unless people consciously make connections between their present conditions of living and larger political events—local, national, and international.

At Mujeres Unidas en Acción, the ideology is explicitly feminist and radical. The stated goal of the organization is that the women members develop critical thinking and question their own oppression. The political message encourages poor Latina women to become conscious of how relations between men and women can subordinate women's needs for personal and political development. The message also encourages women to develop a sense of personal empowerment. Julia Santiago explains:

> *Es como, a la misma vez que tu la estás haciendo a ella consciente . . . tu la estás dando el poder a ella para que ella tome iniciativa—y deje de sentirse como una víctima—para que se entere que no es víctima— es una persona tan completa como cualquier otra persona.*

> It's like, at the same time you are making her conscious . . . you are giving her the *power* so that she can take charge—and stop feeling like a victim—so she can realize that she is *not* a victim—she's a person as complete as any other person.

Helping poor Latina women feel empowered instead of victimized responds to a problem ignored by the larger political system: domestic violence. Many Latina women (especially poor women) suffer from this problem, which is shrouded in public silence. Congress and the president have not defined domestic violence as a political issue to be debated with the same fervor as the budget or foreign affairs. At Mujeres Unidas en Acción, women are encouraged to consider the personal and political impact of this issue.[7]

Developing consciousness is linked to taking action, both as an individual and as a collective—but not as mere followers of a designated leader. Oppressed people can learn to combine critical consciousness with social change; as Freire (1970) explains, "Liberation is a praxis: the action and reflection of men [*sic*] upon their world in order to transform it" (66). Political action is action taken *with* the people, not on their behalf. For the women at Mujeres Unidas en Acción, politics is much more than the visits to the State House, protests, and voting or not voting. Personal problems are social problems—political issues.

Morgen and Bookman (1988) might be writing for these women when they say that "empowerment begins when they change their ideas about the causes of their powerlessness, when they recognize the systemic forces that oppress them, and when they act to change the conditions of their lives" (4). Rather than being told *about* political candidates or events, Latina women talk about development—both political and personal; the two are intertwined. The development of political consciousness—of connecting personal problems to public policy—is one aspect of political education stressed by Latina women, not by Latino men.

Portrait of Teresa Andrade: Consciousness and Political Mobilization

Teresa Andrade, now in her thirties, moved to New York at the age of four. As a young adult, she became involved in "Puerto Rican causes" and moved to Boston in the early 1970s. She had been very active in the Puerto Rican pro-Independence movement and in the Puerto Rican Socialist Party. Her own words best describe the role of consciousness raising in the political development of Boston's Latino community during the mid 1970s:

> We'd have meetings, we'd go house to house, we had study groups, we would hold *charlas*. I sold the newspaper from Puerto Rico that was a bilingual edition *every* Saturday for about five or six years; I would spend my *entire* Saturday from nine in the morning to like four in the afternoon and I would trudge door to door with that newspaper and talk to between forty and sixty families a week, the same ones gener-

ally over and over. . . . We'd talk about what issues they were dealing with. Women would talk to you about their complaints, health complaints, it was a range. Sometimes people didn't even want to bother to talk to me, sometimes they did. . . . We knocked on the door and said, "Here's the newspaper," or "Do you want a newspaper? This is what this newspaper is." We also had newsletters that we put out. One of the organizational structures that we used was little, kind of satellite groupings that emerged around a topic, where someone sponsored a *charla*—a topic discussion at their house. You'd have it maybe on a Friday evening, and it would be a combination between a social gathering and an educational event and it was in somebody's living room and there was Coke and sandwiches or whatever. And kids were all around, you know—no need for child care because it was in people's homes and the kids were sort of hanging out. People were not into, "Oh, this is a formal presentation—you've got to keep the kids quiet." Kids were doing their normal running in and out thing, which is not tolerated in most circles. It made it possible for—like—people to get together. Then what happened was, I'm thinking in one particular case in Jamaica Plain, there were a lot of housing problems and a couple emerged—and kind of developed this leadership. They said, "We really want to see some change around here, we are pro-Independence ourselves." They had had some level of political activism on the island, they began to invite their neighbors, and they kind of took ownership for organizing stuff around the block—and one of those, the woman became very active around the bilingual educational struggle that emerged out of the desegregation suit.

Political consciousness plays a key role in Andrade's political organizing work. Her work typifies a politics of neighborhood relationships and consciousness raising that are *process* not *product* oriented. Political work like voter registration and "get out the vote" drives are product-oriented political behaviors because the sole purpose of the organizer is to get the target to do something the target might otherwise not do, for example. Process-oriented political work might produce fewer voters, but it focuses on political development and the exchange of ideas. One could conceive of a situation, for example, in which "the target" could, through an exchange of ideas, convince the mobilizer to vote for a different candidate. For example, one man told Andrade: "I really like you guys because you come and talk to us about Independence, but we also know that we can count on you when we have housing problems, and—you know, I'm pro-State-hood, but I can count on you because you guys do good work, you provide us with support, you give us information, you work hard—I *trust* you." This relationship implies equal stature of the target and activist (or at least a blurring of these categories); they are equal in their ability to encourage the development of political opinions and decisions to take political action.

This vision of political exchanges in people's homes contrasts greatly with the more typical, and I say male, structure of most political events. The free flow of ideas within informal, ongoing relationships like those described by Andrade was extremely effective in developing political activism in the Jamaica Plain section of Boston. In fact, many people stated that Jamaica Plain is currently the most politically active of the three Latino neighborhoods. I suggest that one of the reasons is the grassroots, women-led, type of political consciousness-raising efforts that took place in the 1970s.[8]

"Becoming Political": *La Chispa Que Prende*

The development of the political self[9] and the sources of politicization have concerned political scientists for decades.[10]Theories of political socialization generally focus on: (1) childhood socialization,[11] (2) adult resocialization and countersocialization (especially through structural changes such as the civil rights movement and the women's movement),[12] and (3) political consciousness.[13] Research on Latino political socialization generally studies Mexican-American children.[14] Few studies empirically examine the process of political socialization for Latina women and Latino men. In addition, our understanding of Latino political consciousness centers on the effects of the Chicano movement on political participation and access to political power[15] or on the development of ethnic consciousness in multiethnic Latino communities.[16] Research on the political consciousness of Latina women other than Mexican Americans is extremely limited.[17]

Latina women and Latino men in Boston had much to share about the politicization process. As I sorted out the threads of many different life experiences, it became clear that all the stories had in common a theme of "becoming political." There is a *process*, for many a contemplative process, of political development. For some, this process is quick—a sudden *chispa que prende* ("the spark that ignites [the fire]") of recognition that a change is needed. For others, political consciousness emerges slowly, from a questioning of the conditions of life and a searching for alternatives within themselves and with others.[18]

Gender differences in the Latino perception of the politicization process abound. *Latino men discussed the politicization process half as much as did the women.* In addition, almost half of the men did

137

not spontaneously refer to the process by which they became political, whereas becoming political was a prominent theme in most of the women's interviews.[19]

Sources of "Becoming Political"

The men and women I interviewed formally and talked with during community observations offered many perspectives on how they became politicized. For some Puerto Ricans, the status of Puerto Rico—Statehood, Independence, socialism—created a political issue that formed their political identity and molded their activism. For others, and for those of other Latino groups, it was *"la necesidad"* (the needs of the community)—being confronted with crushing problems such as a lack of decent housing, AIDS, and a high dropout rate for Latino public school children. For some it was the opportunity to contribute or to achieve personal success through an activist role. A few *decided* to become political, others would have liked to be allowed into politics but felt shut out, and still others felt they emerged gradually despite personal and structural barriers. As in mainstream literature, the role of the family in the political socialization process emerges in the stories of some Latinos.

Childhood Socialization: The Role of the Family. Family background is frequently cited as one of the most influential factors in political development.[20] *"Political socialization* assumes that the political habits of people are formed primarily before adulthood" (Orum et al. 1974, 198; emphasis in original). Political learning in the family supposedly develops partisan attachment, ideology, national loyalty, orientations toward authority, sense of regime legitimacy, and recruitment to bureaucratic and government roles (Hirsch 1971, 4). The family, according to theories of childhood socialization, affects the acquisition of participant values; these values then determine subsequent levels of political activism, party identification, political knowledge, and sense of political efficacy. Exposure in the home to political talk and activism is thus linked to future political behavior. Gender differences in adult women's (supposedly lower levels of) political participation are attributed to sex-linked restrictions, male dominance of the political domain,[21] and feminine characteristics learned as children.[22]

Family traditions of "being political" *do* affect some Latinos in the predicted way.[23] Josefina Ortega and Edwin Colina, for example, agree with earlier researchers that family background is an important component to political socialization. *"Vengo de una familia muy política"* ("I come from a very political family"), says Ortega. Colina recalls: *"Mi abuelita me dice—you're born with it—que es como un microbio que se mete en la sangre"* ("My grandma tells me—you're born with it—that it's like a little bacteria that gets in your blood"). Ortega and Colina locate the roots of their "becoming political" within their family of origin: *"Está en la sangre"* ("It's in the blood").

Becoming political may also come from following a long tradition of activism in the family. Dalia Ruiz, for example, attributes her enjoyment of politics to her family: *"A mi mamá le gusta muchísimo la política. Porque ella se volvía loca con las elecciones, ¡ella se volvía loca! A ella le encantaba la política"* ("My mother likes politics a lot. She would go nuts about the elections; she would just go nuts! She adored politics"). Juanita Fonseca recalls, "I could always remember somehow, somebody always saying things like, I—my family—we had an obligation." Pablo Petillo votes and remembers his mother voting. Manuel Sánchez provides a detailed description of how his family background shaped his political development:

> I'm from Cuba. Both my parents were very much involved, not in political parties, but they were involved in their communities, in Cuba. Then, once they learned English and so forth, they got more involved here. My father was very active in fraternal organizations in Cuba. He was involved with Masons, with the Lions Club in Cuba, and I would go to these things. I would be there, I would see him in action—recruiting, organizing, bringing people together.
>
> My mother was a teacher and a principal. We lived in Havana; we were in a suburb, but she, during a period of her life, went off to work in a very rural district and built a school. It sounds like one of these stories [laughter]. But it's real. They built a school where there was no school. There was no plumbing. Got plumbing into the homes of the people in the area, there was no road, they built a road and all that kind of . . . conservative, but a social activist.

Sánchez's family, in essence, trained him in political participation. In addition, having lived through the Castro revolution provided an intellectual spark to study politics in this country.

Worth noting is the contrast between Sánchez's mother's politics and his father's. His father was active in formally structured organizations, whereas his mother focused on everyday survival: despite her conservative ideology, she worked to build a school, to provide plumbing, to build a road.

Marta Correa also identifies her family as the source of her political interest and her desire to help others.

> Es la forma en que nos han criado—así me criaron a mí. Yo soy de Ecuador; nos criaron con un respeto; nos criaron muy diferente. . . . Mi abuela me decía siempre, "Respeta para que te respeten." . . . O sea, tu cooperas con las personas siempre que te necesiten. Porque en el futuro—esa persona no te va a ayudar a tí pero otra persona te puede dar ayuda. Entonces, a mí me criaron en esa forma—ese respeto—esa ayuda.

> It's the way that we were raised—that's the way they raised me. I am from Ecuador; we were raised with the value of respect, we were raised very differently. . . . My grandmother always told me, "Respect others so they'll respect you." . . . In other words, you help others whenever they need you. Because, in the future—that person is not going to help you but another person may give you help. So, that's the way I was raised—with that kind of respect—that kind of help.

For Correa political participation provides a form of social insurance: being involved in helping others means that, should the need arise, you too will receive help. The value she places on political participation clearly comes from her family.

Marta Rosa feels that the supportiveness of her family gave her the practical means and the emotional strength to weather the demands of her election campaign for a seat on the Chelsea School Committee: "My mother lives in the basement apartment I built for her, and my sister lives on the first floor. I've always had babysitters. . . . It's always been my mother, my husband, my sisters—and they're *really* supportive of what I do, the work that I do. They know it's for a good cause." Her sister was also her campaign manager, and her husband and her children worked on her campaign.

Gender, Socialization, and the Family. It is hard to overlook the gender differences in how Latinos discuss the impact of family tradition and the politicization process. The women are more likely than the men to recall the sharing, giving message from their families. For example, Latinas who come from political or politically supportive families describe the impetus to *compartir*—"to share"—as the basis of working with people. Josefina Ortega talks about how her family communicated the idea that, if they only had one piece of bread, they would share it with others. Catalina Torres says:

> My parents had been migrants and I knew about—we call them *braceros*.[24] My parents, both of them—although we were very poor—

whatever we grew, you could always count on us to get you a hundred pounds of potatoes, a hundred pounds of beans, a hundred pounds of flour, what you needed—staples, to get you through the winter if you didn't have anything, because my dad had a year-round job and it wasn't seasonal and he always would help somebody else, always. I would always say, "Why do you do that? You don't know those people, we need it too." That was my thing, and I was always told, "*Los favores no se cobran*"[25]—don't ever look at a favor and expect that favor to be repaid. Someone else will pay you back and it's a *sin* to ask to be paid back! So, all right, I grew up like that.

Juanita Fonseca recalls the network of Central American women who circulated through her house, helping each other become adjusted to this country and providing both a source of inspiration to her and training in politics. Her first exposure to government institutions came about as a child, while she served as a translator for these women. Another woman traces her interest in influencing political decisions at the government level to her anger at injustice—and to the fact that she comes from a family of social workers.

Despite these testimonies in support of the family as the primary source of participatory political orientation, there are many other examples that illustrate how politicization can occur without a family tradition of political involvement or *despite* inactive and oppressive family conditions. Latina women in Boston, in particular, describe experiences of adult resocialization—"a fundamental reorientation of an *adult* woman's political self" (Rinehart 1986, 13; emphasis in original). By participating in experiences that run counter to female or cultural role expectations, these women, as adults, emerged as political activists. What is important about the portrait of María Luisa Soto, for example, is how she moved from a noninvolved, traditional woman's role into becoming one of the most politically active and influential people in Boston. This process of adult resocialization is somewhat different, although the result may be the same, from childhood experiences that challenge female and cultural role expectations (countersocialization). For example, when, as a young girl, Fonseca acted as a translator for adult Central American women, her exposure to government institutions, the proactive role involved, and a sense of competence in the outside world created a different socialization experience from the more homebound childhoods of many Latina girls. The dynamics of adult resocialization (separate from childhood countersocialization) raise an important question: What is the *process* by which poor women of color become politicized as adults?

Chapter Five

Rising from Oppression: Latina Women and Adult Resocialization

One of the barriers to political participation is the grinding effect of poverty. Virtually all the Latina women and Latino men talked about how difficult it is to think of going to a meeting, challenging a landlord, protesting, or even voting when just trying to survive consumes all one's energy. The participation of poor people—poor Latinos in Boston—hinges on having a reason to participate, whether through personal relationships and connectedness, through the personal appeal of a Latino candidate or friend, or through some combination of factors that pull one into taking action on one's own behalf. For Latina women, "the triple oppression suffered by many women of color has fostered innovative methods and approaches to political organizing" (Morgen and Bookman 1988, 11). To discover how people who are poor, who are oppressed by life and socioeconomic structures, become political, one must examine the life experiences of people who have been there themselves.

Whereas many influential activist Latinos describe the impact of family background, opportunities for activism, and issues such as the status of Puerto Rico as stimulators of their political involvement, *la gente del pueblo* describe a more personal struggle against oppression. For Aracelis Guzmán, the politicization process began when she started working for the Department of Public Health as a nursing outreach worker. She describes the debilitating effects of the poverty she saw when she went into Latino homes:

Creo que lo que yo estaba aprendiendo [measured tone of voice, slower, important] también era que . . . cuando tu no tienes suficiente dinero para tu renta, para alimentar a tus hijos, cuando no tienes dinero para salir ni a un cine o ir a un baile, que estás todo el día encerrada en la casa, cuando tu no estás consciente de que hay otras alternativas en la vida aparte de ser mamá, que puedes ir a la escuela, que puedes sacar un inglés ¿verdad? es muy difícil dar educación preventiva. Que la mente no está abierta para recibir ese conocimiento, está uno embotado—unos lloran, unos tienen diarrea—si están en un relación abusiva con el marido o con el novio, es que . . . son demasiadas presiones.

I believe that what I was learning [measured tone of voice, slower, important] was also that . . . when you don't have enough money for rent, to feed your children, when you don't have money to even go out to a movie or to go to a dance, that you are locked in the house all day long, when you aren't conscious of having other alternatives in life

142

other than being a mother, that you can go to school, that you can learn English, right? it's very difficult to do preventive education. Because the mind isn't open to receiving that knowledge—one is dulled [enervated]—some cry, some have diarrhea—if they are in an abusive relationship with a husband or boyfriend . . . there are too many pressures.

Guzmán goes on to describe how the spark of political awareness transforms poverty and a sense of debilitating oppression into a potential for political participation:

> *Entonces yo creo que para uno poder envolverse políticamente—¿verdad?—tiene que en primer lugar sentir esa necesidad de decir, "Bueno, ¿por qué es que yo estoy así? ¿cómo es que yo puedo cambiar esto? . . . Yo tengo que hacer algo," y entonces uno empieza a preguntar, ¿verdad? o a la vecina, o si hay una agencia dos cuadras cerca de mi casa. . . . Es como una chispa que prende ¿verdad? y que el espíritu de la persona en ese momento está listo* [emphasis added].

So I believe that, for one to be able to get involved politically—right?—one has to first feel that need to say to oneself, "Well, why is it that I'm like this? How can I change this? I have to do something," and then one begins to ask, right? your neighbor, or if there's an agency two blocks away from my house. . . . It's like *a spark that ignites*, right? and, at that moment, the spirit of the person is ready [emphasis added].

For Guzmán, making the initial connection between one's daily problems and larger political issues is the first step toward participation.

The feminist theme of "the personal is political" cannot have a stronger argument than this. Guzmán describes this moment as a spark—*una chispa*—a critical moment in which one begins to question the nature of one's existence. Crucial to the present study of participation is that the spark drives one to venture outward—to other people, other places, first for help, later with others in action for change. This spark can come from a *charla*, like those held at Mujeres Unidas en Acción, from interaction with a new friend, or from a slow process of questioning within the self, as the following portrait of Julia Santiago demonstrates. This portrait shows how, after the spark, there is a slow emergence of increasingly politicized consciousness and behavior.

Portrait of Julia Santiago: From Oppression to "Being Political"

I first met Julia Santiago at the National Puerto Rican Congress Convention, Memorial Day weekend 1989. She was one of a panel of

143

women in a workshop called the Vision of the Woman: Head of the Family, Administrative Tasks of the Household—the Sociopolitical Struggle.[26] At this workshop I heard Santiago tell the story of her development from *una jibarita* to a political person.

A *jíbaro*, as discussed in Chapter 2, is one of the countryfolk of Puerto Rico, a "worker of the cane"—a peasant. Santiago uses the term *jibarita* in its (affectionate) diminutive and feminine form to describe her naivete, her youth, and her oppressive, traditional family. When reading this portrait, it is very important to keep in mind that this is not a woman who comes from the middle class or even the working class. She very much typifies the poor women who make up much of the Latino community. In her language and demeanor, she has not changed into a professional or middle-class person, despite her ability to use such lofty phrases as, *"Yo siempre he estado cuestionando la situación patriarcal"* ("Always I have been challenging the patriarchal system").

What is striking about the story of Julia Santiago is how similar her early life is to that of many Latino people who are the least active politically. In many ways her experiences as a child and young adult sound similar to the description given by Aracelis Guzmán—someone too enervated to think beyond surviving day by day. Santiago came from a family with a rigid, authoritarian father; she left Puerto Rico to *"salir de la dictadura de mi padre"* ("leave the dictatorship of my father") but "like many young women came to live in a house very similar to that of my father." Her husband made her lie to get welfare, and Santiago said, "You have to lie so that they'll serve you." She recalls how alienating and intimidating the experience of "seeking help" was; she describes the welfare workers as *"majadores"*—"real bruisers." After ten months she went to work in a factory and went from *mal en peor* (from bad to worse). She finally decided to put an end to her marriage because: *"Mejor ir sola, que mal acompañada"* ("Better to go it alone than in bad company").

A new period in her life began with the decision to leave her husband. She moved to Boston with her children and got a job as a hospital aide. At first she thought she loved the job so much that she would stay as long as they would keep her. After a while, however, she became aware of discrimination and was the brunt of demeaning jokes against Latinos. At the same time, problems with her building landlord and her children led her to seek solutions in ways she had not thought of before.

During the workshop Santiago passed quickly over how she changed from a woman suffering quietly—alone—to one leading a tenant action, attending college classes, and *"haciendo trabajo político"* ("doing political work"). Only in a later interview were we able to explore the process of her politicization.

Santiago confirms, in many ways, the route to becoming political discussed in Aviel (1981)—through her daily life and the needs of her children.

> *Es bien curioso, precisamente es que todo de momento te encuentras que los hijos te lleguen á tener problemas y tu no sabes que hacer. Porque no importa que tu estás trabajando, cuan honesta tu eres, no se te—no es lo mismo. Tu,—como los niños no entienden y lo único que te queda por él es tirarte por la calle buscar información—de momento.*

> It's really curious, it's just like, all at once you find that your children begin to have problems and you don't know what to do. Because it doesn't matter that you're working, how honest you are, it doesn't— it's not the same. You—like—your children don't understand and the only thing left to you is to throw yourself out into the street looking for help—all of a sudden.

In the process of seeking help for her children, Santiago developed relationships that brought her out of the social isolation common to many Latina women and created social connections and opportunities to go beyond her personal experience into questioning why things had to be the way they were. She says, *"De momento me encuentro con gente que sabía tanto más que yo; de momento, digo, 'Pero, ¡¿qué es lo que pasa conmigo?!'"* ("All of a sudden I find myself with people who knew so much more than me; all of a sudden, I say, 'But, what's going on with me?!'" Like Guzmán, Santiago experienced the spark, the moment of being conscious of the need for change. This consciousness, together with greater social connectedness, is the crucial ingredient in the politicization process of Latina women who move from oppressed backgrounds to political involvement.

Pardo (1990) describes a similar "transformation" process for Mexican-American women in East Los Angeles. She states that "women have transformed organizing experiences and social networks arising from gender-related responsibilities into political resources" and traces this political development to women's concerns (2). "In these processes, women meet other mothers and begin developing a network of acquaintanceships and friendships based on mutual concern for the welfare of their children" (2). This concept of transformation suggests that, in contrast to earlier theories that saw motherhood as a constraint on participation, many poor women are motivated to action precisely out of concern for their children. Marisela Pena, a teacher at Mujeres Unidas en Acción, for example, sees the political education of Latina women as having a greater impact than the education of men because of women's socializing effect on children. She remarks: *"Educar un hombre es educar una persona; educar una mujer es educar una familia"* ("To educate a man is to educate one person; to educate a woman is to educate a family").

Later in the interview, Santiago discussed her tenant organizing experiences; how her new role evolved reveals much about the themes of "being political" and "becoming political." She is able to describe the fine line between the "not conscious" and the "consciously political" as she describes her early days in New York:

> *Es que tu misma no lo sabes que es algo político. Por ejemplo, . . . yo vivía en New York, yo siempre ayudaba a la gente. Yo estaba en welfare y las mujeres, muchas veces me decían: ¿qué yo podría hacer en tal y cual situación?" y siempre yo estaba aclarándoles a ellas, cómo era una manera de saber defenderse—y a la misma vez luchar por lo que ellas querían.*

> It's that *you yourself* don't know that it's political. For example, . . . I lived in New York; I always was helping people. I was on welfare, and the women would often come to me asking what I could do to help them with this and that situation and I was always explaining things to them how there was a way to stick up for oneself—and at the same time fight for what *they* wanted.

Santiago then goes on to link this experience to a point she made at the workshop.

> *Parte de lo que yo dije en mi presentación—que en mi trabajo ahora yo siempre me considero político; yo lo veo como el mismo—de eso de sobrevivir—y no, tu sabes—tu siempre estás haciendo trabajo político y tu no lo sabes.*

> Part of what I was saying in my presentation [at the workshop]—that in the work I do [now] I always consider myself political; I see them as the same thing—that of surviving—and not, you know—you're always working politically and you don't [even] know it.

Julia Santiago's life illustrates that adult resocializing experiences are as important as childhood socialization in the development of the political self. Santiago became political as an adult through a network of personal relationships in her daily life. Her radical feminist ideology is thoroughly entrenched in her worldview but is an ideology clearly learned in adulthood. Her family was part of her oppression, not a source of political strength.

Santiago sees the fine line between political unawareness and political consciousness; she also connects daily survival with politics. Political development is not a fixed characteristic, handed down through the family; it is a process that occurs in interaction with others. In addition, being political and becoming political may develop out of actions begun within women's traditional roles. Latina women's decisions to protest or take other forms of political action may first be stimulated by concerns for children and by family needs. The internal and collective processes that occur by participating in such activities, however, can themselves be politicizing. Within the context of community and connectedness, community empowerment is personal empowerment.

> The process of coming to political consciousness seems to be a process of making connections—between their own lives and those of others, between issues that affect them and their families in the neighborhood or community and those that affect them in the workplace, between the so-called differing spheres of their lives—a process of overcoming precisely the "fragmented consciousness" that, in Katznelson's view, constrains political action in the United States. (Ackelsberg 1988, 305)

The portrait of Julia Santiago provides a counterpoint to the earlier description of Marta Correa. Where Correa says, "I'm not political" and then describes a wealth of conventional political behaviors, here is Santiago, who says, "I'm political" and describes an emphasis on working with others to organize on their own behalf.

The difference seems to have something to do with the focus on working *for* others versus working *with* others. Correa is called upon by the "powers that be" to organize the Latinos for *them*, although she obviously thinks it is to the advantage of the Latino community as well. Santiago, on the other hand, operates in a delicate balance between the traditional political world and the consciousness-focused, personal development politics of Mujeres Unidas en Acción. In fact, Santiago's participation in conventional politics mixes a personal decision not to vote with efforts to offer the women at Mujeres Unidas the chance to learn about the political system. Despite her decision not to vote, Santiago leads women to protests, testimony at the State House, and educational *charlas* on politics to help them learn about the political system. She even invited a group of Latina women to the protest march against Question 3 (a budget-cutting ballot referendum in the 1990 election).

Latinos like Julia Santiago—political activists who do not vote—raise a potentially troubling question: Do community-based, feminist, or radical modes of political participation suppress conventional modes such as voting? It certainly appears that women like Santiago who reject the vote because it does not lead to significant social change, and women like Inez Martínez, Carmen Gómez, and Aracelis Guzmán who eschew citizenship (and thus the vote) favor community-based politics over electoral politics. Most Latina women, however, combine a community focus with traditional political behaviors. And, as the portrait of Santiago shows, even women who do not participate in traditional behaviors like the vote often encourage other women to engage in the full range of political activities. What is more important is that, regardless of the behavioral manifestations of politics that result from the politicization process, the process itself involves the development of personal and political consciousness. In addition, it is consciousness, connections, and collective effort that lead to involvement in politics, especially for Latina women.

Latina Women, Marriage, and the Politicization Process. Julia Santiago is one of several Latina women who marked her entrance into a political life with the decision to leave her husband. María Luisa Soto, is another who became involved in politics only after she moved away from her husband. I did not specifically collect marital status on the people interviewed; however, only nine (37 percent) of the twenty-four women for whom I had marital status were married. The rest were divorced or separated. Three of the nine married women portrayed their husbands as supportive of their political activism; these three are women with higher education levels and income. For the poorer women, not having a husband seems associated with a higher degree of politicization; their political involvement began after separation from their husbands. The Latino men did not mention marriage as having an impact on their degree of political participation or their path to becoming political.

Why poorer Latina women may become more political after separation is a tantalizing question that deserves future research. There is a wide-ranging debate about whether child rearing and homemaking responsibilities limit the time or energy women have available for political participation.[27] Since the politicized Latina women of *la gente del pueblo* all had children, worked, and often went back to school as adults, it may be marriage, not child and home responsibilities per se, that constrains certain groups of women.[28]

Latino Men and the Politicization Process

It may have already occurred to the reader that most of the examples given of the politicization *process* are in Latina women's voices. Why have there been so few examples from the men? The first reason is that, for the most part, Latina women spontaneously brought up their own politicization and discussed it to a much greater degree than did the men. The second reason is that, even when invited, Latino men rarely shared a sense of political development but rather focused on family traditions and formal and organizational affiliations as the source of their politicization. The politicization factors for men merit a deeper look.

As the theme of politicization began to emerge from my analysis of the interviews, I began to question my interview approach. Perhaps I was asking women questions that led them in this direction? Perhaps men "secretly" had many of the same thoughts, but the interview guide was not designed to bring them out? Following the first series of interviews, I explicitly began asking the Latino men: "Tell me what made you become political" and did not rely only on spontaneous revelations. On several occasions I even went back for second interviews when I felt a "hint" about male politicization had been dropped by a man.[29] Surprisingly, or not surprisingly, the additional effort did not yield an increase in discussion around politicizing events, feelings, or stimulating factors. Most of the men who did discuss what led to their living a politically involved life talked about very different things than did the Latina women. The differences stand: *the Latino male talks about becoming political less than the Latina woman and does so in a qualitatively different way.*

Felipe Aviles, for example, describes how he found Boston more open to being shaped by new Latino activists than New York City. He then describes how his first job in the community was an "interesting learning experience. . . . I was excited about that job. . . . It was really a very interesting thing, a way in which people identified me with leadership for the community in education . . . so through there I began to be involved in committees that have to do with public education in Boston. I began to complain with my people of the fact that in the political structure, we have nobody elected anywhere to do anything." Like many of the men, Aviles talks about becoming political in terms of elections, jobs, positions, and opportunities. He also demonstrates the male path to becoming political in his actions: he was one of the men who helped form a major Latino political organization and was appointed to a position in government.

The idea of "opportunity" echoes through many of the Latino men's stories of becoming political. The path to becoming political follows the road of "getting people to participate in holding public offices." Edwin Colina, for example, was a major force in successfully organizing *la gente del pueblo* during the 1970s school desegregation battle, and his activist credentials cannot be faulted. Nevertheless, he speaks of his politicization as an *opportunity*. Boston was, for him, "*unexplored territory*, in terms of Latino politics and Latino presence. . . . There wasn't the infrastructure work that's so necessary in getting a community recognized . . . to come in here and start doing the type of organizing I was used to" [emphasis added]. When pressed, he stated that he felt his political roots were nurtured by being part of the Young Lords and Black Panther movements in New York during the 1960s. He did not elaborate on this theme, however, even when pressed to do so.

When Latino men *did* discuss their politicization, though always less than the women, the theme that emerged over and over again was that they became political through formal affiliations. Juan Vázquez, for example, traces his politicization to the McGovern campaign in Brooklyn and to his work with a local judge. He speaks of wanting to "get into politics" almost as a profession; for him, being political is less wanting to accomplish something for the community and more what he wants to achieve for himself.[30] Aviles talks about committees and organizations. Armando Meléndez, who at first sounded more like some of the women and traced his political life to "*la necesidad*" (need of the community), immediately switched to talk about his role in forming an organization to promote constitutional rights for Hispanics and his work on election campaigns. Later he discussed his own potential for running for office and acknowledged his prominence in the community; he said that although he has no aspirations for elected office he could be elected by Latinos because of his name recognition.

Even Manuel Sánchez who stated, "Not everyone wants to be a politician when they grow up," went on to describe political life as if it meant committees and boards of directors. He said, for example, that one did not have to run for office to be political. I then waited to hear if he would describe some of the more personal aspects, relational aspects, of political life discussed by Latina women. No, his view of alternatives was that "one can be appointed, serve on boards, be involved in community-based organizations; one can be an active member of their community."

Finally, how do Latino men envision stimulating increased politicization? Again, through formal structures. For example, one of the ways some of the influential men try to stimulate politicization in Latino youth is by presenting young Latinos with awards at the Latino Democratic Committee banquet. The male model is the formal organizational model. Even noninfluential Latino men identify political activities with formal affiliations. For example, Luis Hernández, a janitor, describes his political involvement in terms of his role as deacon in the Catholic church. As a deacon of the church he is able to urge people to go to the polls, he offers to take them on election day.

What all these examples share and illustrate is the predominance of formal affiliations in the politicization process of Latino men. The end result seems to be that the Latino men *organize* events, but it is the Latina women who, for the most part, actually achieve participation by the Latino members of the community. Obviously, this role of formal affiliations in the *process* of becoming political is closely related to the male pattern of seeing political participation as achieving positions and status.

Gender differences in the self-perception of "being political" may also explain why some of the Latina women would say, "I'm not political" or "I don't like politics," despite high levels of conventional (e.g., electoral) political activism. Many Latina women seemed to reject the "politicking" within formal political structures that typifies male perceptions of being political. One Puerto Rican woman, for example, had just about decided to give up political work completely. She is an influential Latina who combines election work, party politics, and voter registration with intensive, personal, community-based politics. Her reason? Certain influential men are more intent on maintaining political control than on increasing participation and political awareness. This woman was trying to tell Latinos in various housing developments what their choices were in terms of candidates; certain key men wanted a voting bloc. There was considerable dissension around who was going to control the political participation mechanisms and how individual Latinos were to vote. I suggest that the self-perception of "not being political" involves the rejection of a certain *type* of politics—that of maneuvering for power and control—not of political activism itself.

Gender, Consciousness, and Political Participation

Contrary to a political self derived from a desire for positions, power and autonomy, and competition for status, the political development of Latina women in Boston demonstrates that political consciousness emerges within the social context—in connection with others. The image of political socialization and political consciousness that exists in mainstream literature is revealed to reflect male concerns for power and autonomy, the assertion of the self, and competition— concerns that overshadow what feminists suggest are equally valid political needs: affiliation, connection, and community.

S I X

Constraints on Participation: The Impact of Structure and Sexism

Classic participatory democratic theory is grounded in an appreciation of the mutual interrelationship between political culture and political structure. . . . [Yet,] if the relationship of political culture and political structure is our concern, then some attention must be paid to the impact of structure on culture.[1]

—*Carole Pateman, "The Civic Culture: A Philosophic Critique"*

They would take people who wanted to register to vote to City Hall, and City Hall would treat them like they were nobodies. For some reason, if you don't speak English well, and your name sounds different—if you're José Rivera—people think you're deaf also. So they yell, "What's your name?" and they yell it. It's just an intimidating experience.

—*Marta Rosa, Latina candidate*

One might well ask at this juncture, why, if Latina women's emphasis on connectedness, collectivity, community, and consciousness promotes a participatory model of politics, is political participation in the Latino community not at a higher, more visible level. The major reason continues to be that much of the politics that exists is obscured by the definition of "What is political?" The political-mobilization efforts generally utilized by women—efforts promoting the creation of citizens, political consciousness, and the interpersonal relationships of politics—are reduced to a "lesser" form of politics than are elections and access to positions. Nevertheless, it would be foolish to conclude this book without acknowledging the equally important structural constraints that block Latino efforts to achieve

153

full political participation in the United States. Some of these constraints specifically affect Latina women and reduce their ability to achieve change. Others constrain Latino political participation in general.

In other words, the creation of community, the support of interpersonal connections and collective processes, and the development of political consciousness, however essential in political mobilization, are insufficient in and of themselves to achieve full political empowerment for Latinos. Pervasive constraints on full participation include sexism and racism within the Latino culture and larger Anglo society, limiting Latina women from maximizing their political potential; the lack of concessions from those in power, making political participation seem to be a fruitless expenditure of energy; structural barriers to registration and voting; the changed political system (e.g., the decline of party competition, the demise of the political machine, and the withdrawal of government support for community organizing); and the lack of congruence between cultural expectations for participatory politics and the alienating realities of the current American political system.

Sexism and Racism: Constraints on Latina Women

Connectedness, attention to the interplay between private and public life, development of political consciousness, and collective, nonhierarchical organizational structures are all ways Latina women expand both the meaning of politics and the methods of achieving increased political participation in the community. Even with all that individual Latina activists do and that organizations like Mujeres Unidas illustrate, however, Latina women in politics face constraints *beyond* those facing Latino men.

Latina women, as women, are constrained by sexism within their own culture and within the broader society. Life for Latinas often *is* restrictive, oppressive, and subservient (Guzmán 1976, 231–234). Latina women face pressure to be less assertive and more passive in public than their male counterparts.[2]

There is evidence among Latinos in Boston that women *do* experience constraints on their activism, constraints created by cultural expectations of women's roles and by men's concerns for power and status. According to Teresa Andrade, male concerns for status in public forums and within the family constrain the participation of Latina women. She explains:

> Sometimes I've seen a lot of women get involved and then get pulled back by their partner when they begin to get too involved. It's like,

"Okay, you can go to these meetings but don't get too involved." When they develop a certain level of assuredness and success and self-esteem—sure, when they're recognized by their own peers as doing something good and being of value then the men sometimes get real threatened and say, "You can't come to the meetings, you can't go any more, you can't be there any more, those people are doing bad things to you." It's a loss of control by the men in the household.

Even Latino men notice how Latina women's contributions are stifled by Latino men who are sexist. Juan Vázquez, for example, describes a community meeting:

The majority of those individuals are all men basically, who go to these meetings; they speak and talk about the past and what's happening now and they just basically *talk*. At that meeting what I specifically recall is a gentleman . . . who was one of the old timers and one of the founders of the Puerto Rican Carnival here. He is very well respected, does a lot of work in the community, but he's sexist, period. He was saying a couple of things but not coming up with any concrete solution with how to deal with the particular problem. There was one woman, Juanita, who works now for the state government, who basically proposed something—very articulate, very well thought out. And—*because* she was a woman, the responses from the males that were there were like, "Well it's okay, it's an idea, but we don't want to really participate." There was another woman who said basically the same thing; she was a very articulate woman, Gladys, she was there. The same thing—basically the women that were there were very articulate.

I think, for me, after being here in the community ten years, within Boston, some of the most articulate leaders of our community tend to be women, but the political *power* is invested in men—Armando Meléndez, Tito Morales, and several others I could mention. They tend to *talk* about incorporating women, but actually they don't. So— I remember that specific time women came up with good ideas, but no follow-through—the men won the day and, of course, not too much got done. I remember that specifically.

Subtle forms of racism constrain Latina women's political activism as well. Such a constraint exists in the relationship between Latina women and mainstream feminism. The question might be asked: Can the feminist movement contribute to the politicization of Latina women? The goal of "women reaching women" could overcome many of the barriers facing Latina women, and the concern of the movement about women's rights could rally Latinas around the issues of domestic violence; the impact of AIDS on minority women; the lack of housing, poverty, and inadequate welfare budgets. The relationship between the feminist movement and Latina women, however great its mobilizing potential, is, nevertheless, one of tension and unease. Feminist Latina women in Boston point out that this relationship is much more complex than the potential benefits would indicate. Two sources of tension exist: (1) the ways some Anglo feminist organizations have related to Latina groups and (2) the rights-based focus of the Anglo feminist movement versus the distributive-justice goals of Latina feminists.[3]

Latina feminists pick up quickly on racially denigrating attitudes, however unintentional, that imply Anglo superiority: it is as if women of color need to be *taught* by white women *how* to do politics. Such attitudes are challenged by a long tradition of Latina women who are feminists, hold political positions, and are actively "doing politics." For example, there is a vibrant feminist movement in the Latino community in Boston. Nine of the Latina women identified themselves as feminists. Also, there are three explicitly feminist Latina groups in Boston at the current time: a local chapter of the National Puerto Rican Women's Committee, the Comité de Mujeres Miriam López-Pérez (Miriam López-Pérez Women's Committee), and the women's committee at the Puerto Rican Organizing Resource Center.

In addition, some women cite examples of Latina women holding high national offices in countries like Puerto Rico and Nicaragua. A longtime mayor of San Juan, Puerto Rico, was a woman. Latina women are even presidents of countries (Violeta Chamorro of Nicaragua, for example)—a success American women only dream of. (And Rosario Ibarra de Piedra ran for president of Mexico in 1982.) Andrea del Valle becomes angry when the long tradition of Latina women in Puerto Rican politics is ignored.

> There's a *tradition* of women participation in our history, since the *Indians*, the Tainos. We were a *matriarcado* (a matriarchy). It changed with the Spaniards, but we have *caciques* who were women, *cacicas*— we have women who were sindicalists in the last century, or the beginning of this century. We have women who struggled for the independence of Puerto Rico against the Spaniards—Alejandrina—so it's like, "Why are you talking to me that you're trying to teach me politics?" We have *different* ways to practice that and to participate.

The implication of superiority and the marginalization of Latina women in political life by Anglo women in feminist organizations is illustrated by the following example from del Valle, who is outraged by the unequal status afforded Latina women's groups in developing plans and strategies. Instead of working jointly as equals, they call us like, "Can you cosponsor?" and then we say, "Well, we'll have to meet, we will discuss it, and we have to get back to you." If it's for a flyer, "When are we going to have the flyer so we know that we have to discuss it and give you the information maybe to cosponsor an event." "Oh no, we have the flyer." [Andrea goes on to say,] "So what do you want? A blanket statement, that you can sign my name, so whoever can see that you deal with Latinos?"

What del Valle wants is clear:

To see us as equals. Don't come to me with silly words and trying to be nice. No, let's get serious, let's talk, let's do this, let's strategize. A lot of the participation that they want from us is to show up at an event and when they decide how the event is going to be, where, what time, the decisions, and what the issues are going to be, not the logistics, if it's gonna be Monday versus Wednesday. They don't think that we have to participate. That's why we decided to have our own organization and we don't have to argue if it's important or not, we know it's important so we do it our way [emphasis added].

Thus, conflicts between Latina activists and mainstream feminist organizations stem from implicit messages, however unintentional, of Anglo superiority. Del Valle and others acknowledge that such problems do not occur with every women's organization. There have been examples of racial solidarity, of Latina, black, and white women working together in Boston in common cause. Nevertheless, the uneasy relationship between the Latina women in Boston who are feminists and the mainstream feminist movement reduces potential alliances between the two groups.

In addition to problems of communication and race relations between Anglo and Latina feminists, there are other problems associated with the feminist movement. Ackelsberg (1991), for example, alludes to "the hesitation of many working-class women and women of color in this country to adopt the feminist label" and suggests that this hesitation is due to the perception that "feminism is a white, middle-class movement" that spends "too much attention on abortion, birth control, and sexuality" (3). The Anglo feminist movement's emphasis on protecting the hard-won right to an abortion is troubling to Latina women for several reasons. First, this emphasis on abortion means less attention to Latina issues that have more to do with economic survival. These issues include jobs for Latino men, adequate wages for Latina women who work, sufficient welfare budgets, the availability of day care,[4] quality educational programs, and, as mentioned earlier, protection against domestic violence.

Second, abortion itself is personally and religiously troubling to many Latina women, so that the identification of Anglo feminist organizations with a pro-choice position may alienate some Latinas. Finally, even those Latina women who align themselves with the reproductive-rights stance of Anglo feminist organizations are angry.[5] They feel that when white women's abortion rights were threatened in the Supreme Court, as during the recent assault on reproductive rights, a huge, well-financed mobilization was initiated. However, this same outpouring of women and money did not take place earlier when poor—and Latina—women's rights were threatened by the loss of Medicaid funding for abortions. One woman explains:

I think that people have been confused and, like, we have a lot of problems when we go and meet with all women's organizations because they want us to be like they are, and we're different. They don't take into account socioeconomic issues. . . . Abortion, for example, who cares about abortion if you don't talk about the other rights? Like for us, it's more important to denounce sterilization abuse.[6] To talk just about abortion, the right to abortion? The right to abortion has been an issue for us ten years ago from the Hyde amendment. Now *white* women, or other women from a different class—*her* right to abortion has been affected, but *we* didn't have any funding *years* ago. So, you know, why are you talking to me now that we have to be desperate going crazy around the street talking about abortion? We have been talking about abortion for ten years. But we have to talk about housing, we have to talk about political repression, we have to talk about needing a ceiling over our heads.

Another problem for Latina women is a perceived exclusion of men from the struggle for social change. Many Latina women feel it is critical to work with Latino men to tackle issues that confront the community at large; employment of Latino men, for example, affects Latina women and Latino families so Latina women do not want to isolate themselves in a movement geared toward women alone. Coole (1988) and Dietz (1989) suggest that, when fighting racism, minority men and women may join together and act upon a need for solidarity in ways some Anglo women in the movement seem to eschew. One Latina feminist objects to the exclusion of men:

I think that women's participation—to define it, it has to be viewed in the context of the culture and of class, and where they're coming from because what is political for everyone may be different. For example, a lot of things that we do when we meet with people from NOW, or Mass Choice, is like—what the hell?—that's not feminism. There's a lot of women that think that to be a feminist you have to hate men. . . . We can't have an island of women, that's not realistic.

In other words, Latina women seem to advocate a more inclusive focus: "a commitment to activity of citizenship, which includes and requires the participation of men" (Dietz 1989, 18).

Thus, the Anglo feminist movement and Latina women have an uneasy relationship. There are cultural barriers to be bridged, and Latinas could educate Anglo women about the strength of Latina women in the course of history. Lingering traces of racism continue to affect relations between the movement and Latina feminist groups. Instead of the question, Can the mainstream feminist movement contribute to the politicization of Latina women? a better question might be, Will the Anglo feminist movement learn from Latina women?

Latina women pose a challenge to the movement to broaden its agenda from one focused prominently on the abortion-rights issue to one that tackles the issues of poor women. In addition, given the ability of women in general to consider personal relationships well within the realm of political life, there is a need to address the power balance between Anglo women and Latina women before these two groups can join together for justice and for the participation of all women in all aspects of politics.

Lack of Concessions: The Limitations of Political Activism

Political activism using connectedness, collectivity, community, and consciousness generates participation, but the commitment to a politically participatory life is sorely tested by the unresponsiveness of the political system to the demands of the poor. Piven and Cloward (1979) identify a flaw in the current political system: "The flaw is, quite simply, that it is not possible to compel concessions from elites that can be used as resources to sustain oppositional organizations over time" (xxi). As long as the larger political system fails to respond to the demands of minority groups and the poor, Latinos know there is less reason to participate. As María Luisa Soto explains, *"Somos pobres, pero no somos estúpidos"* ("We're poor, but we're not stupid").

Just as oppositional organizations are worn down by the limited concessions wrested from an unresponsive power structure, Latino activists—even the passionately political—sometimes become depoliticized as a result of their inability to gain concessions from the political system.

Portrait of Inez Martínez: "No Matter What We Do, the Elevators Won't Get Fixed"

Inez Martínez is a fifty-year-old woman who came to Boston from Mexico twenty-five years ago. Although she never became a citizen and does not participate in electoral politics, she personifies the model of participatory democracy based on personal connections and collective action to improve conditions of living for Latinos in Boston. Her basic method has been to keep in touch with residents of the Villa Victoria tower, most of whom are poor and Latino. She describes how she has worked with people for over six years, exhorting them to come to tenant meetings, meetings between tenants and the Boston Housing Authority, and events such as exercise classes for senior citizens. Her sense of politics thus combines participation in communal life and working together to gain improvements in housing. Her imminent depoliticization stems from her inability to wrest improvements from the Housing Authority.

One of the major problems at the tower building of Villa Victoria has been maintenance, especially of the elevators. The elevators, as well as the security system, chronically fail, sometimes due to vandalism, other times because of mechanical problems. For several years Martínez had been successful in rallying members to protests and meetings. She would go door to door:

> *"¡Bajen!" los animaba yo. "¡Bajen! ¡Bajen! Bajen, miren que vamos a tener esto—que se va a hablar de esto, que se va a hablar de otro."* [I ask: *"¿Y cómo respondió la gente?"*] *Pues, más o menos bien, no mucho—pero bajaban, mucha gente. Pero ¡ahora! [I ask, "¿Es diferente?"] ¡Huy! . . . En estos días me he dejado mucho porque yo estoy cansada.*

> "Come on down!" I would encourage them. "Come on down! Come on down! Look we're going to have this—that they're going to talk about such and such." [I ask: "And how did the people respond?" She answers,] Well, more or less okay, not very much—but many people would come downstairs. But now! [I ask: "Is it different?"] Whew! . . . These days I've given up a lot because I'm tired.

Inez Martínez is a woman who has been active in her building, has worked with community groups in Jamaica Plain, and has participated in a protest when a group lobbied at the State House. Now, she is tired and frustrated; she feels like quitting her mobilizing efforts. What is the source of this withdrawal from politics? The lack of concessions. At first, Martínez sounds like she joins the "Latinos are apathetic" bandwagon when she talks about Latinos in her building who reject all overtures, even to the point of insulting the organizers. But upon deeper inquiry, she reveals the real reason for her disillusionment: there has been no response from the institutions that hold the power. "Nothing we do will get the elevators fixed," is how she perceives the feelings of the tenants.

Indeed, the concessions from the Boston Housing Authority are few. Martínez tells her story:

> *Mira, ayer nosotros tuvimos una junta, es por aquí cerca y fuimos allá y yo no sabía porque—esta carta la recibí tarde como siempre* [she shows a letter from the Boston Housing Authority]*—total que yo fui allá pensando en que la reunión iba a ser también por estos pisos en la torre pero dijeron que no. Dijeron que todos los que tenían una pregunta o que querían decir algo, favor lo dijera. Bueno, pues yo empecé a decir a los de Boston Housing que aquí también tenían muchos problemas . . . y dijeron ellos—"Bueno," dice, "eso no se va a hablar aquí—eso no se habla aquí—nada más que las casitas." Y yo me decía, "¿entonces por qué pusieron tantos papeles, y por qué ofrecieron un premio?" A mí me pareció ridículo gastar tantos papeles por todos lados.*

Look, yesterday we had a board meeting near here and we went there and, I didn't know because—I didn't get this letter till late, as usual [she shows a letter from the Boston Housing Authority]—so I went there thinking that the meeting was going to be about these floors in the tower building too, but they said no. They said that if anyone had a question or wanted to say something please say it. Well, I began to say to those of Boston Housing, that here, too, there are many problems . . . and they said, "Well," he said, "We're not going to talk about that here—that's not going to be discussed here—only the garden apartments." And I said to myself, "Then why did they put the notices on the bulletin board and offer a prize for coming?" It seemed ridiculous to me to waste such an amount of paper everywhere.

In other words, the Boston Housing Authority had put up flyers all over the tower building and offered prizes to encourage attendance; she went about mobilizing people to come, only to find out that the meeting would not address the grievances of the residents in the tower.

Martínez then talked about who controlled the agenda of the meeting: the Boston Housing Authority. The Housing Authority's hidden goal for the meeting was to keep people from putting their trash out too early and to inform them that a fine would be given to those found guilty. Another goal of the authority was to stop tenants from repairing cars outside: *"Se ve mal"* ("It looks bad"). Tenants had attended the meeting to voice grievances and seek solutions to chronic problems; they arrived hoping to get the elevators serviced and cleaned. Their issues were not even on the agenda.[7] The people in the building consequently withdrew in disgust and rejected Inez Martínez's entreaties.

Martínez herself has decided it is too frustrating to continue to work on tenant organizing. She feels her health is suffering from the frustration, and she has disengaged from participation. The lack of concessions from the authorities has worn away her dedication to political activism and has depoliticized her. Her story illustrates the interaction between broad structural unresponsiveness and individual decisions to become political or to withdraw from participating.

Such a lack of concessions goes beyond any one government agency, or any one individual, however. The ability of the political institutions to maintain control over any real, substantive redistribution of power also suppresses the ability of Latino organizations to take on explicitly political roles. Nowhere is this more evident than in the relationships between Latino agencies and the larger government institutions that support them.

Structural Constraints on Latino Agencies: The Impact on Political Mobilization

"No society has ever funded its own overthrow," says Jesús Carrillo, co-founder of the Latino Democratic Committee. With this statement, Carrillo identifies a major constraint on the mobilization potential of state-funded agencies: the competition for funds. While there are ample examples of cooperative efforts led by the directors of Latino agencies in Boston[8] and by the (mostly women) staff, as discussed in the last chapters, the competition for funds overwhelms most agency directors and often prevents political mobilization strategies from being included in the agencies' missions.

Agencies are prevented from political activism by four forces: (1) agency survival strategies that stress competition for scarce funds; (2) the withdrawal of government resources and support for political participation; (3) prohibitions against political activism by regulations such as the Hatch Act; and (4) the "lure of the great job," which attracts males away from work within the community into government positions.

Boston's Latino community-based agencies "have been both the results [of] and the avenues for political activism and political power" (Uriarte and Merced 1985, 22). Although Latino agencies have been somewhat successful in organizing among themselves to reduce interagency competition, their dependence on government funding and the dominant power structure has constrained their ability to take independent political action.[9]

Community-based political activism during the 1960s and 1970s created the Latino agencies of Boston. The diminished ability of the agencies today to maintain political mobilizing roles is due to the constraints of a contracting economy, decreasing funds, and a more conservative political climate. In addition, as the agencies became institutionalized their role as mobilizer changed to that of human service provider. In essence, the Latino agencies—as political mobilizers—became depoliticized.[10]

Comunidad Boricua en Acción, for example, has changed from a mobilizer of the community to a human service delivery agency. Under Luz Cuadrado and Julio Herrera, the agency clearly was able to combine agency operations with community mobilization. Gone now, however, are the mass mobilizations led by Cuadrado; gone are the days of Herrera, who on election day turned his staff loose on "get out the vote" drives. Carmen Gómez, the present director, talked about her search for new methods (or old methods, for that matter) to address a problem in the agency's tenant organization: underinvolvement by residents. In the process of deciding what to do, Gómez and her staff spent one day two years ago going door to door to listen to and talk with tenants. She describes what happened:

> The entire staff including myself went out for an afternoon and divided ourselves into the different developments that we have and did door knocking, set up a table, and invited other resources [i.e., staff from other departments of the agency] so that there would be more than us in there and going out there and knocking on doors. When we all came back and shared information, the information was that some staff people felt very frustrated because the general concern was what the management companies are not doing versus what are you [the tenant] doing. Others were very overwhelmed because people received them very warmly and opened the door—it was hard to get out of the house because they wanted us to have coffee—talk and talk and talk, and the time was very limited, and people were very encouraged— "Oh, we haven't seen you in a while, and we're glad to see you! We hope to see more of you." *But we only are able to do that once a year for an afternoon, and we did it a second year, but we didn't do it last year because of no time* [emphasis added].

Although some tenants apparently rejected the overtures of the agency staff and used the visits to complain about housing conditions, many others expressed the desire for connectedness. The La-

163

tino tenants wanted to have coffee, talk about problems, and get to know the staff. At another point in the interview, Gómez described how tenants felt honored at being invited to join the tenant board. The staff, however, was unable to respond as mobilizers: the agency no longer has the time, staff, or ability to maintain connections. People who could have turned into participators are depoliticized. Potential activists are confined to the role of service providers.

What is the process by which agencies created out of mass mobilization retreat from a continued mobilizing role? Structural constraints on the Latino agencies themselves often preclude such a role, and these constraints go beyond the hierarchical orientation of male directors discussed in Chapter 3. These constraints affect even Latina women directors such as Carmen Gómez.

First, Latino agencies today must contend with funding constraints that did not exist during the heady days of the 1960s and early 1970s, when funds flowed from the federal government to the cities—to the Latino community. As resources became more difficult to obtain, community agencies were forced to compete against each other. Eight of the people I interviewed specifically mentioned agency survival as a major reason for the decline in political activism.

Gómez, for example, is facing financial constraints that cause staff and program cutbacks. Political mobilizing, according to Felipe Aviles, can get an agency into trouble and use up resources needed for other agency priorities that are funded by outside sources. On the other hand, when an agency focuses on maintenance of the organization, community goals get less attention. Edwin Colina, for example, contrasts a group he had worked with during the early 1970s and today's Comité de Familias Latinas de Boston: "We saw that if we received money from any source, . . . then we would be in the same position as the agency sponsoring El Comité—having to balance the interest of continuing the momentum for building an agency or an organization versus the actual desires and interest of a community. So, by not being tied to the funding resources, we could take risks that others couldn't." The concern for safety and survival at El Comité has led to less outreach to community members and more reliance on impersonal recruitment such as flyers.

Just as survival becomes a priority for poor people and poses a barrier to participation, survival as an agency takes precedence over political activism. Pedro Contreras explains, "You could do all the planning you want—if the funding is not being allocated to those areas, it doesn't matter what you do. So what people do is chase requests for proposals."

Competition for funds and the survival of the agency have supplanted loftier goals of political activism and neutralized much of the Latino political force in Boston.[11] Of course, the struggle for institutional legitimacy, funding security, and even organizational status is not unique to the Latino community in Boston, or to Latinos in other communities. As Schattschneider (1975) says, "The substitution of conflicts is the most devastating kind of political strategy" (71). In other words, it is not that the competition for funds stems from some internal flaw within the Latino (or other community) agencies. Rather, the institutions in power are able to stimulate such competition and other interagency conflicts as a strategic political move that, to a great extent, assures their continued hegemony.

Second, historical events such as the War on Poverty and the withdrawal of federal funds during the Reagan administration created conditions that first stimulated and then constrained the ability of Latino agencies to take on political-mobilization roles. Manuel Sánchez, for example, describes the changes since he was at the Concilio Latino. Compared to the "maximum feasible participation" of the War on Poverty years, current contracts have a "product-processing" flavor in which clients are hurried through a program that will produce a job holder in the shortest possible time. Whereas in the 1970s, the Concilio Latino could build civic education into the program (e.g., clients joined the board of the organization, were helped to take out library cards, worked to build a business association, and were part of candidate nights at the agency), current practices at the same agency stress short-term employment-placement contracts. The reduction of funds for operating expenses also translates into not having the staff time to do voter registration or many of the other activities that were possible earlier.[12]

It should be pointed out that the effects of government antipoverty programs on Latino agencies is complex (Andrews and Wikstrom 1991). During the 1970s, antipoverty programs targeted to Latino and black agencies provided financial resources and stimulated organizational and leadership development that translated into political resources. At the same time, however, community residents changed from being clients to recipients of services. By replacing clientelist politics with a recipient model, new members could get benefits directly without using the intermediary step of political participation (Hamilton 1979; Rivera 1984; and Piven and Cloward 1989, 170–172). In contrast to earlier immigrants, who were clients with obligations to political bosses, Latinos today are recipients with rights to benefits. Naturally, this change has affected other groups besides Latinos. Hamilton (1979), for example, suggests that black communities were depoliticized when benefits were no longer linked to vot-

165

ing: "This process is 'depoliticizing' precisely because it fails to take into account the very important fact that it is the *elective* political offices that ultimately control the fate of these 'soft-money' programs" (218; emphasis in original). In addition, Morone (1990) describes in great detail how during the War on Poverty black leaders moved from protests to lobbying efforts and legal suits directed at gaining access to sociopolitical institutions. In a process common to many movements, the organizations began to resemble the urban institutions they tried to change, marking "the evolution from mass participation to administrative consolidation" (244).

Even the problem of the male focus on positions in government as the goal of politics may be reexamined within a structural constraint context. One of the most effective ways to protect the balance of power from shifting to another ethnic group, such as Latinos in Boston, is for those in power to develop alliances with key leaders and at least attempt to co-opt them. Jones (1972) and Jennings (1986, 73), for example, suggest that leaders in the black community are often selected for nominal positions *precisely* to defuse their mobilizing power and then are prevented from continuing the community efforts that brought them to the attention of the Anglo elites in the first place. A similar process may have occurred with Latino leaders in Boston, especially the men. As Latinos began to press for more influence (via protests and election campaigns), during the mid 1960s to mid 1970s, their key leaders were invited to join the existing government.

Juan Maldonado, for example, laments the pattern of frequent job moves by many Latino leaders; by moving on to other positions, a vacuum in leadership develops, and by protecting turf, new leaders are not encouraged to emerge. In addition, Latinos who are appointed to government positions have limited influence on public policy. Jesús Carrillo states that the men in "high" positions are actually only at the middle-management level; once they become appointed to positions in government, their actual influence on government policies and the benefits they can wrest from the public institutions they work for are extremely limited. Nevertheless, the community members feel abandoned and may withdraw from participation.

A third constraint on political-mobilization efforts by Latino agencies stems from legal regulations against political activity by public employees. Latino agencies, when they receive public funds—as most do—are constrained from offering political education and serving as political mobilizers. Angel Pérez, an agency director from South America, feels that getting involved in politics at the agency would create divisiveness among his staff. Since he has to serve all the ethnic and racial groups that attend his agency, he cannot be seen as favoring Latinos.[13] He is also aware of the Hatch Act and its prohibition against political activities in government-funded agencies such as his.

Finally, there is evidence that Latino appointed officials are torn between the loyalty (in the guise of neutrality) demanded by the people that hired them and their deep desire to support community struggles. The "lure of the good job" constrains those who achieve positions from acting politically, especially when their actions challenge those who appointed them. Bruno and Gaston (1984), for example, state that during the Mel King/Ray Flynn mayoral campaign discussed in Chapter 4, the power, visibility, and prestige of Latino appointed officials in the Dukakis administration could have made them a political force in the community's support of Mel King. However, when they were approached, "they were in fact unable to move politically because the politicians at the state level were requiring neutrality in the mayoral election from their 'troops.' . . . We were thus given concrete evidence that democratic reforms won from the state . . . can actually weaken popular efforts" (Bruno and Gaston 1984, 70).

The competition for funds and the decreased resources in a shrinking economy thus decrease the leverage of Latino leaders in determining public policy. The retreat of agencies from political-mobilization efforts on a broad scale during the 1980s (and the decline in the economy) have contributed to a decrease in participation by Latino residents. While the agencies have continued to advocate for the community by means of their connections to key Latino and Anglo individuals in city and state government, they have generally and increasingly concentrated on service delivery. Of course, service delivery—even when it operates in place of political education or political mobilization—should not be minimized as a worthwhile endeavor. After all, improved service was the goal of the political struggles that created the agencies in the first place: the desire for bilingual, culturally sensitive social services located in the neighborhoods where Latinos live. In addition, as Uriarte and Merced (1985) explain, "In a community that has nothing, social services are often everything: they represent the first line of defense for the survival of the community. For this alone they deserve to be defended" (23).

Nevertheless, the constraints on Latino agencies and their concomitant retreat from mass political-mobilization efforts have had a suppressive effect on Latino political participation. One such effect has been a decline in voter participation. It must be pointed out, however, that other structural obstacles to registration and voting often create even more unsurmountable barriers to political participation in electoral politics.

Obstacles to Registration and Voting

Why don't more Latinos vote? The structural context again informs the debate about the causes of supposed political apathy in Latino communities. Nonvoting, as the statistics provided in Chapter 1 indicate, is a widespread problem for the American polity in general, not just for Latinos. The vast literature on the reasons people in America do not vote focuses on individual attitudes, preferences, and a lack of personal or political resources. This individualistic, "rational-choice" theory suggests that a cost/benefit analysis is conducted by each individual and that "people abstain because, given their attitudes, the 'costs' of voting outweigh the perceived benefits" (Piven and Cloward 1989, 114).[14]

The attitudes supposedly responsible for the decision not to vote include a lack of a sense of political effectiveness (Almond and Verba 1963, chaps. 11 and 12; Shaffer 1981), a lack of a sense of civic obligation (Almond and Verba 1963; Verba and Nie 1972, 125–137), and psychosocial predispositions associated with demographic characteristics (socioenomic status, age, and ethnicity, for the most part) (Banfield and Wilson 1963, Wilson and Banfield 1971, Verba and Nie 1972).

Inherent in such a focus on individual attitudes is a perception that the vote should be treated as a privilege; people are expected to prove their interest and willingness to expend energy to gain access to the privilege. Kimball (1972) and Piven and Cloward (1989) challenge such a focus on individual characteristics as the source of voter behavior. Instead, they urge attention to the legal–institutional–procedural obstacles to voter registration. These obstacles include, for example, cutoff dates for registration and re-registration; residency; inconvenient times and locations of registration offices; and in-person registration, among others. Obvious obstacles such as poll taxes and literacy requirements are no longer legal, but many other, more subtle, obstacles have taken their places for persons of color and non-English-speaking immigrants.

Under the cumbersome regulations that surround the right to vote—regulations that are more restrictive and exclusionary than in most Western democracies—voters must "demonstrate suitable qualifications. Elsewhere in the world, voter enrollment is the responsibility of the state, not the individual" (Burnham 1987, 79).

Latino Experiences with Structural Barriers to Electoral Politics.
Actual experiences of Latinos in the United States illustrate how
structure affects Latino political participation, especially voter participation. The first example is the dramatic difference between the voting rates of Puerto Ricans in Puerto Rico compared to their voting
rates in the mainland United States. In Puerto Rico, Puerto Ricans
have a voting rate that has averaged 80 percent of eligible adults
since 1952, whereas on the mainland their voting rate has been estimated to be as low as 20 percent in some elections (Jennings 1988b,
72). While this difference could reflect a lack of investment in local
politics, stress following migration, and difficulties with the English
language, structuralists point instead to the differences between election procedures here and in Puerto Rico. Puerto Rican politics features easy registration, Sunday elections, clearly differentiated parties, and direct benefits for participation.

Superior Anglo economic and legal resources are a second type of
structural barrier. Fuentes (1984) describes efforts by Puerto Rican
parents in Brooklyn to elect a Puerto Rican to the school board. The
parents collected the requisite number of signatures, duly notarized,
and attempted to register the petition with the board. The Anglo
school board members hired lawyers to block the petition. Having
more money and a lawyers' network within the Anglo community
enabled the Anglo members to wage a protracted legal fight. Fuentes
concludes that it was not apathy but legal and economic obstructionism on the part of Anglo school committee members that prevented
New York City Latinos from having input into school policy.
Clearly, political processes, procedures, and resources are dominated
by groups with an investment in maintaining the power that accrues
from holding government positions. Voting alone does not affect
these processes, and access to the vote can be blocked procedurally as
well as legally.

For Latinos, access to the vote is impeded as well by language
barriers. The American myth of the model immigrant expects Latinos
to learn to speak or read sufficient English to register and vote; if he
or she does not, the lack of access to the franchise is, to a great
extent, his or her fault. In fact, decisions at the structural, institutional level turn a lack of English into an obstacle to political participation, especially to voting. For example, the government decision
not to provide bilingual voting materials and machines is a structural
barrier that specifically blocks access to the vote for non-English-
speaking groups like Latinos (Kimball 1972, 297; Camayd-Freixas
and Lopez 1983, 54–56).[15] In addition, when local, state, and federal
governments fail to fund ESL courses *with long waiting lists* of those

eager to learn English, the language barrier to political participation is clearly located within the political structure, not the individual.

Other obstacles, such as distance, language, and rudeness of the staff at polling places, are often dismissed as trivial matters. For the poor, however, as well as for racial and ethnic groups, the energy needed to vote is greater than it is for others. Inconvenient places and times of registration (Willis 1988, 3), lack of transportation, and other practicalities pose greater barriers to voting for Latinos (as well as other poor immigrant groups) than for other Americans.

Registration Procedures in Boston. My own odyssey through the offices and halls of the City of Boston Elections Department and the Office of the Secretary of the Commonwealth Elections Division shows how subtle, yet daunting, the obstacles to Latino voter registration can be. The first obstacle to registering to vote in Boston involves proof of residence. The "Information for Voters" from the Office of the Secretary of the Commonwealth Elections Division says clearly:

> Go to any registration place and complete an affidavit of registration, which must be answered truthfully under the penalty of perjury. The questions on the affidavit will include your name, residence and date of birth.
>
> Upon registration, your name, address and party preference will be added to the voting list of your city or town. This list is used on election day to identify and check off the names of registered voters when they come to the polling place to vote (Office of the Secretary of the Commonwealth Elections Division 1990b, 24).

No proof of residence or citizenship seems to be required. To verify this, I specifically called both the Office of the Secretary of the Commonwealth Elections Division and the Elections Department at Boston City Hall to ask if any papers are required to prove residence or citizenship. The response was, "Oh, no! The fact that they sign under penalty of perjury is enough!"

Once at the Elections Department at City Hall, however, I observed one of the registrars meticulously scrutinizing a woman's lease and checking her address. I inquired, "I thought you didn't have to bring any proof?" The registrar indicated that any person wanting to register *should* bring proof that she or he actually lives at the stated address. This proof might be, for example, a driver's license, a lease, or a utility bill. If such proof is *not* supplied at the time of registration, the person does not actually leave the office as a registered voter. Instead, the Elections Department mails the pink registration verification slip inside a postcard that has instructions written in English. When (and if) the postcard packet arrives at the individual's home, the upper half of the postcard must be signed and returned to the Elections Department.

This procedure presents many obstacles to Latinos. First, the rule about proof is not made explicit. A person could negotiate the corridors of City Hall, fill out the form, and leave thinking he or she is registered; the postcard that arrives days later could easily be ignored or might not be understood, especially given the language barriers discussed above. Second, the rule favors those with driver's licenses and leases,[16] thus excluding young adults, multiple adults living in one household, and persons living in postal zones considered unsafe by postal service letter carriers. Most Latino young adults do not have driver's licenses, leases, or utility bills in their names, and they would have to respond to the postcard. Many poor families "double up" in one apartment; not all adults at a single address can provide proof of residence. Mail delivery to certain housing projects and areas of the city where Latinos live is not reliable; the postcard may not reach the person who tried to register.

The third obstacle to voter registration is the need to re-register every year. Even though the election law clearly states that "registration is permanent in Massachusetts" (Office of the Secretary of the Commonwealth Elections Division 1990b, 24), if a registered person is not found at the same address during the Boston city census, he or she is automatically dropped from the registration list. Theoretically, a postcard notification is sent (to the old address, again, in English), but this procedure *clearly* favors those who are able to have residential stability *and* is not well publicized. The "Information for Voters" does say that one must notify the Elections Department in writing if one moves within the city of Boston, but it does not say one's name will be dropped from the rolls if this procedure is not followed.

It is common knowledge that Latinos and other minority groups are distrustful of census takers and that the census workers chronically undercount people who live in projects, poor neighborhoods, and "dangerous" neighborhoods—neighborhoods commonly called home by many Latinos in Boston. Therefore, even if every Latino in Boston registered tomorrow, a substantial proportion would be dropped from the voting lists a year later without even knowing it.

Amazingly enough, *citizenship* does not have to be proved. "Illegal aliens" (i.e., undocumented Latinos) who have residential stability could vote more easily than could legal citizens who move frequently. Within the Election Department, there seems to be more concern over protecting the distribution of potential voters in the various districts and the type of people who live there than about the possibility of an influx of voters who are not citizens.

Marta Rosa describes her experience with voter registration:

The most depressing thing was that before the primaries, they come out with a list of voters—we had begun with eight hundred registered voters and we had registered by the primaries, we felt, about five hundred. When the list came out—the updated list before the end of the time line—there were four hundred people registered. What happened to the other eight hundred plus all the new ones we had registered? What happened is that they had all been thrown off the list, all the people that were registered prior to our effort were mostly thrown off the list. Because of the yearly census. They have to send in a yearly form and most people don't send them in. So that was really depressing.

She links these experiences with the suppression of political participation by describing the Latino experience with voter registration: "Every single year you get thrown off—and people get disgusted and they don't go—or you move and get thrown off."

The experience of registering in Boston (or neighboring Chelsea in this case) can pose psychological barriers as well as structural obstacles; Rosa describes how Latino campaign workers "would take people who wanted to register to vote to City Hall, and City Hall would treat them like they were nobodies. For some reason, if you don't speak English well, and your name sounds different—if you're José Rivera—people think you're deaf also. So they [Election Department Officials] yell, 'What's your name?' and they yell it. It's just an intimidating experience."

Other Latinos connect voting obstacles to the distribution of power. Juan Vázquez, for example, states, "I'm sure the powers that be don't want us to develop, and they try to do anything and everything they can to keep the community the way it is." And Rosa herself recalls, "It threatened them out of their minds that we were registering so many people." Apathy is created by the personal experience of structural obstacles.

Restrictive voter registration and voting regulations were one of the consequences of election reform at the turn of the century; an intended or unintended side effect was the decline in voting, especially by immigrants and the working class.[17] As registration procedures increasingly excluded immigrants, blacks, and the working class, the political parties turned away from the issues that affected these constituencies. This process further suppressed voting participation by the poor and the working class—and, more recently, Latino immigrants. The history of more restrictive American voting regulation for immigrants and blacks coincides with another series of historical events and processes: the decline of party competition and the demise of the political machine.

Decline of Party Politics and the Political Machine

Burnham (1965) explicitly challenges assumptions about the evolution of a pluralistic democratic system in America when he associates the decline of party competition with lower rates of political participation. He says that the "transformations over the past century have involved *devolution*, a disassociation from politics as such among a growing segment of the eligible electorate and an apparent deterioration of the bonds of party linkage between electorate and government" (10; emphasis added). Devolution, not evolution, resulted from a structural realignment by class and ethnicity. The white, elite-organized reform movement replaced the political machines (which had stimulated immigrant participation in politics) with "good government." Voter participation decreased, and "the functional result . . . was the conversion of a fairly democratic regime into a rather broadly based oligarchy" (Burnham 1965, 23).

Much is made of the relatively rapid integration of European immigrants into the American political system and their readiness to use the vote; political machines contributed to their political development. There is ample evidence that the situation facing Latinos migrating to the United States today is substantially different from that which faced European immigrants during the period 1870 to 1930. Within this context, the role of political parties and political machines as structures that stimulated immigrant participation cannot be ignored, if only because of the power of myth and the symbol that is the political machine.

The lack of party competition and the subsequent unresponsiveness of political parties to certain groups contribute to the suppression of Latino political participation in the United States. Juana Oviedo, for example, has been able to overcome the barriers of language and lack of information regarding voting in this country. To the best of her ability, she follows the candidates and the issues. (The tenuousness of her grasp on political candidates and issues is demonstrated by the way she decides for whom to vote. She goes to the polls, "hangs around," and eavesdrops on other voters to hear whom they are planning to vote for.) And yet, at this time, Oviedo is contemplating exiting from electoral politics completely. The source of her proposed rejection of political participation in its simplest form?

The retreat of the political parties from the issues that affect her and her community. For Juana Oviedo, the Democratic Party has been the party of the poor, the party that responded to injustice. For her, as for many Puerto Ricans raised on the island, voting meant following her family tradition and hoping that Democratic public servants would protect her interests. Over the years, Oviedo has seen the erosion of what the party stands for and an abandonment of people like her. She has no knowledge of Schattschneider's (1975) theory of the mobilization of bias; nevertheless, as she looked at the gubernatorial candidates and the issues of the 1990 election, she recognized that the political system was developing policies that work to her disadvantage. What was on the political agenda was no longer poverty, affordable housing, and human services (as had been, albeit in a weak form, on the agenda during the 1960s and early 1970s) but rather budget cuts, welfare reductions, and how to reduce benefits for people like Oviedo. She perceived the government, and the Democratic Party, as turning its back on the poor; she eloquently exclaimed:

Ahora—si están cortando los servicios, y van a—deso[18]—¡Yo no voto este año! ¿Por qué? ¿Para qué? ¡A los que están perjudicando son a los pobres! Porque yo voto para ayuda, para que—deso—para la ayuda de nosotros los pobres que no tenemos nada. *Pero si yo veo que las cosas están así, ¿quién nos está perjudicando? A nosotros, los pobres. Porque esa gente tiene dinero, él que tiene dinero—esto no le afecta nada. Tiene buen trabajo, buena casa. Pero ¿quieren cortar el dinero de* disability? *Entonces, ¿cómo uno va a vivir? Dígame usted—si cortan eso? . . . Ay, ¡no! ¡Yo no voto* nada!

Now—they're cutting services, and they're going to—you know—I'm not going to vote this year! *Why?* What *for?* The ones that they're hurting are the poor! Because I vote for assistance, so that—you know—for help for us, the poor, who don't have *anything.* But if I see that things are like they are, who is it that is being hurt? It's us, the poor people. Because *those* people have money—the one who has money—this doesn't affect him at all. He has a good job, a nice house. But they want to cut the disability funds? Then, *how* is one supposed to survive? You tell me that—if they cut that money? . . . Ay! *No!* I won't vote—*no way!*

The anger in her voice, the vehemence and strength of feeling are not the signs of an apathetic person but the sounds of a party loyalist. She has participated for years but is now exiting the political system. While Hirschman (1970) sees exit as being less effective in the political arena than voice (protest) and less constructive than loyal working for change, Oviedo sees few options other than refusal to participate in an unresponsive political system. Her issues are not even on the table any more. And the fact that no candidate ever comes to where she lives is a clear message to Oviedo that her concerns are *not* on the political agenda. Another Latino participator lost to electoral politics: labeled as apathetic.

The demise of the political machine has also created structural conditions that suppress political participation for Latinos and other immigrant groups. The image of the urban political machine is no longer one of corruption, fraud, scandal, graft, and greed. Social and political scientists such as Merton (1957), Teaford (1982), and Bridges (1988) now identify the urban machines as having been key socializing structures in immigrant political development. Political machines were directly responsible for drawing immigrants into electoral politics by giving "the new immigrants both physical and psychic rewards in return for their votes" (Pachon 1985, 250). The machines and their ward bosses politicized new immigrants through the exchange of favors, patronage, and a network of personal and political relationships that bridged the gulf between the immigrant and public officials. The machines brought immigrants into the political parties, exacted party loyalty, and rewarded cooperation with tangible, material benefits. Immigrants were, on occasion, paid to vote; received direct personal favors in return for campaign support; and were actively wooed in the competition for votes.

Do political machines still exist?[19] Pachon (1985) denies a major role for machines in most Mexican-American communities, and Jennings (1984b) declares that Anglo machines, in their weakened state, *use* Latinos to support their candidates but dismiss Latinos at other times. The apparent demise of the political machine has created a different climate in which new immigrants are seen as threats to political careers rather than as assets. Elected officials no longer direct their efforts to gaining votes from new immigrants but rather to soliciting funds from wealthier campaign contributors.[20]

The impact of urban machines on Puerto Rican politics is a more complex matter. The urban machines of New York and Chicago did not enlist or try to mobilize Puerto Rican residents during the 1930s and 1940s (Jennings 1984b, 7). Analyses of the Puerto Rican and black communities in Boston during the 1960s and 1970s indicate, however, that there was, in fact, a "Kevin White machine" (Jennings 1984c, 1986; Travis 1990). This machine first ignored Latinos, then wooed them when their votes were needed. White gained support in part by appointing Latino spokespersons to government positions as a form of patronage reminiscent of old-style party machines. The

Chicago machine also continues to exert its influence on local politics in that city.

There is also some evidence that Puerto Rican politicians have developed small-scale, machine-type politics within the Latino communities in New York City and New Haven, Connecticut. Baver (1984) and Rogler (1974) suggest that Latino politicians turn to machine politics, at least *stylistically*, in certain circumstances. New York's Ramon Velez, for example, "became a local notable using the political style of a machine boss . . . a 'Plunkett' [*sic*] of the South Bronx" during the 1960s; the plums of patronage dispersed during this apparent renaissance of urban machine politics, albeit on a small scale, involved antipoverty funds, grants, and control of agencies (Baver 1984, 47–48).

Rogler (1974) describes a Puerto Rican "political boss" in New Haven, Connecticut. This man lived in the community for thirty years and served as an intermediary between the "welfare system and the grassroot level of ethnic life" (58). This boss exerted his power, on the one hand, by controlling the emergence and loyalty of any new Latino organization. On the other hand, he maintained control within the community with his intimate and personal contacts with Puerto Rican residents.

The stories of Latinos in Boston, especially of *la gente del pueblo*, seem to suggest that the lack of clear-cut party politics and of the personal connectedness inherent in machine politics are structural constraints on political participation. Latinos from Puerto Rico and the Dominican Republic hold cultural expectations of party and machine politics that contrast sharply with the dearth of these structures in the United States. For many Latinos from these countries, the absence of strong parties and political machines contrasts unfavorably with their more inclusive experiences of politics in their home countries—experiences that include the concrete benefits, the personal-style politics, and the lively festival-like atmosphere of party politics and political machines. At the same time, Latinos from countries in Central America often arrive in the United States from home-country political experiences based on fear and danger—experiences that then constrain their ability to become involved in American politics.

Home-Country Politics: The Impact on Latino Participation in Boston

One of the commonly held beliefs in Latino participation literature is that "ties to the homeland" constrain political participation.[21] Puerto Ricans in particular are portrayed as making endless trips to "the island." The term *circular migration* describes the back and forth flow of Latinos between the United States and Puerto Rico, Mexico, and other homelands. The pattern of circular migration is supposedly (1) a change from the pattern of earlier immigrants; (2) the source of weakened attachment to the United States; and (3) the explanation for lower naturalization rates and, therefore, political participation. According to this view, Latinos in the United States do not vote, or participate in politics, because of these strong ties to their homelands.

Homeland ties as an explanation of low participation has its roots in the sociopsychological explanations of lower levels of political participation by certain groups discussed in the section of Chapter 1 on culture and political participation (Piven and Cloward 1989, 96–121). Latinos supposedly differ from earlier immigrants, who, according to the theory, arrived with a more participant political culture.

Certainly, Latinos in Boston voice deep ties to their countries of origin, and these ties do create a tension of loyalty to two countries, particularly for first-generation Latinos. Juana Oviedo, for example, firmly believes that if Puerto Rico became the fifty-first state of the United States with the same social service benefits as the mainland, *"Todo el mundo se vaya para Puerto Rico"* ("Everyone would be off to Puerto Rico"). Even María Ramírez, who has spent much of her life in political endeavors, says that home ties constrain voting participation here: "Well, Puerto Ricans are citizens; we're allowed to vote. We don't exercise that as we should—here. Basically, I think, because we still have a love for our island. . . . Our hearts and thoughts are really back on our little island south of Florida." About one-third of the people I interviewed made some allusion to the ties that bind people to their home country as a constraint on participation in the United States.[22] Nevertheless, there did not seem to be an automatic association between the strength of homeland ties and the level of participation in the United States. For example, Carlos García, a thirty-nine-year-old, illiterate, Puerto Rican house painter, has lived here since he was eighteen years old. He is quite clear that Boston is his home and that he no longer feels comfortable in Puerto Rico. Nevertheless, he does not vote, does not follow the issues, and seems isolated from social and political events, despite his low degree of attachment to Puerto Rico. On the other hand, Inez Martínez, who has lived here for half her life, feels strong ties to Mexico and plans to retire there in a few years. In spite of her ties to her homeland, she has been an indefatigable tenant organizer. She does not vote, but she is passionately political.

Home ties may affect participation but probably play a much smaller role than the contrast—the *incongruence*—between politics in one's homeland and politics in the mainland United States. What emerges most strongly from the data is the power of the contrast between the two countries—homeland and the United States—in shaping the decision to become involved in this country.

Theorists of the political-culture school draw conclusions about homeland politics from immigrant-group participation rates in this country and then conclude that lower rates of participation here are caused by low participant cultural values. Or, as Banfield (1958) did, they ignore the impact of structure on culture.[23]

The actual effect of homeland politics on immigrant behavior may depend on how closely the structural conditions in the United States match or contrast with conditions in the home country. If structural conditions in the home country favor participation, but the immigrant finds political conditions unfavorable here, the immigrant may participate less in this country. Puerto Ricans vote in tremendous numbers in Puerto Rico but have the lowest voting rates of any Latino group in the mainland United States.[24] For them, participatory structures in Puerto Rico encourage participation, but American political structures discourage participation. In other words, home-country patterns do affect the participation of Latinos in the United States, but one cannot assume that lower rates here are caused by deficient home-country politics or by apathy.

Latinos in Boston consider structural constraints to be extremely important in explaining lower participation by Latinos in the United States. For example, *twice as many Latinos discussed how the participatory structures in Puerto Rico and the Dominican Republic encourage political participation in those countries as the number of Latinos who discussed home-country ties as a constraint on participation.* Puerto Ricans compared the well-organized, issue-specific, and party-dominated politics in Puerto Rico with politics here and said they find Anglo politics disorganized, bland, and unwelcoming.

Dominicans, likewise, contrast the vibrant political life in Santo Domingo[25] with the tepid political climate of the United States and find little reason for participating here. The lack of material or psychological rewards here, compared with those gained through the systems in those two countries, creates a disincentive to participation for Puerto Ricans and Dominicans in this country. Certain *individuals* from Latino countries are indeed apathetic. Even the passionately political, however, find it difficult to act politically in the United States given the contrast between Anglo politics and the politics of Puerto Rico and the Dominican Republic.

In a somewhat different vein, Latinos coming to the United States from home countries with repressive government systems in which political activism is punished even unto death may avoid political participation here because of residual fears stemming from their experiences in their countries of origin. In other words, the fear and danger associated with home-country politics in many countries in Central and South America inhibit the political inclinations of Boston Latinos whose origins are in Central and South America. For example, it may be particularly difficult to overcome the fear of danger for people from places like Guatemala and El Salvador. Yet these fears do not stem so much from innate individual characteristics or from cultural deficiencies, but rather from external realities embedded in the political structure.

In addition, the myth of the model immigrant is tarnished somewhat by the true migration practices of earlier immigrant groups. Gage (1989) and Vecoli (1972), for example, challenge the notion of the model immigrant who came here to stay and who therefore invested energy in joining American politics. Gage (1989) makes the case that most of the Greeks who migrated to Worcester, Massachusetts, during the early decades of the twentieth century through the 1940s continued to feel they would ultimately return to their villages even after living in the United States for decades. Vecoli (1972) states that "as many as a third of the [Italian] immigrants returned to their homelands" (411). Thus, Puerto Ricans, Mexican Americans, Dominicans, and other Latinos may not differ much from earlier immigrants in terms of ties to the homeland. What may be more important is the political structure that affects their decision to participate.

Puerto Rican Politics in Puerto Rico. The Puerto Ricans I interviewed were unanimous in their opinion that Puerto Ricans, as a *people,* are extremely political. Armando Meléndez enthusiastically declares that Puerto Ricans love politics. He goes on to identify the differences between political practices here and in Puerto Rico: "In Puerto Rico, the election is the fourth of November. And, on the fifth of November they're out campaigning again. So it's a constant working in politics. Here people don't go out and vote because they feel that their vote is not important; they feel that, 'Who am I gonna give my vote to? Who is going to do for me? Who wants to champion my cause?'" A lack of attention to Latino concerns—having no one "champion their cause"—creates an obstacle to participation. An even more important obstacle discussed by virtually everyone is the contrast between politics here and in Puerto Rico.

Kernstock (1972) claims that Puerto Rican political behavior in Hartford, Connecticut, shows evidence of "their basically passive

character" (189). Juanita Fonseca, in contrast, insists cultural deficiencies do not affect Puerto Rican voting patterns. Her reaction is
worth repeating.

> I'm not an expert in terms of politics from Puerto Rico, but I *do* know
> that everybody votes in Puerto Rico. I *do* know those who are regis-
> tered, those who are of age—people vote in Puerto Rico. So it's not
> like somehow there's a genetic missing link here that somehow Puerto
> Ricans just can't seem to get it together, they just come from such a
> culturally deprived area that they're just not capable of mentally get-
> ting involved in the voting process. Bullshit! In Puerto Rico everybody
> votes and politics is a big issue!

And recall Beatriz Bustillo, at the end of Chapter 1, who exclaims
that in Puerto Rico, "If you don't vote, well, you're *nobody!*"
    What explains the difference in electoral participation of essen-
tially the same people in Puerto Rico and the mainland United
States? Pachon (1981, 7) provides an alternative explanation to the
cultural model: structural differences such as government-sponsored
registration procedures, holiday election dates, and ceremonious social events at election time. The answer lies, then, not in what is
culturally missing from Latinos but what is missing in this country:
the lack of personal connectedness in the political process, the excitement associated with what have been called tribalistic political styles
(Piven and Cloward 1989, 31–35), and the failure to provide concrete benefits for political participation.
    In Puerto Rico, political parties are extremely strong, with loyal
members and with clearly differentiated agendas. Party politics domi-
nates Puerto Rican politics in Puerto Rico. The three parties—*Pava,
Palma, Independentista*—are clearly distinguished by their stance on
the status of Puerto Rico in relation to the United States: continued
commonwealth status, statehood, or independence. Party differences
on the long-term status of Puerto Rico serve as party identifiers and
issues around which people can rally. Bustillo compares the two
systems:

> *O eres de la Pava, o eres de la Palma, o eres Independentista, y, pues,
> la gente sabe quién tu eres. . . . Allá los partidos son mucho más
> fuertes que aquí. Allá si eres republicano—eres* republicano. *Bueno,
> diríamos—de la Palma. Si eres demócrata, eres de la Pava—eres de la
> Pava* [she reiterates]. *Aquí, yo creo, que últimamente no se está dando
> la definición de qué realmente eres.*

> You're either with the Pava [Party], or you're with the Palma, or
> you're a pro-Independence person, and, well, people know who you

are. . . . There the parties are much stronger than here. There, if you're Republican—you're *Republican*. Well, we would say, of the Palma [Party]. If you're a Democrat, you're with the Pava—with the *Pava* [she reiterates]. Here, I think, lately it's not really clear what you are.

The contrast between this system and the U.S. system is striking. In Puerto Rico, party politics, political machines, easy registration, and lively political campaigns yield high levels of participation. In contrast, Boston's Puerto Ricans have not been invited or encouraged to become part of party structures and processes. In addition, the Democratic Party virtually controls the Boston scene and, in essence, does not need Latinos; in fact, maintenance of the status quo requires the exclusion of potentially unpredictable voters.

Party machines are also extremely strong in Puerto Rico but relatively inactive in Boston. The barrios of Puerto Rico are well organized with ward leaders and cadres of political workers who work year round. Election periods are filled with parties, festivals, street marches, singing, and rallies. Piven and Cloward (1989), in describing nineteenth-century politics in the United States, might be describing Puerto Rican politics today: "The pageantry, the marching bands, the rallies, the hoarsely shouted slogans, the fury and excitement—in short, the extraordinary popular enthusiasms that marked election campaigns" (31).

Juana Oviedo, who feels abandoned by the Democratic Party in the United States, echoes this image as she describes politics in Puerto Rico: *"Para mí era como una fiesta—porque a mí me gustaba ver a la gente votando, y ¡se pelearon! . . . ¡Se mataban por la política!"* ("For me, it was like a festival—because I, myself, liked to see people voting, and—did they fight! . . . They'd *kill* for politics!"). She contrasts this excitement with the disappointing drabness here: *"Aquí es muy distinta. Ni se sabe—deso—porque son tan calladitos"* ("Here it is very different. You can hardly tell—about that—because they're so subdued").[26]

Oviedo ties in the *revolú* (lively uproar)[27] with another difference—that of political media saturation in Puerto Rico versus non-election year silence here: *"Allí en Puerto Rico—desde que entra el año y sale el año—están hablando política. Y en los diarios es todo—hablando de Fulano de Tal—¡eso siempre!—¡Ay! Yo—de sobra. Se cansa uno"* ("Over there in Puerto Rico—from *day one* of the year till the *end* of the year—they're talking politics. And in the newspapers it's all—talking about So-and-So—all the time!—Oh! I—it's *too much*. You get tired of it").

This theme of the constant political debates that occur in Puerto

Rico and how politics is the topic of everyday conversations permeated the interviews in Boston. In contrast, American politics features a peak of media coverage immediately preceding an election, and little excitement or useful information is provided about politics the rest of the year.

While I did not explicitly examine the content of Latino news media, it seems that the Spanish-language radio in the United States contributes to this problem. Whereas in Puerto Rico the airwaves and news media reverberate with the political goings-on, the radio news here, which is what is most attended to by the common folk, is missing an opportunity to inform about local issues. Here, Latinos depend on "an extremely limited Hispanic media for information on political candidates and elections" (Camayd-Freixas and Lopez 1983, 56). In addition, Spanish-language radio focuses heavily on news about the countries of origin, not on local politics. This lack of media coverage of politics again contrasts starkly with political expectations generated by home-country political experiences and poses an additional constraint on participation.

The failure to provide concrete benefits for political participation, or at least to make explicit campaign promises, is another feature of the U.S. political system that is different from politics in Puerto Rico. The failure to "get something back"—to receive some community benefit from political participation—was a major theme in all the interviews and observations I conducted. Three people from Puerto Rico specifically used the term *villas y castillos* ("villas and castles," meaning something akin to "promised them the moon") to indicate that they expected candidates to identify benefits that will accrue to the community in exchange for its vote. Promises are not necessarily fulfilled once the election is over, but a concrete platform is expected. Here, campaigns have deteriorated into issueless and promiseless poll watching. Reports in the media concern the percentage points by which one candidate is ahead of another. Many Americans, regardless of ethnic background, find little of substance on which to base their vote and thus fail to engage in electoral participation.

Even Marisa Robles, who to some extent operates in the world of establishment politics, expresses what many Americans feel is a barrier to voting: the lack of substance in political campaigns. She recalls one campaign: "They give us some papers—if I hear from two candidates—that still doesn't give me enough information because there's like ten or whatever running for the same office. What I get is like—he's married, he has two kids, lived in Massachusetts for so many years, and this and that—it's just not enough for me." Contrast this with the story recounted by María Luisa Wilson Portuondo of the longtime mayor of San Juan, Puerto Rico, a woman named Felisa Rincón-de Gautier. The mayor once had an airplane flown to the United States; it picked up a planeload of snow, which it brought back to Puerto Rico "so the kids could see what snow was."[28]

Political Expectations and Politics in the Dominican Republic: "Bring Back Tammany Hall." Dominicans in Santo Domingo have some of the same experiences with politics as Puerto Ricans: the strength of party and political machines, the excitement of political campaigns, and the constancy of political debates. Contrary to Nelson's (1979) portrayal of Dominicans in New York as apolitical, Dominicans in Boston describe enthusiastic political participation in their country. In the Dominican Republic, party machines rally the voters. Jobs and patronage assure loyalty and active participation, and political involvement generates concrete benefits.

Francisco Salamanca is a thirty-seven-year-old illiterate mechanic who in the five years since his migration has been able to build his own automobile repair business. He says simply that, to get a job in the Dominican Republic, one has to vote.[29] Jobs are distributed on the basis of political participation and the level of activity on behalf of the party in power. When a party is ousted following an election, most jobs change hands to loyalists of the winning party. Salamanca states that proof of voting is technically required prior to obtaining one's *cédula* (identity card). In addition, shopkeepers often display their proof of voting in a prominent place to enhance their business.

Aurelia Rivera is twenty-six years old and has four years of university training in Santo Domingo. She has been here three years, is married, and now has two young children. She describes how, in anticipation of the need for an engineering job following college, she joined the party apparatus while at the university. Being part of the governing party—attending its meetings, being part of a youth group, doing campaign work—counts favorably when good jobs are being dispensed.

Fraud, corruption, and manipulation of the media were common features of American political machines, features that ultimately led to the reform movement at the turn of the century in the United States. Dominicans in Boston complained as well about the existence of fraud in home-country politics. Aurelia Rivera tells a story about how the provision of electricity has been manipulated as a vote-getting technique. During one election, the out-party interrupted the power supply. The out-party candidates blamed the outages on the party in office and promised that reliable service would be restored if votes were cast for the out-party. Silvia Barajas, Francisco Salamanca, and Juan Betances also decried fraudulent election returns and told stories about how customs regulations are bypassed when one has party connections. While the morality of these tactics is dubious, if not outright corrupt, the impact on participation was clear: voters respond to obtain improved services.

Party machines rally the voters, jobs and patronage assure loyalty and active participation, and political participation generates concrete benefits. In Boston today, civil service provisions and the politics of reform prohibit political patronage at the community level. Of course, many political appointments are still party dominated, but they typically generate benefits to the professional or upper classes alone. In many ways, for poor immigrants in this country, Plunkitt was right: civil service *did* ruin politics (Riordon 1963, 11–17). People need a reason to participate, and that reason often must be tangible.

The influence of party politics and political machines on participation in Puerto Rico and the Dominican Republic raises anew the question whether hierarchical or collective organizations stimulate political participation. If political parties and machines play such a prominent role in generating participation in these countries, why stress the importance of collective organization as I did in Chapter 3? I suggest several answers to this apparent paradox.

First, it may be that what generates participation is the collective *methods* inherent in, and perhaps despite, the hierarchical organizational *structures* of political machines. In other words, what Latinos report as the source of their involvement is the *interpersonal* connection—doing things together—that is the hallmark of "old-time" politics, the *revolú* referred to by Juana Oviedo. It is also possible that research less oriented toward hierarchical relationships as a given social condition might uncover collectively organized clusters or groups operating simultaneously within parties and political machines that would explain the participation-generating qualities of these structures. Second, the perceived tangible benefits of participation in political parties, especially in the Dominican Republic, generate participation in a way that, again, overshadows the effects of the hierarchical organizational structure. Third, in the day-to-day activities that form the basis of political participation, people may not perceive, or respond to, the hierarchical organization as much as the relationships in which those activities are embedded. Thus, participatory experiences may exist despite hierarchical organizational structures; however, collective structures promote these participatory experiences to a greater extent than do hierarchical structures. Nevertheless, a certain paradox remains: high levels of participation despite essentially hierarchical structures.

Fear and Danger: The Impact of Central American Politics. I interviewed ten people from a variety of countries in Central and South America.[30] Because of the small number of people from a variety of countries, my analysis of the impact of Central American politics on participation in Boston is only suggestive. It is impossible to generalize to all Central Americans living in Boston; neither their opinions about politics in their own countries nor their political experiences can be seen as having any statistical reliability or validity. The interviews with Latinos about Central American politics and with people from Central America were so laden with the theme of danger, however, that a discussion of the impact of home-country politics on Latino participation in the United States would be deficient if this theme were not included.

Teresa Andrade describes how the fear of danger blocks political participation: "People's politics in their own countries of origin are *highly* charged. People might be quiet. People may have learned to express their opinions in very guarded situations because it's not even *safe* for them to talk about politics, in particular—in people who are coming from countries where there has been a lot of fascism—I mean—where you know that you can *disappear* because you say the wrong thing to the wrong person." Salamon and Evera (1973) identify fear of physical or bodily harm, or economic vulnerability as a more accurate cause of low participation by blacks in the South than apathy. Eighteen of the Latinos interviewed in Boston described similar feelings of economic and physical vulnerability.[31] The association of danger with home-country politics was an even more prominent theme for people from countries like Guatemala.

A sense of danger was obvious in the interviews with Octavio González. González is a sixty-three-year-old man from Guatemala who finished the sixth grade in school. He has been in this country six years. He identifies himself as an *"obrero—de la clase trabajador"* ("laborer—of the working class"); although he had been in construction in Guatemala, he now works in office cleaning. When asked whether he thought he would attend a hypothetical meeting to deal with the crime problem in Boston's neighborhoods, he responded by focusing on the potential danger of community political activism.

Bueno, como solo es para opinar respecto a esas cosas ¿verdad?—no lo van a involucrar a uno en nada de eso porque también es peligroso, porque esas pandillas son muy vengativas, y que si a uno ven que está actuando y participando directamente en una cosa de esas, es posible que lo eliminen. Porque son capaces. ¿No cree usted?

Well, if it's just to talk about those things, right?—but one shouldn't get involved in those kinds of things because they're also dangerous, because those gangs are very vindictive, and if they see you participating directly in something like that, it's likely that they'll kill [eliminate] you. Because they're capable of that. Don't you agree?

When asked if he would talk to his boss to address the discrimination he felt existed in factory salaries for Latinos, González told a story about what happens to *sindicalistas* (labor organizers) in Guatemala:

> *Allá hay sindicatos. Y a veces surgen esos líderes que enfrentan esos problemas, los reunen y les hablan. . . . Hay veces que si es mucho lo que está hostigando el líder, a veces lo desaparecen. . . . Es peligroso. Peligroso porque lo desaparecen. Desaparecen a los líderes.*

> There [in Guatemala] there are unions. And sometimes leaders rise up to confront those problems; they gather people together and talk to them. . . . A lot of times they harass the leader, sometimes they disappear him. They disappear the leaders.[32]

The fear of physical danger—of being "disappeared"—and the sense of economic vulnerability pose considerable barriers for Latino immigrants to political participation in the United States, especially for those who come from dangerous political situations in their home countries. To overcome this constraint, immigrants and refugees must begin to experience politics in America as safe; politics must also reach out to communicate a sense of relevance, a sense of commonality and community, and a sense of efficacy. Ultimately, in the case of Central American refugees, their experience of American politics as safe may be conducive to increased participation. Once the message of relative safety is communicated, however, Latinos, including those from Central America, still face the *structural* barriers discussed above: sexism and racism, the lack of concessions, barriers to voter registration and voting, and the decline of party politics and the political machine.

In any analysis of gender differences, culture, and political structure, the relative weight of these different forces in stimulating or suppressing political participation is difficult to determine. If it is true that, as Pateman urges, "some attention must be paid to the impact of structure on culture," one must conclude that structural constraints create a heavy burden for activists in their struggle to nurture and generate Latino political participation. The constraints of sexist attitudes on women and the constraints on Latinos in the United States, generally—racism, the lack of concessions, structural barriers to voting, the changed political system, and the lack of congruence between cultural expectations and U.S. politics—all serve to limit the effectiveness of a participatory model of political life. On the other hand, if the experiences of Latina women in Boston suggest that an understanding of politics as connectedness, collectivity, community, and consciousness can promote more participation, and if the political mobilization of growing numbers of Latinos in communities across the country could create a movement toward changing the political structure, then Latina women may hold a key that addresses both the structural and cultural dimensions of politics.

Conclusion

Despite the constraints that face them as women, and in the process of challenging the constraints that face Latinos in the United States as a group, Latina women in Boston envision a political life that is more participatory than that envisioned by Latino men. The vision of Latina women is based on connectedness rather than personal advancement; collective methods and collective organization rather than hierarchy; community and citizenship generated from personal ties rather than from formal structures; and consciousness raising rather than a response to opportunity. The story of Latina women in politics in Boston is one that deserves to be told, if only because it challenges myths about their supposed passivity and submissiveness and because it counters their invisibility in mainstream political science.

If this were only a story about Latina women who overcame the constraints of sexism and racism to become political mobilizers, however, the broader implications for our understanding of culture, gender, and political participation in America would be missed. In this conclusion, I explore some of the ways the experiences of Latina women and Latino men in Boston inform several key debates in political science today, debates about the meaning of gender differences for political theory, about the nature of politics, and about the interaction of culture and gender in political participation. The stories of Latina women and Latino men in Boston have much to teach us not only about engendering political participation in Latino communities but also about addressing the cynicism and disaffiliation in American politics today.

Latina Politics, Latino Politics:
Implications for Political Theory

Latinos in Boston provide substantial support for feminist theories that differences exist between women and men in how they view politics. The relational–positional debate posits that women stress relationships, whereas men are more focused on gaining and maintaining positions—positions as elected office, as government appointments, and as status. Feminist theories have suggested that relationships play an important role in women's psychological development; connection—connectedness—emerges as central to women's politics as well.

The relational aspects of political life dominate the stories of Latina women in Boston and are observable in their political work within the Latino community. For Latina women in Boston, politics is an interpersonal, interactive process—building bridges and making connections between people. In contrast, Latino men emphasize access to political positions and status, the development of formal political structures, hierarchical organizations, and politics as an opportunity—an opportunity for community advancement, yes, but for personal advancement as well.

A key issue within the debate about gender differences is whether there is an essential divide between the public and private dimensions of politics. For Latina women, much more than men, the boundary between these supposedly distinct spheres of life is blurred, indistinct. With their emphasis on grassroots politics, survival politics, the politics of everyday life and through their emphasis on the development of political consciousness, Latina women see connections between the problems they face personally and community issues stemming from government policies.

For Latina women, making connections between problems in their daily lives and institutional policies, "taking a stand" against oppression from any source, is the first step toward a political life; it creates a *chispa*—a spark—a passion for politics. The development of the personal self, as a woman, as a person with new capacities, as someone who can take action with others, is intimately linked with the development of the political self. Political mobilization occurs when the desire to *desenvolverse*—to develop oneself—is linked to working with other people on the government policies that affect one's ability to achieve personal and community goals.

A similar process occurs in relation to the debate about the nature of power. Latina women differ substantially from Latino men in how they perceive the meaning of power. Latino men talk more about power than do Latina women; they also reflect the mainstream, perhaps male, view of power as "power over," whereas Latina women see power as the "power to"—especially the power to achieve change. This finding lends support for feminist theories of gender differences in the meaning of power and suggests that these differences are valid cross-culturally. As Rosa López says, "It's promoting change. . . . That's political, that's what I mean by politics, that's what politics means to me."

Feminist contributions to political theory—contributions about gender differences, the public–private dimensions of politics, and power—are sometimes limited, unfortunately, by a lack of attention to diversity. Hurtado (1989), for example, contends that "most contemporary published feminist theory in the United States has been written by white, educated women" and that "the experiences of other women . . . are absent in much of white academic feminist theory" (838). Latina women in Boston lend considerable support for contemporary feminist theories that women—as women—are more focused on the relational aspects of politics than are men. Nevertheless, Latina women in Boston, like many black women and Latinas in other parts of the United States (Hurtado 1989, 842), are highly critical of Anglo feminism for not paying more attention to struggles faced by poor women of color. Economic subordination and racism have not been addressed within the feminist movement to the extent desirable for the mobilization of Latina women as women. Thus, while Latina women in Boston provide support for feminist theories about gender differences, they also help explain the dilemma of why some groups of women of color hesitate to embrace—or lend active support for—feminist causes.

An even more complex theoretical dilemma exists, however. In contending, as I do, that substantial differences exist between Latina women and Latino men around connectedness, collectivity, community, and consciousness, I am treading on dangerous ground. The contention that the politics of women differs in some essential way from the politics of men comes perilously close to the biological determinism and the "separate spheres" arguments of the nineteenth century, notions that contributed to the subordination of women. Dietz (1989), Flanagan and Jackson (1990), and Deutchman (1991) caution against any tendency toward what Dietz calls "binary opposition," in other words, against seeing women and men as promoting diametrically opposed visions of society and politics.

Many potential dangers exist when theory or empirical research concludes that there are intrinsic differences between women and men: (1) the truth may be distorted; even though Latina women are twice as likely as Latino men to focus on connectedness, and Latino men are five times as likely as women to emphasize politics as positions, some women and men share a common view of politics—a view that represents a meeting ground, a potential for common understanding and common action, a view that might be obscured when differences are highlighted. (2) The role of patriarchal social structures consequently receives less attention. (3) Essentialist explanations of observed gender differences may contribute to antifeminist policies (Deutchman 1991) and the imposition of greater constraints on women.

In other words, when I couch observed gender differences as connectedness *versus* positions and status, collectivity *versus* hierarchy, community *versus* formal structures, and consciousness *versus* opportunity and formal affiliations, the occasions of common political understanding shared by Latino men and Latina women retreat from view. In addition, as I discussed in Chapter 2, the reasons Latina women do not stress positions more, for example, may originate in the sociopolitical structure: subordination, social conditioning, and blocked opportunities. Finally, by promoting a vision of Latina women's politics as more participatory, as superior, their potential activism in areas currently dominated by men may be further inhibited.

What purpose is served, then, by asserting and highlighting the gender differences? First, the differences exist; they cannot be ignored or rationalized away. Second, regardless of the source, the differences reveal a contribution by Latina women to a model of participatory politics, a model that may hold a key for political mobilization and political empowerment, especially in communities of color. By pointing to the differences, then, I do not wish to create the impression that these participatory qualities are the unique realm of women—there were indeed Latino men who exhibited some of them as well; in each analysis, some men responded like the women and some women resembled the men.

Nevertheless, by highlighting the different, more participatory, vision of politics voiced and acted upon by Latina women, participatory skills and values are likewise highlighted, brought to the forefront of political analysis. It is obviously possible that these skills and values are within the abilities of men—who may be constrained from their expression or may suppress their expression in action or words because of another kind of sexism that stifles men's relational abilities. Finally, by highlighting observed gender differences among Latinos, a vision of politics, of "What is political?" takes shape, a vision that holds promise for a revitalization of political participation.

When Andrea del Valle, Barber (1984), and Dietz (1989) argue for participation, it is a participation of all, a revitalization of the truer image of citizenship.

What Is Political?

What emerges from the stories of Latina women and Latino men is that the traditional focus on politics as positions, on politics as elections and interest groups, that frames much of our understanding of politics may be a gendered construct. It may be that the emphasis on the hierarchical organizations, elected offices, and formal structures that constitute the system of representative democracy prevalent in American politics reflects its origins in male concerns about positions, hierarchy, and formally organized structures. The dominance of these concerns in political *analysis* may also reflect the dominance of males in the profession of political science.

It is not my goal to dismiss the importance of elections, of voting, of promoting legal citizenship, and of traditional modes of political participation. As indicated previously, what Latino men do politically may contribute as much to the realignment of political power for Latinos in this country as what Latina women do. Redistricting challenges by Latino men, for example, were directly responsible for the election of the first Latino to statewide office in Massachusetts. In addition, this book begins by documenting the actions of Latina women in these traditional political roles. The fact that Latina women in Boston have run for office as often as Latino men, and in greater proportion than their non-Latina counterparts, shows that a more participatory vision of politics does not in any way preclude support for the electoral side of politics. Latina women are candidates; they also figure prominently in voter registration, in party politics, and in political education. Latina women even discuss voting slightly more than do Latino men. What Latina women contribute to our understanding of "What is political?" then, is not a dilution of support for electoral politics but a specification of the interactive process of political mobilization and a reexamination of the nature of politics.

Strategies built on an interpersonal, interactive, *process-oriented* type of politics involve mutuality, the *intercambio de ideas* (exchange of ideas), and the ability to truly listen. Organizational structures that encourage members to take on new roles, including political roles, and those that encourage participation in defining and implementing organizational goals enhance political participation. Building community through face-to-face, door-to-door conversations and discussion groups does more to create a sense of citizenship among neighbors—a sense of citizenship that transcends legal status—than campaign flyers and voting instructions. While elections and redistricting decisions in the courts determine representation and are important vehicles for Latino political success in *electoral* politics, political strategies built on interpersonal relationships may in fact contribute far more to mass *participation* within Latino communities.

Finally, a reexamination of the nature of politics via a study of Latina women and Latino men in Boston addresses the question whether gender affects the definition and study of politics in America. Too often, political analysis ignores the gender of the political actors involved in political mobilization; when women's political behavior is ignored, their politics and their ideas about "the political" are marginalized. When, for example, Uriarte-Gaston (1988) follows convention and does not identify the gender of many of the leaders and participants in the community development activism of Boston's Puerto Rican community during the 1960s and 1970s, many readers might assume the community organizers were men, or that the gender of the participators was unimportant. The contribution of the many women active in that period is thus lost. It is not sufficient, therefore, to discuss the roles of women only in research or theoretical works on women or, in a sense, to contain the politics of women within the bounds of feminist political theory and research; gender must be identified and included in general political analysis as well.

Politics as an Interactive Process: "Everybody Wants Personal Politics"

When I claim that connection, collectivity, community, and consciousness are the ingredients that create a passion for politics and translate political passion into political activity, am I somehow claiming that Latinos are unique, in other words, that they have a cultural need for a more personal politics? Or is there an implicit class dimension: Do poorer Latino groups, like Puerto Ricans and Dominicans, require personal politics because of a parochial, private-regarding, ethos? Finally, am I claiming that Latina women are unique in their ability to generate mobilization because they use connection, collectivity, community, and consciousness as mobilization methods? All these questions revolve around a central issue: What is the relationship between culture, class, and gender in the study of Latino politics?

On the surface, it seems clear that the Latino cultural value of *personalismo* could explain much of the need for a more personal style of political mobilization. A class perspective also seems suggested by my findings: traditional theories see lower-class people as having a parochial, private-regarding, view of politics; the consensus of Latinos in Boston is that they want something concrete for the community as a result of their political efforts. But then, where does the fact that Latina women focus on connectedness and personal politics to a much greater degree than Latino men fit into a culture–class model of Latino political participation? Obviously, culture, class, and gender all interact in some way.

Latinos clearly do have cultural traditions that point to an expectation of personal politics, concrete benefits, and group-centered mobilization strategies. The discussion in Chapter 6 on home-country politics in Puerto Rico and the Dominican Republic, for example, demonstrates that men and women alike expect politicians and political organizers to "come and find out," to listen, to shake hands, and to promise benefits and respond to community needs.

Of course, this is not just a cultural tradition (in the sense of shared values transmitted through generations) but an expectation based on a different political structure. Latino countries such as Puerto Rico and the Dominican Republic have strong parties, dynamic campaigns, and a political style that integrates affiliative needs into political events. Latino politics in the United States, when compared to home-country politics, clearly demonstrates how culture alone does not determine political participation in a linear way—structure creates the conditions in which cultural values develop.

At the same time, the political-culture school implies that class determines political participation. There did seem to be a class gap between influential Latinos in Boston (*los profesionales*) and their mobilization targets (*la gente del pueblo*). Many Latinos, however, bridged that gap using a political style that blended culture and politics; many of these were Latina women. In addition, there may be a flaw in the argument that lower-status groups or different cultures require certain types of politics (i.e., private-regarding, personal politics). Perhaps the real reason higher socioeconomic groups seem to focus on more than concrete benefits is that, in comparison to poorer groups like Latinos, they already receive the benefits; their dominance of Congress, state legislatures, and other government decision-making bodies assures that their concrete needs are met, again, at least in comparison to poorer groups. Middle-class, white neighborhoods have better schools, cleaner streets, and more responsive police departments. The difference in political styles and political ethos between the upper and lower classes may be less the result of innate

194

differences within the lower classes and more the consequence of who controls the economic resources. As the pained cry of Juana Oviedo, who is facing cuts in her disability allotment, shows, she knows who benefits from this control: "Who is it that is being hurt? It's us, the poor people. Because *those* people have money—the one who has money—this doesn't affect him at all. *He* has a good job, a nice house. . . . How is one supposed to survive? You tell me *that!*" Oviedo recognizes that having money, a good job, and a nice house protects people from the exigencies of life; I suggest that already having many of these concrete benefits also protects the higher socio-economic groups from the need to engage in "parochial" politics.

Some would argue that middle- or upper-class people have received these benefits precisely because of their political activism and political talents. The socioeconomic model implies, however, that the middle- and upper-class groups are, in a sense, less concerned with these private benefits and more concerned with broader social or community needs. I suggest that concrete benefits are concrete benefits and that lower-status groups are not the only ones with "parochial needs." They are simply demanding what they do not have.

What about gender? Latina women in Boston clearly perceive politics differently from Latino men. But do they perceive politics differently from white women, or from black women? Mine was not a comparative study. Only future research can answer the question of culture-specific gender differences between Latina women and women of other ethnic or racial groups. However, the gender differences between Latino men and Latina women add another layer to the already complex task of sorting out culture and class. If Latino men value *personalismo* because of cultural expectations and because most people respond to a politics embedded in interpersonal relationships, why is it that Latina *women* are the ones in the community who are most successful at integrating personal politics into their political mobilization efforts? And if Latino men of *la gente del pueblo*—as men—prefer formal affiliations, hierarchical structures, and access to positions, why do they not respond in greater numbers to the appeals of like-minded Latino male leaders? Is it possible that Latino men are also looking for a more personal style of politics, albeit with a male slant? From the gender differences that form the foundation of the themes of this book, almost as many questions are raised as the book answers.

It is not entirely clear why what would seem to be a shared orientation of Latino male leaders and men of *la gente del pueblo* would not mobilize more Latino men in Boston and other Latino communities. I tentatively suggest several possible reasons. The first is that in Puerto Rico and other Latin countries there seems to be a greater connection between the classes around male political affiliative organizations, possibly because of vestigial paternalistic relationships between the professional/upper-class men and the working-class/ lower-class men. Also, as Johvanil (1989) suggests, cultural clubs and sports clubs play an important role in male socialization in Latin countries but are underdeveloped in both their socialization and political roles in Boston.

The second reason Latino male activists may not have more success at mobilizing Latino men, despite shared politicization patterns, stems from the gender-related constraints on participation discussed in the previous chapter. Men like Luis Hernández, among others, want leaders to come into the community, and Tito Morales demonstrates that maintaining connections (within a male-style hierarchical structure) can be effective. The expectation of *personalismo* is thwarted, however, when male Latino leaders, due to their greater access to "good jobs" in the mostly Anglo government, move up the success ladder of government appointments, leaving behind a vacuum. Juan Maldonado, for example, believes being political means formal affiliations, political structures, and, especially, positions in government. He nevertheless voices the negative impact of Latino male leaders moving into new jobs: "There was a down side because none of these leaders had the time or the vision to basically nurture other leadership, or mentor other leadership to take their place. So Nelson leaves—vacuum! Manuel leaves—vacuum! Julio dies—vacuum!" Previous research on Chicana politics suggests that, while some women are constrained by their multiple roles as workers, mothers, and family members, Latina women develop politically in the context of these roles. They cannot go off to a "good job" and leave family responsibilities behind: these responsibilities stimulate a search for change, a connection with others, and an integration of informal and formal community action. For this reason, Latina women may transmit and maintain cultural traditions (including political traditions) in ways that are difficult for the Latino men who have achieved (somewhat limited) access to the power structure. Community ties blend the politics of culture, class, and gender.

In addition, Latino men's sense that the way they contribute to the community is by being role models does not translate into either the concrete benefits or the personal connections needed (because of *personalismo*) for Latino men to feel part of the political system. In other words, Latino men who are of *la gente del pueblo*, like Latina women in general, may require politics to be built upon personal connections—in the case of men, within formal structures like political parties and clubs—but Latino male leaders, having moved into the Anglo power structure, may fail in, or be constrained from, building or maintaining those connections.

While a few men like Tito Morales integrate the need for concrete benefits and cultural expectations into a male version of personal politics, he is outnumbered by the large number of Latina women who draw others into political events by their emphasis on connection, collectivity, and political consciousness. Women like Josefina Ortega, María Luisa Soto, Inez Martínez, Julia Santiago, and Marta Correa represent a blending of culture and politics and constitute an important political resource for successful mobilization in the Latino community.

Finally, is it not possible that on a smaller scale Latino politics mirrors American politics? Is it not possible that, contrary to the implicit ideological bias of the political-culture school (and class bias of the progressive movement), *all* people want personal politics?— that what Latinos want from politics reflects a universal need? I have already discussed the view that the decline of American political participation since the early part of the century was due, in great part, to the decline in the political party and the demise of the political machine. What these structural changes really involved, however, was the simultaneous decline in politics as an interactive *process*. It may be that what Latinos want from politics is a model for what Americans in general want from their political system.

It is time for the voices of Latina women to be heard. Latina women have long been a source of strength in the Latino community. Their skills at building networks, their experiences blending culture, personal relationships, and political participation have too long been ignored. Latino political empowerment begins in the community; it depends on the engagement of large numbers of Latino people. Many of those who can engage Latinos—who can make connections, work collectively, build community, and raise political consciousness within Latino communities, are Latina women. As Ivelisse Rodríguez and Luis Hernández said so simply, *"Hay que escuchar."* It *is* time to listen to the women.

Notes

The quote by Julia de Burgos, "*Somos la vida, la fuerza, la mujer*" (We are the life, the strength [force], the women), on the dedication page of this book, was printed on a flyer distributed by the Comité de Mujeres Puertorriqueñas Miriam López-Pérez to announce a conference that included a series of workshops on such topics as domestic violence, women and work, friendship, AIDS, and organizing for basic human rights (Comité de Mujeres Puertorriqueñas Miriam López-Pérez 1988).

Portions of Chapters One, Two, and Six appeared in an abbreviated form in papers titled "Latina Women, Latino Men, and Political Participation in Boston: *La chispa que prende*" (Hardy-Fanta 1991b), "Latina Women and Politics in Boston: *Somos la vida, la fuerza, la mujer*" (Hardy-Fanta 1992), and "Discovering Latina Women in Politics" (Hardy-Fanta 1993).

Preface

1. *La gente del pueblo* literally translates to "the people of the village." The term is generally used to mean the common folk or the masses.

2. It should be noted that even highly quantitative studies often include extensive qualitative research that is hidden to some extent by the numbers. A good example of this is the book by Browning, Marshall, and Tabb (1984). In their work, the quantitative results take center stage but serve to support findings generated in large part by qualitative methods.

3. Prior to each interview I asked each participant for permission to conduct the interview and discussed issues of confidentiality. I tape-recorded interviews and field notes of community events, and later coded and analyzed the transcripts for patterns and themes. For a complete discussion of the research methodology on which this book is based, see Chapter 2 and the appendixes in Hardy-Fanta (1991a).

4. And some obvious disadvantages. By limiting myself to people associated with the same three centers, it is likely that some common factors led to their selection. They also may have shared perceptions about, or experiences with, politics precisely because of being at the same center and participating in the same events. They were not friends, however, and they came from a

199

variety of backgrounds and countries. (There was one exception: Jaime Romero was the son of Carlos García's girlfriend.)

5. I am creating very general attributes for the three neighborhoods. There is considerable variation within each of the neighborhoods, and I welcome evidence that my designation of a neighborhood as being a certain "type" is wrong or exaggerated. My sense, however, is that North Dorchester is, in fact, the newcomer and poorer neighborhood (despite the exceptions), Jamaica Plain has more political involvement and more Latino businesses, and the South End has the more established Latino institutions. For a general discussion of potential selection bias see Hardy-Fanta (1991a, 89).

6. I look at the dogeared paper with three columns of names; hundreds of arrows in red, blue, and black; and circles identifying people suggested for future interviews. I worry, What if I had interviewed Camila Alvarado? Why didn't I interview Doña Petra as well as Doña Fina? Maybe my findings would be different if I had been able to contact Carlos Irizarry and Arturo Jiménez? The problem I faced was the perennial "just one more interview." However, it should be pointed out that random samples without an adequate response rate are no better statistically than nonrandom samples. Hochschild (1981), for example, used a time-consuming and sophisticated sampling strategy but achieved a response rate of only 33 to 37 percent. Her findings, while not statistically generalizable, nevertheless provide important information about Americans' views on distributive justice.

Introduction

1. A literal translation would be: "Well, to finish this. . . ." Her tone and meaning, however, communicated a more assertive stance, which I translated as noted in the text.

2. For a discussion of the impact of religion, including Pentecostal religions, on politics, see Hardy-Fanta (1991a, 199–204).

3. In fact, a third of the women specifically used the phrase, "It depends on what you mean," when I asked them to tell me what they did politically. None of the men questioned the definition of "What is political?"

4. See, for example, Jennings and Rivera (1984), Falcón (1988), and Jennings (1988a, 1988b).

5. Data are based on the 1990 U.S. Census as reported by Northeastern University Center for Labor Market Studies; preliminary report in the Boston Globe (1991b).

6. Osterman's study puts the Puerto Rican population at 47 percent, compared to the 42 percent census tabulation; thus, his data on the other subgroups may also vary from the 1990 Census reports. One explanation is that his population sample consisted of those 18 to 60 years of age and thus undercounts what may be more non–Puerto Rican youth and elder populations. Nevertheless, I include his data on non–Puerto Ricans because he is

the only source of data that breaks down the "other" category to show population size of the Central Americans, South Americans, and Dominicans.

7. East Boston is now 17.6 percent and Roslindale is 10.4 percent Latino. In 1990 Allston/Brighton became 9.1 percent Latino (*Boston Globe* 1991a).

8. Santillan (1988a) identifies the drawing of district lines to be a major barrier in the history of Latino communities across the country.

9. This poem was published in Chile as a broadside. A rough translation might be "Forgive me if I speak of foolish things / on a lovely afternoon in February / and if your heart should wander off to Santo Domingo . . ."

10. Data in this section are from the 1990 U.S. Census as reported in the *Boston Globe*. Nationally, Puerto Ricans have the highest poverty rate of all the Latino groups: 37.9 percent of Puerto Rican families were below the federal poverty line in 1988 compared to 25.5 percent of Mexican Americans, 13.8 percent of Cubans, and 18.9 percent of Central and South Americans. The poverty rate for families not of Hispanic origin was only 9.7 percent (U.S. Bureau of the Census 1988, 8).

11. Recent research suggests, however, that residential stability has improved considerably in recent years (Jennings 1984c; Osterman 1992, 60).

12. This literature will be critiqued in the next chapter.

Chapter One

1. Diana Lam's candidacy lasted only three days because of extensive news coverage of her family's failure to submit recent IRS tax returns until shortly before she declared she was running for office. This news coverage overshadowed her campaign platform, and she withdrew. It was only after her withdrawal that the *Globe* began praising her appeal to many dissatisfied constituencies in the city. In addition, even *before* her financial difficulties were exposed, the *Globe* downplayed her candidacy—the announcement that she was challenging Mayor Flynn appeared "below the fold." For an analysis of how the news media treats minority candidacies, see, for example, Alberts (1986).

2. The percentage of women candidates was calculated using the pink and blue "strip sheets"—the lists of candidates for nomination for the Democratic and Republican 1990 state primaries—provided by the Office of the Secretary of the Commonwealth Elections Division (1990a). Nationally, the total number of women running for public office at the city or state level is difficult to gauge. Clark et al. (1984, 152) provide data from New Mexico, Oklahoma, Nebraska, and Wyoming: during the period 1968 to 1974 no more than 12.1 percent of the candidates for the lower house of the state legislatures were women. Between 1976 and 1980, the numbers rose slightly:

between 11.3 and 17.0 percent of lower-house candidates were women. Rule (1981, 61) cites a study by Darcy and Schramm (1977) showing that in 1974 women ran for state legislative seats in 8 percent of the congressional districts. According to Rule (1981, 61), Karnig and Walker (1976) find similar results in city elections.

Black women, like Latina women in Boston, may run for public office in greater numbers than their white counterparts. Darcy and Hadley (1988, 638) find, for example, that 31.1 percent of the black women delegates to the Democratic Party Convention of 1984 aspired to elected public office, whereas only 19.7 percent of the white women delegates wanted to hold public office.

3. These women do not represent the totality of Latina women active in party politics in Boston. I interviewed María Luisa Soto and Josefina Ortega not because of their roles in party politics but because they were identified by others as being "good at organizing Latinos." Their party political activities emerged in the interviews.

4. Sacks (1988) and Garland (1988) would call them "centerwomen." *Cassell's Spanish Dictionary* (1968, 43) defines *alcadesa* as "wife of an *alcalde*," but Latinas in Boston clearly use the term to mean much more than a wifely role.

5. See, for example, Sánchez Korrol (1983, 85–117).

6. Pachon (1987, xvi) states, for example, that "while there is a large underrepresentation of Hispanic women in public offices, the proportion of Hispanic women in elected office is larger than for society in general. Nationally, women hold only 12 percent of all elected offices. In the Hispanic community, women hold 18 percent of the offices." Vigil (1987, 50) mentions the campaign of Linda Chavez for the U.S. Senate from the state of Maryland in 1986 and notes that, in running against Barbara Mikulski, this campaign "marked only the second time in U.S. history when two women faced each other in a U.S. Senate race."

7. Pachon (1987, xvi) states that, despite the stereotype of *machismo* in the Latino community, "more Hispanic women vote than men." In the 1988 presidential election, Latina women were registered and voted at rates slightly higher than those of Latino men: 37.4 percent of women compared to 33.5 percent of men were registered; 30.1 percent of women voted compared to 27.4 percent of men (U.S. Bureau of the Census 1989, 17). In the 1984 presidential election, Latina women in New York City were registered at a substantially higher rate than were Latino men: 59 percent to 41 percent (Falcón 1988, 183). This gender gap was the same as for blacks but is greater than for whites; white women in the same election were registered at the rate of 55.7 percent, compared to 44.3 percent for white men. (Data are percentages of voting-age population.) Vigil (1987, 38) summarizes exit polls during the 1984 presidential election that show the same pattern: Latina women outvoted Latino men 59 percent to 41 percent in New York and 55 percent to 45 percent in Texas. The only contrary evidence seems to be in

California, where Latino men outvoted Latina women 55 percent to 45 percent.

8. See, for example, Carrillo (1986), Pardo (1990), and Rose (1990). These articles will be discussed later in this chapter.

9. The bibliographic essay by Lillian Castillo-Speed (1990), "Chicana Studies: A Selected List of Materials Since 1980," includes only about ten explicitly political references out of several hundred. Much of the work on Chicana women and politics focuses on organizing in the makeup and cannery factories, situations less pertinent to Puerto Rican, Dominican, and Central American women in the Northeast. In addition, a search of major computer databases confirms my observation that the vast majority of literature on Latina women concentrates on women in their reproductive, social, and labor-market roles.

10. Obscuring the role of Latina women in politics by the exclusive focus on "designated" leaders may be similar to a process that occurs for black women. According to Ferguson (1989, 13), for example, in Sacks's (1988) study of black women's union organizing at Duke University Medical Center, Sacks "discovered that the equation of political leadership with public spokespersons 'obscured an equally crucial aspect of leadership, that of *network centers*, who were almost all Black women.' The women were at the center of family-like networks formed around everyday relationships among friends, neighbors and colleagues. They drew upon organizing skills honed at home. . . . They stood at the center of their community and on-the-job networks, tapping and directing the groups' collective energies while remaining responsible to them."

11. Wilson and Banfield (1971, 1050) state that "for every ethnic group other than Irish and Negroes, the percentage of female respondents did not exceed 24." Their data suggest, however, that Yankee respondents were primarily male. Non-Yankees had substantially larger numbers of women in the samples: up to one-quarter of the Jews, Italians, and Poles, and a third or more of the Irish and black Americans were women.

12. See, for example, Pateman (1970) and Ackelsberg (1991). Barber (1984) provides prescriptions for what he calls "strong democracy" but is weak in providing empirical examples. A problem with Pateman's and Ackelsberg's research is that it focuses on participatory experiences in Yugoslavia and Spain, respectively.

13. I acknowledge the existence of a great deal of literature about women getting elected. See, for example, Amundsen (1971), Tolchin and Tolchin (1976), Githens and Prestage (1977), Baxter and Lansing (1981), Klein (1984). I am, however, specifically looking at the feminist literature that expands the notion of the nature of political participation beyond conventional, behavioral definitions.

14. Obviously, feminism encompasses a wide range of political ideologies. Liberal feminism strives to gain access to the jobs, elected offices, and power held by men in the American political system. Marxist feminism at-

tempts to locate women's oppression within capitalistic economic structures. Coole (1988, 260–261) describes how radical feminists emphasize the "gendered rule of women by men" and concludes that the so-called feminine personality is a social construction. There is a strain within feminist theory between ideologies that imply women and men are not inherently different versus those that attempt to "revalorize" women—to celebrate the differences. In the latter perspective, women as women can contribute to a more cooperative world order. The problem with this radical perspective is that it contains within it a "biology is destiny" component that has been used to disempower women in the social/economic/political arena.

I do not ascribe to liberal feminist goals of access to male power circles, and my data suggest that women do have different perspectives on power and political relationships. When I speak of feminist theorists, therefore, I am referring not to liberal women seeking equality with men in a male-defined political world but rather to the more radical perspective. The issue of the sources of gender differences (i.e., biology or social construction) and the theoretical problems implicit in this discussion will be addressed in the Conclusion.

15. See Almond and Verba (1963) and Verba and Nie (1972).

16. See also the literature on women in politics in Latin America, for example, Aviel (1981), Carrillo (1986), and Letelier (1989). Carrillo reveals the role of Latina women as presidential candidates when she describes the candidacy of Doña Rosario Ibarra in the 1982 Mexican presidential election. Carrillo "focuses on Rosario's candidacy and evaluates the impact of her campaign on women's political participation and organization within the Mexican Left" (96).

17. For a discussion of the debate about the social construction of gender differences and a caution against seeing male and female visions of politics in oppositional terms, see Dietz (1989).

18. *Doña* is a form of address used in conjunction with a woman's first name; it, like its male version, *Don*, connotes friendly respectfulness.

19. Women challenge Banfield and Wilson's (1963) artificial distinction between public-regarding and private-regarding behaviors with a declaration that "the personal is political" (Evans 1980). For a discussion of the feminist critique of this distinction between public and private spheres of politics, see Jones (1990).

20. Of course, there are men for whom politics, especially for the poor, involves something besides electoral, formal, organizational processes. Scott (1985, xv–xvi), for example, claims that "formal, organized political activity, even if clandestine and revolutionary, is typically the preserve of the middle class and the intelligentsia. . . . [The everyday forms of] resistance are often the most significant and the most effective over the long run."

21. The way political silence is orchestrated in formal organizations is not discussed only by feminist theorists. Lukes (1974) and Bachrach and Baratz (1962) detail the subtle ways people's awareness of their own needs and interests gets shaped. People may have grievances and needs that are

unarticulated, covert, or latent, and the power structure may work to suppress these grievances and needs.

22. See, for example, Carr (1989) and Pantoja and Martell (1989–90) for alternative visions of political activism.

23. All voting rates are the percentage of the total voting-age population for each group and are based on U.S. Census data. Latino rates are based on the U.S. Census count of "persons of Hispanic origin." (See U.S. Bureau of the Census 1989, 78.)

24. They are careful to point out that only *eligible* Latinos (i.e., citizens) should be counted as the denominator in determining voting rates. As noted before, however, given Boston's influx of Dominicans who are not citizens, the number of Latinos eligible to vote as a percentage of the total Latino adult population will become smaller.

25. See, for example, Browning, Marshall, and Tabb (1984); and Jennings, in Falcón (1984, 40). Torres-Gil (1976) and Garcia and Arce (1988) suggest that Latino political attitudes support community organization and the utilization of the vote as important political tools but that these attitudes are not translated into increased voter participation.

26. See, for example, Watson and Samora (1954), Kernstock (1972), and Jennings, in Falcón (1984, 15). A survey by MacManus and Cassel (1988, 203) finds that Mexican Americans are less interested in politics than blacks and Anglos. Nelson (1979, 1037) suggests that Dominicans and Puerto Ricans in New York City come from a "weak participant culture." For a dissenting view, see Garcia and de la Garza (1977, especially chap. 3), Santillan (1988a), and Hardy-Fanta (1991a).

27. See Piven and Cloward (1971). They provide numerous examples of nineteenth-century objections to the quality of socialization of these early immigrants.

28. See also Morone's (1990) *The Democratic Wish.* He states that the progressive movement at the turn of the century had a "coherent vision of democratic participation. Their democratic reforms were all aimed at minimizing, even spurning, the role of the representational intermediaries that stood between the public and its government—parties, legislators, private interests, ultimately politics itself. . . . [Nevertheless,] the many devices designed to empower the people proved unwieldy in operation and élitist in effect" (112, 123). (The specific devices Morone refers to are the direct primary, the secret [Australian] ballot, and, in a broader sense, civil service.)

29. In the area of black politics, for example, Walton (1985, 2–3) finds that "a focus on the individual leads inevitably and logically to the weaknesses and imperfections inherent in man and away from the imperfections and weaknesses of the political system"; the wealth of black political participation becomes obscured.

30. Dahl (1961, 224–225), quoted in Pateman (1980, 66; emphasis in Dahl).

31. Of course, Latina women may share certain capabilities with other women, especially black women activists. In her study of black hospital

workers, Sacks (1988), for example, discusses the idea of "centerwomen"—women who organize others. These are women who "[are] at the center of family-like networks formed around everyday relationships among friends, neighbors and colleagues" (Ferguson 1989, 13).

Chapter Two

1. Granovetter (1973, 1982) asserts that the weaker ties between strangers who are connected only because of a specific issue have the potential of creating more bridges because weak ties are not limited by the number of people one knows intimately. I suggest that he sees weak ties between officials and members of organizations as more effective because these are the ties that men prefer, encourage, and feel more comfortable utilizing for personal and political purposes. I thank Hillard Pouncy for alerting me to this literature and for redirecting my thinking toward participatory theories of politics.

2. "You can immediately identify with . . ."

3. Thirteen of the twenty influential Latina women discussed connectedness a total of twenty-four times (for an average of 1.2). In contrast, only seven of eighteen influential men discussed connectedness a total of eleven times (for an average of 0.6). Note that I calculate the average number of coded segments for the men and women *as a group*. In other words, an individual man or woman is counted as mentioning a specific topic 0, 1, 2, . . . , x times. All the counts are added up, and the average is calculated with the total number of men and women in the subset as the denominator. I used this average rather than a simple average (i.e., the number of mentions by the people who mentioned a topic at least once) because I did not want the "score" for each sex overly weighted by one or two individuals who spoke extensively on a given topic that was not considered important by the rest of the group. In addition, the analysis of some themes was based on my interviews with the thirty-eight influential (including *gente*/influential) Latinos. It is also important to keep in mind that the numbers I provide do not represent a quantitative or statistical statement of validity or reliability. They are provided to support findings generated qualitatively and to give a general sense of the magnitude of difference between the women and the men.

4. *Cacica* is the female form of *cacique*—the name of the original Taino Indian rulers. The Tainos were one of the indigenous people of Puerto Rico.

5. Guzmán (1976, 199) found the same pattern in Mexican Americans, who had "little or no knowledge of leaders of organizations and of others recognized *externally*, by the Anglo community as ethnic leaders. But they were knowledgeable about neighborhood leaders."

6. Sixteen of the twenty influential and *gente*/influential women identified survival as a crucial issue affecting political participation a total of twenty-seven times (for an average of 1.4). Men discussed survival politics very little: only three men mentioned survival three times (for an average of 0.2).

7. Nelson (1979) identifies the following behaviors as "subsistence politics": contacting government agencies like welfare, social security, housing boards, and so on, and seeking personal services. He distinguishes these behaviors from what he implies are higher-level politics: voting, joining organizations, and "contacting officials." His primary distinguishing factor is that subsistence politics "does not exhibit the 'voluntarism' characteristic of [the other types], and is therefore best conceived as 'non-participatory' political activity" (1030). Stone (1989) points out, however, that when Lee Iacocca appealed to the government for the Chrysler bailout, the process was indeed political and not any more "voluntary" than a person seeking a housing judgment following an eviction.

8. See Scott's (1985) book *Weapons of the Weak: Everyday Forms of Peasant Resistance.*

9. Grassroots politics implies that the people who are directly affected by a given social problem develop their own goals, methods, and solutions— from the grass roots up rather than from outside organizations or leaders down. I discuss gender differences in the Latino emphasis on grassroots politics in Chapter 4.

10. MCAD is the Massachusetts Commission Against Discrimination; MDC is the Massachusetts District Commission; DSS is the Department of Social Services; and DYS is the Department of Youth Services.

11. Thirteen of the eighteen influential or *gente*/influential men discussed politics in terms of positions and status for a total of fifty-five times; the average number of mentions was 3.0. Only six of twenty influential or *gente*/ influential Latina women, in contrast, discussed positions and status. They mentioned this theme only twelve times in total, and the average was 0.6.

12. Quote is from Chodorow (1974; in Gilligan 1982, 16). See also Gilligan (1982), and *Women's Growth in Connection: Writings from the Stone Center* (Jordan et al. 1991).

13. For a fuller discussion of these theoretical points, see Miller (1991).

14. Note that many of the human needs that Lane (1969) claims lead to involvement in politics can, in fact, be traced to male rather than female social orientations. For example, he connects politics to the need for power and the need to express or control aggression, but he downplays social relations and affiliative needs (31). Lane's conclusions that politics is more about power and control than affiliation and social connectedness most likely result from the fact that the subjects of his research were male and not from an accurate analysis that reflects both male and female perspectives.

15. Flanagan and Jackson (1990, 39), in discussing research on Gilligan's "ethics of care," state that "recent research shows that . . . men and women distribute themselves bimodally on the justice and care ends of the scale."

16. Eleven of eighteen influential and *gente*/influential men discussed politics as power, for an average of 1.8. Only eight of twenty influential and *gente*/influential women discussed politics as power, for an average of 0.8. For women, in general, power means achieving change; for men, it is control

and dominion (Miller 1983, 3–4). This seems to be true for Latina women and Latino men, as well.

17. I am painting an excessively rosy picture of personal–public relationships in Latin American countries. Fraud and corruption contaminate these relationships: in Mexico, for example, police stop motorists at will and exact a payment. Of course, police payoffs (personal as well as business) are not uncommon in America—despite our "value" of impersonal public service.

18. Guzmán (1976) points to certain Anglo outsiders (namely Fred Ross, Saul Alinsky, and other white liberals) who "turned to the [Mexican-American] *barrios* to promote social change. . . . These well-meaning Anglo outsiders, many of them left-wing ideologists, identified the roots of poverty: they provided arguments and important political options. There was great resistance to these aggressive *auslanders*. Their manner was considered abrasive and insensitive" (217–218).

19. *Averigüar* implies an active, investigative, type of finding out.

20. I interviewed only four Dominican individuals (although I spoke informally with others), but I found that Dominican women were more politically aware and enthusiastic than the men. Both men I met had rejected political participation in the Dominican Republic (although they did vote there) and were too busy working here to engage in political discussions or activities.

21. I am uncomfortable ending this section with the appearance of a lively, responsive, or even democratic government in the Dominican Republic. Corruption and political machinations abound in its political system. Mota (1976) adds an even more damning portrayal of Dominican politics; she points to the brutality of the Trujillo regime during the 1930s and the stranglehold the present party seems to have on the country. In such an analysis the question always arises whether the participatory processes can be (or should be) separated from the power structure in a given country.

22. In Puerto Rico, a seventeen-year-old may register to vote in the primary if he or she will be eighteen by the time of the general election.

23. See, for example, Guzmán (1976, 205–219) and Gómez-Quiñones (1990, 166).

24. I discuss this literature at length in Chapter 5. See Almond and Verba (1963), Verba and Nie (1972), and Miyares (1974). Even Sigel (1989), who concludes that adult political socialization is "an interactive process" (458), includes few articles in her book that examine interpersonal interactions as sources of political behavior. And Walton (1985), who purports to uncover "invisible politics" in the black experience, continues to focus on measurable political activities. (He also ignores, unfortunately, the political life of black women.) Morrison (1987), on the other hand, provides an excellent recounting of Unita Blackwell, a black female leader in Mississippi during the 1970s. Morrison describes in considerable detail Blackwell's interpersonal mobilization methods (95–122).

25. See, for example, Walton (1985), Morris, Hatchett, and Brown (1989) (civil rights); Klein (1984), Carroll (1989) (women's movement).

26. Latina women yielded forty-eight coded segments of interview transcripts that referred to personal relationships in political mobilization; Latino men, only sixteen.

27. For a discussion of talking and mutualistic listening as essential components of participatory politics, see Barber (1984, esp. 173–198).

28. The political history of Puerto Rico is steeped in colonial experiences of displacement. Operation Bootstrap, a U.S. industrial policy implemented during the 1950s, encouraged the abandonment of small agricultural plots by rural Puerto Ricans to create a workforce for industries; the industries received tax breaks so they would locate on the island. The loss of land by the *jíbaros* still resonates with many Puerto Ricans.

29. See Gregg (1991) for an excellent discussion of the complexities of "choice" for women.

30. For example, Latina women and Latino men are in a unique situation because of the language they speak; the geographical proximity of Puerto Rico, the Dominican Republic, and Mexico; the impact of homeland politics and U.S. foreign policy on mainland politics; and cultural traditions that affect participation. Cultural traditions in particular have gender-linked consequences for political participation. (See the discussion on *personalismo* earlier in this chapter.)

31. Divisible benefits can be delivered to individuals, families, small groups; indivisible benefits are the result of government policies that target benefits to segments, or categories, of the population (Dahl 1961, 51). Flammang (1984a) compares the service provision in Chicana, black, and white women's networks in Santa Clara County, California, to ward-heeler practices: "The parallel between female activists and ward heelers most certainly does hold for providing services not offered elsewhere" (91). Flammang also points, however, to critical differences between today's women activists and machine politicos: (1) the services are not exchanged for partisan votes, and (2) the services are not contingent on Who sent you? (95) as they were in the days of the urban machine.

32. Only two of the Latina women interviewed were appointed officials, and they seemed less active in mobilizer roles.

33. Only eight women, compared to eleven men, discussed power, and the number of times women mentioned power was half that of men (seventeen compared to thirty-four).

34. Nine of the twenty influential and *gente*/influential women share the connectedness of Josefina Ortega, María Luisa Soto, and Marta Correa but are concerned more with personal and political development than with party politics and the vote.

35. I discuss the way the political style of certain men resembles machine politics in the portrait of Julio Herrera in the next chapter.

36. Another crucial difference is that machine bosses had the wherewithal to grant utility and other city contracts and to exact "assessments" from those who were appointed to plum jobs. Morone (1990) calls these assessments "the cornerstone of party finance" (101).

Chapter Three

1. The organization is frequently referred to as just Mujeres (Women) or Mujeres Unidas (Women United).

2. Pateman (1970) promotes the development of democratic experiences in the workplace as training for participatory democracy, instead of the undemocratic and hierarchical, experiences of current workplace environments which contribute to alienation from government institutions built on a representative system. I suspect that Pateman would include participatory experiences at Latino agencies as a way of increasing true democratic participation for Latino groups, since Latinos spend considerable time at their agencies.

3. When using the term *group*, I am not necessarily referring to the kinds of political organizations that traditional studies of political participation count under "organizational membership." Few of the more participatory of the individuals who took part in this study would claim membership in a formal organization. Most of the groups they participate in are informal or social, not explicitly political. These groups, however, represent an important potential mechanism by which political participation can be introduced into the lives of new immigrants. For a discussion on the role of primary groups (especially the family) and secondary groups (peer groups and organizations) in political learning, see Dawson and Prewitt (1969, esp. chaps. 8 and 9, 181–194). For a more recent analysis of women's groups, see, for example, Conover (1988).

4. This is an inadequate translation of the phrase *me oriento con ellas*. The phrase in Spanish implies the joining of the self and the group. "Being with others, I get myself together" is an awkward translation, but one that captures the true meaning. The verb *orientarse* literally means "to find one's bearings" or "to consider the course to be taken" (*Cassell's Spanish Dictionary* 1968, 593).

5. I am struck by the inadequacy of the written word to recapture the feelings behind such a statement. Her sense of connectedness to a common humanity of the poor came out in speech through the richness of the way she stressed certain words and used pauses between others for drama. I am also saddened that the English-speaking reader loses the beauty of the Spanish language and must make due with a mere translation.

6. Again a problem with translation. *Distraerse* translates to "to amuse oneself" or "enjoy oneself"; however, there is an element of leaving behind preoccupations, distracting oneself from troubles. I will add an only slightly tangential note on another word that means "to amuse" or "to enjoy" oneself. *Entretenerse* is also a way of saying "to amuse" or "to enjoy" oneself. However, *entretenerse* implies connection with others; it literally translates to "to have [put] oneself between [with]" others. Enjoyment, in the Spanish language, occurs in connection with other people. Thus, linguistic differences express cultural beliefs about the importance of connectedness and social relationships.

7. I suspect, although I did not gather data to support my suspicion, that the great majority of the agency staff who got out the vote during the days of Julio Herrera were women as well. Front-line staff at most human service agencies are female.

8. Young (1990) suggests that, without group representation, disadvantaged groups are effectively silenced in public forums. In discussing research by Mansbridge (1980), Young demonstrates that "women, blacks, working-class people, and poor people tend to participate less and have their interests represented less than whites, middle-class professionals, and men. . . . White middle-class men assume authority more than others and they are more practiced at speaking persuasively; mothers and old people often find it more difficult than others to get to meetings" (Young 1990, 125). Of course, even supposedly participatory democratic structures still tend to silence disadvantaged groups (Young 1990, esp. 125–126). Changing the structure is not enough; assuring the diversity of voices, irrespective of class, color, and gender, is critical. What Barber (1984, 269–272) suggests is neighborhood assemblies to assure convenient meeting times, public discussion, citizen-generated agenda, and time for questions, debates, and the venting of grievances. A facilitator (not a "leader") would assure rules of fair discussion and open debate, maintain decorum, and encourage participants to raise questions.

9. Replacing people without replacing organizational structure does not necessarily increase participation or create change. In Boston, for example, the recent replacement of an elected school committee (with no Latino representation) to one appointed by the mayor (with two Latinos) has created a new problem. Despite more Latino representation, the focus is still on school closings, decisions are still made hierarchically without discussion, the audience is still in an audience role, and the agenda is set from the top.

10. There were almost one hundred mentions of the "*envidia*" codeword reflecting disunity, dissension, one-upmanship, and turf conflicts. A subcode of not getting enough back from designated leaders was part of the "*envidia*" theme and was discussed eighty times. For a complete discussion of this topic, see chap. 4 in Hardy-Fanta (1991a).

11. *Caciques* were the Taino Indian chiefs in pre-Columbian Puerto Rico. In English this would be expressed as "Everyone wants to be a chief, not an Indian." Armando Meléndez actually used those words in English to discuss the problem of how the drive to be in charge of something interferes with cooperation for a larger community goal.

12. Several exceptions are works on black community politics by Jones (1972), Jennings (1982), and Travis (1990); in addition, Rivera (1984, 69f.) discusses some aspects of internal politics in Puerto Rican organizations in New York City during the War on Poverty. Foley et al. (1977) discuss how Anglo politicians stimulated internal conflict as a way of suppressing the emerging Chicano movement in southwestern Texas.

13. Jennings (1986) states that "the political vulnerability of blacks working for city hall produced the . . . [following] effect: independent black political behavior was discouraged and punished" (63). He goes on to describe

how black appointees were threatened with the loss of their jobs after having refused to follow the mayor's dictates.

14. Seven interviewees specifically mentioned prohibitions such as the Hatch Act. Fourteen others discussed inhibitions about acting politically at their places of employment.

15. When discussing such a loaded subject as this, it is very important to clarify certain points. When I talk about Latino men and women and say "most men" or "in general, men" display certain patterns that are different from those of "most women," I am opening myself up to the criticism of excessive generalization or of lumping individuals into diffuse groupings. It is necessary to affirm that I am speaking of general patterns that occur by gender—an "ideal type." While there were certainly exceptions among both the men and women I talked with and heard about, the data definitely showed clear patterns by gender.

16. See the discussion in Chapter 1 on the invisibility of women in political science literature.

17. In addition to the major, broad-based agencies, there are a few organizations or agencies directed by women (e.g., a battered-women's shelter and a day care center).

18. Six of the seven people identified as being of *la gente del pueblo* and who were also extremely influential within the community were women. In addition, several other women who were well known within the community as effective and influential organizers were not affiliated with agencies or City Hall departments.

19. Guzmán (1976) echoes this theme when he describes "the failure of the [Mexican-American] leadership to deliver the goods." He explains: "In many ways Mexican American leaders were emissaries to Anglo centers of power" (99). Also, the class gap that is stimulated by key Latinos moving into "good jobs" in government creates anger at social achievers (Guzmán 1976).

20. For a discussion of how agency-based political careers evolve and how they are different from the "independent or personal" and "bureaucrat-politician" paths, see Jennings (1984c).

21. I should point out that Paolo Freire's model is part of the formal, stated ideology of the agency. In other words, I am not intuiting a relationship between observed ideology and intellectual ideology. On the contrary, staff and students used Freire's name, his key points, and his vocabulary in discussions with me.

Chapter Four

1. Dietz (1989, 17) draws upon chap. 6 in Hannah Arendt's *On Revolution* (1963).

2. Seven of the twenty influential or *gente*/influential women specifically used the term *grassroots organizing* to describe Latino political history. Only

three men mentioned the term. In addition, the women overwhelmingly described events coded as grassroots efforts, while men stressed elections and formal political structures.

3. Uriarte-Gaston (1988, 156–161) states that Puerto Ricans became such a strong force in this movement that the Puerto Rican nationalist slogan, Awake Puerto Ricans! became the slogan of the group. Boriquen was the original Taino Indian name for Puerto Rico; Puerto Rican people often refer to themselves as being Boricua, in other words, from Boriquen.

4. For a discussion of this change in emphasis, see Uriarte (1992, 21).

5. Thirteen of the eighteen influential or *gente*/influential men discussed elections a total of forty-three times (an average of 2.4). Twelve of the Latina women discussed elections a total of nineteen times; Latina women discussed elections less than half as much as the men did, with only 1.0 on average for the group.

6. In 1967 Puerto Ricans made up about 20 percent of the South End neighborhood (Uriarte-Gaston 1988, 140); in 1980 Jamaica Plain–Mission Hill was about 25 percent Latino (Camayd-Freixas and Lopez 1983, 83).

7. Just prior to the completion of this book, Arroyo was appointed to the newly restructured school committee. The committee is no longer an elected body; members are appointed by the mayor. The decision to sacrifice electoral representation in favor of better educational leadership (and the inclusion of more racial/ethnic groups) was determined in a citywide vote. Arroyo received much acclaim when, to avoid any conflict of interest between his job and the school committee appointment, he resigned from his position as director of personnel.

8. This trend is not unique to Latinos. The decline in protest and mass movements, of course, must be viewed in the larger sociopolitical context; times changed, mass movements by any ethnic group became virtually nonexistent in the United States during the 1980s (see, for example, Browning, Marshall, and Tabb 1984).

9. Chelsea is in a unique position at the present time: it is in receivership due to fiscal and political mismanagement. In addition, the poor management of its schools led to a "takeover" by Boston University in a ten-year plan to improve the quality of education. Current efforts to improve its fiscal and governance functions are underway by consultants from the McCormack and Gastón Institutes, of the Boston campus of the University of Massachusetts, as well as other Boston groups, thus solidifying the influence of Boston on many institutions in Chelsea.

10. The male average was 0.77 while the female average was only 0.05.

11. Alex Rodriguez and Carmen Pola, Latino candidates mentioned earlier, were two of the Latino residents who joined the suit as Boston residents.

12. Jennings (1986) discusses the pattern of disenfranchising blacks and Latinos by attaching portions of minority neighborhoods to white districts. He states, "Thus, even under a district-based system of voting, thousands of blacks and Latinos in locations like the South End and North Dorchester

were in effect disenfranchised because they were placed in virtually all-white, hostile districts in neighborhoods like South Boston, South Dorchester, Savin Hill, and Neponset" (67).

13. Sixteen of the twenty influential and *gente*/influential women discussed voting a total of forty-eight times (an average for the group of 2.4); twelve of the eighteen men discussed voting a total of thirty-four times (an average for the group of 1.9).

14. For a discussion of Gastón's conception of community and his efforts to build coalitions between dispossessed Latino and black residents of Boston in the 1960s to 1980s, see Gaston and Kennedy (1985, 1986a, 1986b, 1987); Kennedy, Gaston, and Tilly (1990); and Kennedy and Tilly (1990).

15. The Rafael Hernández magnet school offers English language instruction to non-English-speaking students and Spanish as a second language to non-Spanish-speaking students; this school has developed into a model of bilingual education. Its principal is a Latina woman.

16. Juan Maldonado did mention Villa Victoria, but only in passing; he did not discuss politics in terms of creating community but was one of the men who focused almost exclusively on politics as access to positions.

17. See, for example, Portes and Truelove (1987), who found Mexican Americans to have one of the lowest naturalization rates of U.S. immigrant groups; Pachon (1987, x) found that, in the 1986 congressional elections, 52 percent of Hispanic nonvoters were noncitizens, compared to only 8 percent of blacks and whites. By the 1990 congressional elections, 56 percent of Latino nonvoters were not citizens compared to only 9 percent of blacks and 13 percent of whites (U.S. Bureau of the Census 1991, 16–17). See also Garcia and Arce (1988), Jennings (1988b), Pierce and Hagstrom (1988), and other articles in Garcia (1988).

18. Somewhat surprisingly, only four of the thirty-eight influential Latinos discussed citizenship as a cause of low political participation. *La gente del pueblo* were less likely to be citizens and more likely to identify the lack of citizenship as a constraint: six of the fifteen noninfluential *gente* identified their own lack of citizenship as a reason for not participating in Boston politics.

19. Camayd-Freixas and Lopez (1983) found that, in 1983, 77.6 percent of the Latinos in Boston were citizens. Forty-four of the fifty-three individuals I interviewed (83 percent) were U.S. citizens. I specifically oversampled activists and Puerto Ricans, however, all of whom were more likely to be citizens; 73 percent of the twenty-two *gente* were citizens.

20. See Schuck and Smith (1985), who argue for a change in the birthright citizenship law so as to decrease the incentive for illegal immigration; this proposed change would prohibit the children of undocumented immigrants from being citizens even if they were born and raised in this country.

21. When the U.S. government was eager for settlers, noncitizen franchise was permitted: "In a number of states west of the original thirteen— for example, in Michigan until 1894 and in Wisconsin until 1908—aliens

who had merely declared their intention to become citizens were permitted to vote" (Burnham 1965, 9).

22. It should be noted that in Boston, as in many U.S. cities, relations between the police and the Latino Community (or for that matter the black community) are characterized more by tension than by cooperation. In fact, this same neighborhood was shaken into a more confrontational stance when, about a year later, the police shot a Latino youth under questionable circumstances.

Chapter Five

1. I interviewed Silvia Barajas almost by mistake. I had handed out my card to women at the *charla* at Mujeres Unidas en Acción. That same evening I received a call from her—but she thought I was offering a course in *costura* (sewing). When I explained I was interviewing people about politics, she enthusiastically agreed to be interviewed.

2. Three of the four women who explicitly used those words (in Spanish) were *gente*/influentials. The men who denied participating in politics were *la gente del pueblo* who actually were not involved in any type of political activity.

3. At that moment I almost decided to end the interview. I felt, however, that it would be rude to pack up my tape recorder and go home. After all, she had opened up her home to me on a Saturday morning, so I decided to listen to what she did feel she had to say.

4. Mota (1976) suggests that such programs were developed by elite women; precluded a feminist agenda; and served essentially conservative, even reactionary, purposes. Despite the truth of these criticisms, my research documents the effects of such participatory programs on broad-based female political participation in the Dominican Republic.

5. Twelve of the eighteen influential and *gente*/influential men discussed this need a total of thirty times (for an average of 1.7). Eleven of the influential and *gente*/influential women discussed this need about as often, twenty-six times (for an average of 1.4).

6. *La gente del pueblo* identified lack of information as a major barrier to participation; all twenty-two mentioned this problem a total of thirty-nine times (for an average of 1.9 times).

7. For an excellent discussion of the political issues involved in, and the police treatment of, domestic violence, see Martin's (1990) compelling work titled *Arresting Violence*.

8. This is, as Coles (1986) stressed, a tentative suggestion—even a speculation that should be explored at a later date. Many other factors contribute to the strength of the Latino presence in Jamaica Plain. Edwin Colina suggests, for example, that many Latinos moved to the area following the gentrification of the South End; Jamaica Plain has had more opportunities for housing for middle-income Latinos. A higher socioeconomic base is often

associated with higher levels of participation. In addition, the founding of the Latino Democratic Committee and Carmen Pola's campaign (discussed in the previous chapter) should not be ignored. Based on what I was told, however, I believe that Latina women's consciousness raising played a role in the political development of the neighborhood. How much of a role is the subject for future research.

9. For a discussion of the concept of "the political self" see, for example, Dawson and Prewitt (1969, 15–24).

10. Herbert Hyman (1959), the "originator of the concept of political socialization" (Walton 1985, 43), began to systematically review the process of political learning over thirty years ago.

11. See, for example, Dawson and Prewitt (1969) and Jaros (1973); for a review of early literature on black political socialization in childhood, see, for example, Abramson (1977). A few studies compare the interaction of gender and race in the political socialization of children (see, for example, Orum et al. 1974).

12. See, for example, the articles in Sigel (1989); for an example of the adult socialization of immigrants, see Hoskin (1989). For the impact of the civil rights movement on black political socialization, see chap. 3 in Walton (1985) and Morris, Hatchett, and Brown (1989). Many works focus on the women's movement as a socializing force; see, for example, chap. 5 in Klein (1984) and Carroll (1989).

13. Robert Lane has played a major role in shaping the study of political consciousness; see Lane (1959, 1962, 1969, 1972). For a discussion of the role of black consciousness on political thinking, see Shingles (1981), Jackson (1987), and Morris, Hatchett, and Brown (1989, 283–292). It would be impossible to note all the research and writings on political consciousness and the women's movement; see, for example, Klein (1984), Chapman (1987), Conover (1988), Kelly and Burgess (1989).

14. See, for example, Garcia (1971) and Howell-Martinez (1982).

15. See, for example, Garcia and de la Garza (1977) and Guzmán (1976).

16. See, for example, Padilla (1985) and Uriarte-Gaston (1988).

17. See Carr (1989) and Mota (1976). Mota is particularly relevant to my study because she explored the interaction of class and feminism in the Dominican Republic.

18. Chapman (1987) describes how out-groups (such as women and minorities) need to develop "political consciousness and the commitment which gives courage to confront their marginality" (318).

19. The twenty influential and *gente*/influential women spontaneously described the way they became political a total of sixty-seven times for an average of 3.4. The men, on the other hand, were less likely to discuss their politicization process (only twelve men discussed it), and they did so less often (a total of only thirty-one mentions, for an average of 1.7). Thus, the men talked about positions and status five times more than the women but about their politicization process only half as much. Men and women who

were noninfluential *gente* displayed the same pattern. Five women of nine discussed their politicization process a total of fourteen times. Only one of the noninfluential *gente* men discussed his politicization, and he mentioned it only once.

20. See note 11.

21. See, for example, Lane (1959) and Campbell et al. (1960).

22. These characteristics supposedly include passivity, less interest in politics, belief that politics is for men, and, in the infamous words of Duverger (1955), the "mentality of minors" (129). For a review of the literature on gender differences in political socialization, see, for example, Bourque and Grossholtz (1974), Orum et al. (1974), and Randall (1987). For examples of research dismissing gender differences in children on scales of political efficacy, see, for example, Easton and Dennis (1967) and Orum et al. (1974).

23. Twelve of my total sample of fifty-three mentioned family background as playing a role in their political development.

24. The bracero program was a U.S. government labor agreement with Mexico to import Mexican agricultural laborers during the 1940s and 1950s.

25. This phrase is hard to translate directly. It means one does not ask to be repaid for a favor: no "tit for tat"; one is not owed something in return. Doing things for others may result in others helping when one is in need; however, there is no exchange or promise of repayment.

26. *La visión de la mujer: Jefe de la familia, las tareas administradores del hogar—la lucha política-social.*

27. See, for example, Lipset (1963), Jaros (1973), Pomper (1975), and the discussion from a feminist perspective in Randall (1987, 85–88).

28. Rinehart (1986) suggests that "the expected constraints [of marriage and child rearing] on adult women's political development may be overemphasized" (23). Data in Flora (1977, 90) suggest, however, that marriage does constrain political efficacy in (nonindustrial) blue-collar women. The number of married women who scored high on a political efficacy scale was 20-percentage-points lower than the number of men. Divorced women and men, however, showed an opposite tendency: 14.3 percent of divorced blue-collar (nonindustrial) women had high political efficacy scores compared to only 7.1 percent of the men. This difference was not true for white-collar or industrial workers.

29. I even went back and recoded some male transcripts to be sure I had not missed discussions during an earlier reading.

30. Again, Lane's view of politicization is not as incongruous when looking at Latino men as when examining the Latina woman's experience. Lane (1969) identifies the need for achievement and confirmation of a sense of self as one of the motivators for political participation. I say it is not *the* need, but more a *male* need. Women have additional or alternative needs that must be included in any theory of political development. Lane only *mentions* the need for affiliation, for example, although Latina women stress this need as critical in the process of political development.

Chapter Six

1. Pateman (1989, 144, 159).

2. See, for example, Mirandé and Enríquez (1979), Barragán (1980), and Melville (1980) for discussions of how racism, sexism, and cultural factors oppress Mexican-American women, specifically.

3. I thank Jennifer Jackman for sharing her excellent analysis of the tension between a rights-focused and a distribution-focused agenda within the women's movement. See also Dietz (1989, 12).

4. For a discussion of the inequities in the history of child-care benefits in the United States, see Miller (1992).

5. There are indeed Latina feminists who are pro-choice. On October 2 in 1988 and 1989, for example, Latina members of the Rosie Jiménez Committee met in Boston to commemorate the life of Rosie Jiménez, a Chicana woman who "was the first known victim of the Hyde Amendment" (unpublished flyer). Jiménez died following a back-alley abortion shortly after the Hyde Amendment denied federal funding of abortions.

6. Many Puerto Rican women have suffered excessive sterilization and contraceptive testing abuses with the acquiescence or encouragement of the U.S. government.

7. Control of the agenda is at the heart of the debate among Dahl (1961), Bachrach and Baratz (1962), and Lukes (1974) over the nature of power.

8. CAHA, the Council of Administrators of Hispanic Agencies, was set up to minimize competition for contract funds. The Latino Network was established by a Puerto Rican man at the mayor's office to develop better communication links and job connections for Latino professionals.

9. Rogler (1974), Cardona (1976), Baver (1984), and Jennings (1984c) found different patterns in New Haven, Connecticut; Philadelphia; and New York City, where independent politicians rose to politics through their grassroots activities and were able to become independent political forces within their Puerto Rican communities.

10. I refer to the depoliticization of the agencies that concerns their role as political mobilizers. Most agency directors see themselves as engaged in political work vis-à-vis government offices. In addition, agencies also stimulate participation by encouraging groups of clients to lobby for continued funds. Community activism is not a primary goal of the Latino agencies, however, and they are considerably less politicized than during the 1970s.

11. Jennings (1984c, 92), in writing about New York Puerto Rican politics, suggests that agency dependence on "soft money" suppresses the emergence of actual power. In another article, he states that "for many Puerto Rican activists, the antipoverty programs were the only available channels for political mobilization, and these were used extensively to enter the electoral arena. But . . . these structures were also functional in discouraging

independent and uncontrolled community activism, which could possibly lead to mobilization around systemic demands" (1984a, 140).

12. Although the federal government never planned for the policies implemented during the 1960s and 1970s to challenge the status quo to the extent they did, the role of the federal government in funding the "maximum feasible participation of the poor" certainly contributed to the political mobilization and protests that characterized that period of time. And in the case of Latinos in Boston, it is possible to see the effects of the support—and then the withdrawal—of the federal government for political participation. Arnstein (1969) and Daley and Kobak (1990) admit that the actual benefits of the antipoverty programs' emphasis on client participation in program administration, goal setting, and organization were more limited than hoped for. Nevertheless, the overall push for participation led to some of the most successful political efforts in the Latino community in Boston. Villa Victoria, described in chap. 4, is a case in point.

13. Jennings (1988b, 71) found a similar concern in New York Puerto Rican politics.

14. Piven and Cloward (1989) base their description of the rationalchoice theory on an earlier analysis by Aldrich and Simon (1986, 271–301), Anthony Downs's (1957) model of political choice, and Riker and Ordeshook's (1968) "calculus of voting." For a discussion of how costs and benefits have affected black women and men, and white women differently from white men, see Welch and Secret (1981, esp. 15–16).

15. In 1983, 62 percent of the precincts in Boston with Latino populations of 5 percent or more did not have Spanish-language voting machines. One precinct with a Latino population of 39.1 percent in 1983 did not have Spanish-language voting machines (Camayd-Freixas and Lopez 1983, 56).

16. Several Latinos in Boston decried the problems associated with not having leases on apartments: evictions, instability, and rent increases. Not having a lease turns out to have the additional effect of creating barriers to political participation.

17. For a discussion of the impact of reform on these groups, see Piven and Cloward (1989, 89–95) and Morone (1990, 123–125).

18. *Deso* is a contraction (commonly used in Puerto Rico) of *de* and *eso*, "of that"; in the current context *deso* is a "filler word." A comparable phrase in English would be "you know."

19. In addition to the writers mentioned above who answer this question with a definitive yes (Merton 1957; Teaford 1982; and Bridges 1988), Gross and Kraus (1982) add that "the political machine is alive and well." Travis (1990) discusses the Kevin White machine in Boston, and Torres (1991) points to the persistence of political machines in Chicago today.

20. See Stern (1988).

21. See, for example, Jennings (1988b, 68–70, 75).

22. Twelve of the thirty-eight influentials or *gente*/influentials considered homeland ties as a factor that suppresses participation. More women (thir-

teen of twenty) than men (three of eighteen) mentioned homeland ties as a constraint. Six of the women in the noninfluential *gente* category believed that their feelings about their home countries affected their political participation in the United States. The six men who were of the noninfluential *gente* group did not specifically discuss this effect.

23. Banfield's (1958) condemnation of Italian peasants completely ignored the structural roots of their self-absorption; their inability to think beyond their immediate family; and their concern with present, as opposed to future, needs. He failed to discuss the impact of the larger context. Southern Italy was the fighting ground in a world war that had ended only a few years before. The additional struggle between communist and fascist forces *within* the country made lack of trust beyond the family a logical reaction. In addition, people starved in this area of the country. The war and the internal struggles created an understandable concern for subsistence. Thus, the concern for subsistence (rather than for future or altruistic goals) is consistent with a structural explanation. Furthermore, to compare the "political culture" of people living under these conditions with Kansas farmers living in the "breadbasket of the world," as Banfield does, reflects a blindness about the impact of structure on culture.

24. Jennings (1988b) states that "Puerto Ricans, in Puerto Rico, have a much higher turnout rate for elections than is the case for all voters in the United States. Between 80 and 90 percent of Puerto Ricans vote in Puerto Rican elections, while in New York City some important elections have experienced less than 20 percent turnout from this group." In addition, compared to the United States, where the voting rate gap between lower- and middle-class Americans is substantial, in Puerto Rico "the 80 to 90 percent figure is a cross class figure, that is, lower-income Puerto Ricans vote as frequently as higher-income Puerto Ricans" (72).

25. A reminder: people from the Dominican Republic refer to their homeland as the *República Dominicana* (the Dominican Republic) and as *Santo Domingo* with equal frequency. As discussed earlier in the Introduction, I use the two names interchangeably.

26. Of course, not all political analysts agree with the viewpoint held by the people I interviewed in Boston. García-Passalacqua (1984), for example, describes the same realities in exceedingly negative terms. He acknowledges that "the degree of political alertness and militancy has become high, and with it, the electoral power of the masses"; however, he goes on to complain that "the average voter, the individual person, is catered to by politicians." He acknowledges as well the extremely well organized political machines and barrio leaders that guarantee turnout for elections and yet decries "the horizontal and alienating nature of the political system." He views the panoply and excitement that draws people into participation as a situation in which "the people are manipulated into rabid political tribalism, engineered from above and opposed only by the emerging group of unaffiliated voters" (64–68).

While García-Passalacqua may long for a populace that is either better informed or more questioning of the political arrangements in their country, he seems unable to acknowledge that in terms of pure *participation*, Puerto Rico could be considered a model for the United States. He also ignores the historical context: nineteenth- and early twentieth-century politics in the United States was very similar to current affairs in Puerto Rico and is sometimes referred to as "the golden age of politics."

27. Also, hullabaloo, commotion.

28. Note: the Anglo politician in Boston with the biggest Latino following is the state representative from the Jamaica Plain–Mission Hill district, who, among other things, holds a free, day-long fishing outing at the Jamaica Pond—free food, free equipment—a very effective constituent strategy.

29. I acknowledge the problem of reaching conclusions about the politics of the entire country based on interviews with four Dominicans in Boston. However, the effect of party politics on political participation in the Dominican Republic was the focal point of all four interviews and should not be dismissed simply because of a small sample. In addition, my informal interviews and community observations support my findings.

30. I interviewed four individuals whose roots are Mexican, two Guatemalans, two Ecuadoreans, one Honduran, and one Colombian. Two of the people of Mexican origin were born in the United States to families that migrated to western states several generations ago. My conclusions are based, however, not only on the limited number of interviews with individuals from Central America but also from observation data and interviews with activists who currently work with recent immigrants from Central and South America.

31. A total of forty-three separate discussions of fear or danger occurred during my formal interviews. While physical danger was the dominant theme in the political views of the Central Americans, a sense of general vulnerability emerged from the interviews with *la gente del pueblo*. The latter were more likely than *los profesionales* to feel that the expression of negative opinions could cause the government to withdraw benefits or to get them into some kind of trouble. People who were poor were also more likely to choose to have their interviews remain anonymous for the same reason.

32. Those readers familiar with the human rights abuses in various countries in Central and South America will understand how *to disappear* has become a transitive, as well as an intransitive, verb.

References

Abramson, Paul R. 1977. *The Political Socialization of Black Americans: A Critical Evaluation of Research on Efficacy and Trust.* New York: Free Press.

Ackelsberg, Martha A. 1984. "Women's Collaborative Activities and City Life: Politics and Policy." In *Political Women: Current Roles in State and Local Government,* ed. Janet A. Flammang, 242–259. Beverly Hills, Calif.: Sage Publications.

———. 1988. "Communities, Resistance, and Women's Activism: Some Implications for a Democratic Polity." In *Women and the Politics of Empowerment,* ed. Ann Bookman and Sandra Morgen, 297–313. Philadelphia: Temple University Press.

———. 1991. *Free Women of Spain: Anarchism and the Struggle for the Emancipation of Women.* Bloomington and Indianapolis: Indiana University Press.

Alberts, William E. 1986. "What's Black, White, and Racist All Over?" In *From Access to Power: Black Politics in Boston,* ed. James Jennings and Mel King, 137–174. Rochester, Vt.: Schenkman Books.

Aldrich, John H., and Dennis M. Simon. 1986. "Turnout in American National Elections." *Research in Micropolitics,* Vol. 1, 271–310. Greenwich, Conn.: JAI Press.

Almond, Gabriel A., and Sidney Verba. 1963. *The Civic Culture.* Boston: Little, Brown.

Amundsen, Kirsten. 1971. *The Silenced Majority: Women and American Democracy.* Englewood Cliffs, N.J.: Prentice Hall.

Andrews, Joseph E., and Nelson Wikstrom. 1991. "The Lasting Impact of the War on Poverty." Paper presented at the annual meeting of the American Political Science Association, 29 August–1 September, Washington, D.C.

Arendt, Hannah. 1963. *On Revolution.* New York: Viking Press.

Arnstein, Sherry R. 1969. "Ladders of Citizen Participation." *Journal of the American Institute of Planners* (July): 216–224.

Aviel, JoAnn Fagot. 1981. "Political Participation of Women in Latin America." *Western Political Quarterly* 34, no. 1 (March): 156–173.

Bachrach, Peter, and Morton S. Baratz. 1962. "Two Faces of Power." *American Political Science Review* 56, no. 4 (December): 947–952.

Banfield, Edward. 1958. *The Moral Basis of a Backward Society.* Glencoe, Ill.: Free Press.

Banfield, Edward C., and James Q. Wilson. 1963. *City Politics.* Cambridge, Mass.: Harvard University Press and MIT Press.

Barber, Benjamin. 1984. *Strong Democracy: Participatory Politics for a New Age.* Berkeley: University of California Press.

Barragán, Polly Baca. 1980, September. "The Lack of Political Involvement of Hispanic Women as It Relates to Their Educational Background and Occupational Opportunities." In *Conference on the Educational and Occupational Needs of Hispanic Women,* ed. National Institute of Education, 39–46. Washington, D.C.: National Institute of Education.

Baver, Sherrie. 1984. "Puerto Rican Politics in New York City: The Post–World War II Period." In *Puerto Rican Politics in Urban America,* ed. James Jennings and Monte Rivera, 44–59. Westport, Conn.: Greenwood Press.

Baxter, Sandra, and Marjorie Lansing. 1981. *Women and Politics: The Visible Majority.* Ann Arbor: University of Michigan Press.

Bayes, Jane. 1982. *Minority Politics and Ideologies in the United States.* Novato, Calif.: Chandler and Sharp.

Beauvoir, Simone de. 1952. *The Second Sex.* New York: Knopf.

Boneparth, Ellen. 1981. "Women and Politics: Introduction." *Western Political Quarterly* 34, no. 1 (March): 3–4.

Bonilla-Santiago, Gloria. 1989. "Legislating Progress for Hispanic Women in New Jersey." *Social Work* 34, no. 3 (May): 193–288.

———. 1990. Speech given at the National Association of Social Workers Conference, 15 November, Boston, Mass.

———. 1991. "Hispanic Women Breaking New Ground Through Leadership." *Latino Studies Journal* 2, no. 1 (January): 19–37.

Boston Globe. 1991a. "The Changing Face of Boston." 4 April, p. 8.

———. 1991b. "Increased Diversity Shown in Census." 1 July, pp. 17, 22.

———. 1992a. "It Was No 'Miracle' for Poor Children." 11 June, pp. 31–32.

———. 1992b. "Recent Arrivals: Influx Changed Boston, Data Show." 17 June, pp. 1, 32.

Bourque, Susan C., and Jean Grossholtz. 1974. "Politics an Unnatural Practice: Political Science Looks at Female Participation." *Politics and Society* (Winter): 225–266.

Bridges, Amy. 1988. "Rethinking the Origins of Machine Politics." In *Power, Culture, and Place,* ed. John Hull Mollenkopf, 53–73. New York: Russell Sage Foundation.

Browning, Rufus P., Dale Rogers Marshall, and David Tabb. 1984. *Protest Is Not Enough: The Struggle of Blacks and Hispanics for Equality in Urban Politics.* Berkeley: University of California Press.

———, eds. 1990. *Racial Politics in American Cities.* White Plains, N.Y.: Longman.

Bruno, Melania, and Mauricio Gaston. 1984. "Latinos for Mel King: Some Reflections." *Radical America* 17, no. 6, and 18, no. 1: 67–79.

Burnham, Walter Dean. 1965. "The Changing Shape of the American Political Universe." *American Political Science Review* 59, no. 1 (March): 7–28.

———. 1979. *The Disappearance of the American Voter.* Washington, D.C.: American Bar Association.

———. 1982. *The Current Crisis in American Politics.* New York: Oxford University Press.

———. 1987. "Electing Not To: Why Americans Are Staying Away from the Polls in Droves." *Boston Sunday Globe,* 6 September, pp. 79, 82.

Camayd-Freixas, Yohel, and Russell Paul Lopez. 1983, September. *Gaps in Representative Democracy: Redistricting, Political Participation and the Latino Vote in Boston.* Boston: Hispanic Office of Planning and Evaluation, Inc.

Campbell, Angus, Philip E. Converse, Warren E. Miller, and Donald E. Stokes. 1960. *The American Voter.* New York: Wiley.

Cardona, Luis. 1976. *The Coming of the Puerto Ricans.* Washington, D.C.: Unidos Publications.

Carr, Irene Campos. 1989. "Proyecto la mujer: Latina Women Shaping Consciousness." *Women's Studies International Forum* 12, no. 1: 45–49.

Carrillo, Teresa. 1986. "The Women's Movement and the Left in Mexico: The Presidential Candidacy of Doña Rosario Ibarra." In *Chicana Voices: Intersections of Class, Race, and Gender,* ed. Teresa Córdova, Norma Cantú, Gilberto Cardenas, Juan García, and Christine M. Sierra, 96–113. Austin, Tex.: CMAS Publications [Center for Mexican American Studies, University of Texas, Austin].

Carroll, Susan J. 1989. "Gender Politics and the Socializing Impact of the Women's Movement." In *Political Learning in Adulthood,* ed. Roberta S. Sigel, 306–339. Chicago: University of Chicago Press.

Cassell's Spanish Dictionary. 1968 ed. New York: MacMillan Publishing Co.

Castillo-Speed, Lillian. 1990. "Chicana Studies: A Selected List of Materials Since 1980." *Frontiers* 11, no. 1: 66–84.

Cerullo, Margaret, and Marla Erlien. 1984. "Women Hold Up More Than Half the Rainbow: Notes on Feminism and the Mel King Campaign." *Radical America* 17, no. 6, and 18, no. 1: 49–58.

Chapman, Jenny. 1987. "Adult Socialization and Out-Group Politicization: An Empirical Study of Consciousness-Raising." *British Journal of Political Science* 17, pt. 3 (July): 315–340.

Chodorow, Nancy. 1974. "Family Structure and Feminine Personality." In *Woman, Culture and Society,* ed. Michelle Zimbalist Rosaldo, Louise Lamphere, and Joan Bamberger. Stanford, Calif.: Stanford University Press. Quoted in Carol Gilligan, *In a Different Voice,* 16. Cambridge: Harvard University Press, 1982.

Christy, Carol A. 1987. *Sex Differences in Political Participation: Processes of Change in Fourteen Nations.* New York: Praeger.

Clark, Janet, R. Darcy, Susan Welch, and Margery Ambrosius. 1984. "Women as Legislative Candidates in Six States." In *Political Women:*

Current Roles in State and Local Government, ed. Janet A. Flammang, 141–155. Beverly Hills, Calif.: Sage Publications.

Coles, Robert. 1986. *The Political Life of Children*. Boston: Houghton Mifflin.

Comité de Mujeres Puertorriqueñas Miriam López-Pérez. 1988. Conference flyer. Encuentro de Mujeres Latinas en Massachusetts, 6 August, University of Massachusetts, Boston.

Conover, Pamela Johnston. 1988. "The Role of Social Groups in Political Thinking." *British Journal of Political Science* 18, pt. 1 (January): 51–76.

Coole, Diana H. 1988. *Women in Political Theory: From Ancient Misogyny to Contemporary Feminism*. Brighton, England: Wheatsheaf Books; Boulder, Colo.: Lynne Rienner.

Dahl, Robert. 1957. "The Concept of Power." *Behavioral Science* 2:201–215.

———. 1961. *Who Governs?* New Haven, Conn.: Yale University Press.

Daley, Nelda Knelson, and Sue Ella Kobak. 1990. "The Paradox of the 'Familiar Outsider.'" *Appalachian Journal* 17, no. 3 (Spring): 248–260.

Darcy, R., and Charles D. Hadley. 1988. "Black Women in Politics: The Puzzle of Success." *Social Science Quarterly* 69, no. 3 (September): 629–645.

Darcy, R., and Sarah Slavin Schramm. 1977. "When Women Run Against Men: The Electorate's Response to Congressional Contests." *Public Opinion Quarterly* 41 (Spring): 1–12.

Dawson, Richard E., and Kenneth Prewitt. 1969. *Political Socialization*. Boston: Little, Brown.

Deutchman, Iva Ellen. 1991. "The Politics of Empowerment." *Women and Politics* 11, no. 2: 1–18.

Dietz, Mary G. 1989. "Context Is All: Feminism and Theories of Citizenship." In *Learning About Women: Gender, Politics, and Power*, ed. Jill K. Conway, Susan C. Bourque, and Joan W. Scott, 1–24. Ann Arbor: University of Michigan Press.

Dill, Bonnie Thornton. 1988. "'Making Your Job Good Yourself': Domestic Service and the Construction of Personal Dignity." In *Women and the Politics of Empowerment*, ed. Ann Bookman and Sandra Morgen, 33–52. Philadelphia: Temple University Press.

Downs, Anthony. 1957. *An Economic Theory of Democracy*. New York: Harper.

Duverger, Maurice. 1955. *The Political Role of Women*. New York: UNESCO.

Easton, David, and Jack Dennis. 1967. "The Child's Acquisition of Regime Norms: Political Efficacy." *American Political Science Review* 61 (March): 25–38.

Eisinger, Peter K. 1980. *The Politics of Displacement: Racial and Ethnic Transition in Three American Cities*. New York: Academic Press.

The Ethnograph Version 3.0. Qualis Research Associates, Littleton, Colo.

Evans, Sara. 1980. *Personal Politics*. New York: Vintage Books.

Falcón, Angelo. 1984. "A History of Puerto Rican Politics in New York

City: 1860s to 1945." In *Puerto Rican Politics in Urban America*, ed. James Jennings and Monte Rivera, 15–42. Westport, Conn.: Greenwood Press.

————. 1988. "Black and Latino Politics in New York City: Race and Ethnicity in a Changing Urban Context." In *Latinos and the Political System*, ed. F. Chris Garcia, 171–194. Notre Dame, Ind.: University of Notre Dame Press.

Ferguson, Kathy E. 1987. "Male-Ordered Politics: Feminism and Political Science." In *Idioms of Inquiry: Critique and Renewal in Political Science*, ed. Terence Ball, 209–229. New York: State University of New York Press.

————. 1989. "Grass Roots, New Routes." Review of *Women and the Politics of Empowerment*, ed. Ann Bookman and Sandra Morgen, and *Women Activists: Challenging the Abuse of Power*, by Anne Witte Garland. In *Women's Review of Books* 6, no. 6 (March): 13–14.

Flammang, Janet A. 1983. "Feminist Theory: The Question of Power." In *Current Perspectives in Social Theory*, ed. Scott G. McNall and John Wilson. Greenwich, Conn.: JAI Press.

————. 1984a. "Filling the Party Vacuum: Women at the Grassroots Level in Local Politics." In *Political Women: Current Roles in State and Local Government*, 87–113. Beverly Hills, Calif.: Sage Publications.

————, ed. 1984b. *Political Women: Current Roles in State and Local Government.* Beverly Hills, Calif.: Sage Publications.

Flanagan, Owen, and Kathryn Jackson. 1990. "Justice, Care, and Gender: The Kohlberg–Gilligan Debate Revisited." In *Feminism and Political Theory*, ed. Cass R. Sunstein, 37–52. Chicago: University of Chicago Press.

Flora, Cornelia Butler. 1977. "Working-Class Women's Political Participation: Its Potential in Developed Countries." In *A Portrait of Marginality*, ed. Marianne Githens and Jewel L. Prestage, 75–95. New York: David McKay.

Foley, Douglas E., Clarice Mota, Donald E. Post, and Ignacio Lozano. 1977. *From Peones to Politicos: Ethnic Relations in a South Texas Town, 1900 to 1977.* Austin, Tex.: Center for Mexican American Studies, University of Texas, Austin.

Fowlkes, Diane L. 1984. "Conceptions of the 'Political': White Activists in Atlanta." In *Political Women: Current Roles in State and Local Government*, ed. Janet A. Flammang, 66–86. Beverly Hills, Calif.: Sage Publications.

Freire, Paolo. 1970. *Pedagogy of the Oppressed.* New York: Continuum.

Friedman, Marilyn. 1990. "Feminism and Modern Friendship: Dislocating the Community." In *Feminism and Political Theory*, ed. Cass R. Sunstein, 143–158. Chicago: University of Chicago Press.

Fuentes, Luis. 1984. "Puerto Ricans and New York City School Board Elections: Apathy or Obstructionism?" In *Puerto Rican Politics in Urban*

America, ed. James Jennings and Monte Rivera, 127–137. Westport, Conn.: Greenwood Press.

Gage, Nicholas. 1989. *A Place for Us: Eleni's Children in America.* Boston: Houghton Mifflin.

Garcia, F. Chris. 1971. *The Political Life of Chicano Children.* New York: Free Press.

———, ed. 1988. *Latinos and the Political System.* Notre Dame, Ind.: University of Notre Dame Press.

Garcia, F. Chris, and Rudolph O. de la Garza. 1977. *The Chicano Political Experience: Three Perspectives.* North Scituate, Mass.: Duxbury Press.

Garcia, John A., and Carlos H. Arce. 1988. "Political Orientations and Behaviors of Chicanos: Trying to Make Sense out of Attitudes and Participation." In *Latinos and the Political System*, ed. F. Chris Garcia, 125–151. Notre Dame, Ind.: University of Notre Dame Press.

García-Passalacqua, Juan M. 1984. *Puerto Rico: Equality and Freedom at Issue.* New York: Praeger.

Garland, Anne Witte. 1988. *Women Activists: Challenging the Abuse of Power.* New York: Feminist Press.

Garza, Rodolfo de la, ed. 1987. *Ignored Voices: Public Opinion Polls and the Latino Community.* Austin, Tex.: CMAS Publications [Center for Mexican American Studies, University of Texas, Austin].

Gaston, Mauricio, and Marie Kennedy. 1985. "Roxbury: From Disinvestment to Displacement." *North Star* 2 (Fall): 17–22.

———. 1986a. "Blueprint for Tomorrow: The Fight for Community Control in Boston's Black and Latino Neighborhoods." *Radical America* 20, no. 5 (September–October): 7–22.

———. 1986b. "A Neighborhood Under Pressure: From Disinvestment to Displacement in Roxbury." *Shelterforce* 9, no. 3 (September–October): 12–17.

———. 1987. "Capital Investment or Community Development? The Struggle for Control of Turf by Boston's Black and Latino Community." *Antipode* 19, no. 2 (September): 178–209.

Gerlach, Luther, and Virginia Hine. 1970. *People, Power, Change: Movements of Social Transformation.* New York: Bobbs-Merrill.

Gilligan, Carol. 1982. *In a Different Voice: Psychological Theory and Women's Development.* Cambridge, Mass.: Harvard University Press.

Githens, Marianne, and Jewel L. Prestage, eds. 1977. *A Portrait of Marginality: The Political Behavior of the American Woman.* New York: Longman.

Glazer, Nathan. 1985. "The Political Distinctiveness of the Mexican-Americans." In *Mexican-Americans in Comparative Perspective*, ed. Walker Connor, 207–226. Washington, D.C.: Urban Institute.

Goetze, Rolf. 1991. "Boston's 1990 Population from U.S. Census Tract and Census District Boundaries: Racial and Age Characteristics of Boston's Population." Boston: Boston Redevelopment Authority Research Department, Publication No. 407, June.

References

Gómez-Quiñones, Juan. 1990. *Chicano Politics: Reality and Promise, 1940–1990*. Albuquerque: University of New Mexico Press.

Granovetter, Mark S. 1973. "The Strength of Weak Ties." *American Journal of Sociology* 78, no. 6 (May): 1360–1380.

———. 1982. "The Strength of Weak Ties: A Network Theory Revisited." In *Social Structure and Network Analysis*, ed. Peter V. Marsden and Nan Lin, 105–130. Beverly Hills, Calif.: Sage Publications.

Gregg, Robin. 1991. "Pregnancy in a High-Tech Age: Paradoxes of Choice." Ph.D. diss., Brandeis University; New York: Paragon House, forthcoming.

Gross, Bertram M., and Jeffrey F. Kraus. 1982. "The Political Machine Is Alive and Well." *Social Policy* 12, no. 3 (Winter): 38–46.

Guzmán, Ralph C. 1976. *The Political Socialization of the Mexican American People*. New York: Arno Press.

Hamilton, Charles V. 1979. "The Patron–Recipient Relationship and Minority Politics in New York City." *Political Science Quarterly* 94, no. 2 (Summer): 211–227.

Hamilton, Cynthia. 1989. "Women in Politics: Methods of Resistance and Change." *Women's Studies International Forum* 12, no. 1: 129–135.

Hardy-Fanta, Carol. 1991a. "Latina Women, Latino Men, and Political Participation in Boston: La chispa que prende." Ph.D. diss., Brandeis University.

———. 1991b. "Latina Women, Latino Men, and Political Participation in Boston: *La chispa que prende.*" Paper presented at the annual meeting of the American Political Science Association, 29 August–1 September, Washington, D.C.

———. 1992. "Latina Women and Politics in Boston: *Somos la vida, la fuerza, la mujer.*" *Latino Studies Journal* 3, no. 2 (May): 38–54.

———. 1993. "Discovering Latina Women in Politics." *Journal of Hispanic Policy.*" Forthcoming.

Hekman, Susan. 1991. "Moral Voices, Moral Selves: An Epistemological Analysis of the 'Different Voice.'" Paper presented at the annual meeting of the American Political Science Association, 29 August–1 September, Washington, D.C.

Hero, Rodney. 1992. *Latinos and the U.S. Political System*. Philadelphia: Temple University Press.

Hertz, Susan Handley. 1981. *The Welfare Mothers Movement: A Decade of Change for Poor Women?* Lanham, Md.: University Press of America.

Hirsch, Herbert. 1971. *Poverty and Politicization: Political Socialization in an American Sub-culture*. New York: Free Press.

Hirschman, Albert O. 1970. *Exit, Voice and Loyalty*. Cambridge, Mass.: Harvard University Press.

Hochschild, Jennifer L. 1981. *What's Fair? American Beliefs About Distributive Justice*. Cambridge, Mass.: Harvard University Press.

———. 1989. Interview with author, Princeton University, Princeton, N.J., 19 April.

Hoskin, Marilyn. 1989. "Socialization and Anti-socialization: The Case of Immigrants." In *Political Learning in Adulthood*, ed. Roberta S. Sigel, 340–377. Chicago: University of Chicago Press.

Howell-Martinez, Vicky. 1982. "The Influence of Gender Roles on Political Socialization: An Experimental Study of Mexican-American Children." *Women and Politics* 2, no. 3 (Fall): 33–46.

Hunter, Floyd. 1953. *Community Power Structure: A Study of Decision-Makers*. Chapel Hill: University of North Carolina Press.

Hurtado, Aída. 1989. "Relating to Privilege: Seduction and Rejection in the Subordination of White Women and Women of Color." *Signs* 14, no. 4 (Summer): 833–855.

Hyman, Herbert. 1959. *Political Socialization*. New York: Free Press.

Infante, Isa María. 1977. "Politicization of Immigrant Women from Puerto Rico and the Dominican Republic." Ph.D. diss., University of California, Riverside.

Jackson, Byran O. 1987. "The Effects of Racial Group Consciousness on Political Mobilization in American Cities." *Western Political Quarterly* 40, no. 4 (December): 631–646.

Jaros, Dean. 1973. *Socialization to Politics*. New York: Praeger.

Jennings, James. 1982. "Race, Class, and Politics in the Black Community of Boston." *Review of Black Political Economy* 12, no. 1 (Fall): 47–63.

———. 1984a. "Conclusion: Puerto Rican Politics in Urban America—Toward Progressive Electoral Activism." In *Puerto Rican Politics in Urban America*, ed. James Jennings and Monte Rivera, 139–143. Westport, Conn.: Greenwood Press.

———. 1984b. "Introduction: The Emergence of Puerto Rican Electoral Activism." In *Puerto Rican Politics in Urban America*, ed. James Jennings and Monte Rivera, 3–12. Westport, Conn.: Greenwood Press.

———. 1984c. "Puerto Rican Politics in Two Cities: New York and Boston." In *Puerto Rican Politics in Urban America*, ed. James Jennings and Monte Rivera, 75–98. Westport, Conn.: Greenwood Press.

———. 1986. "Urban Machinism and the Black Voter: The Kevin White Years." In *From Access to Power: Black Politics in Boston*, ed. James Jennings and Mel King, 57–86. Rochester, Vt.: Schenkman Books.

———. 1988a. "Future Directions for Puerto Rican Politics in the U.S. and Puerto Rico." In *Latinos and the Political System*, ed. F. Chris Garcia, 480–497. Notre Dame, Ind.: University of Notre Dame Press.

———. 1988b. "The Puerto Rican Community: Its Political Background." In *Latinos and the Political System*, ed. F. Chris Garcia, 65–80. Notre Dame, Ind.: University of Notre Dame Press.

Jennings, James, and Monte Rivera, eds. 1984. *Puerto Rican Politics in Urban America*. Westport, Conn.: Greenwood Press.

Johvanil, Luis. 1989. "Los clubes culturales y deportivos: Su papel ante la comunidad." *El Mundo*, 14–20 September, p. 7.

Jones, Kathleen B. 1990. "Citizenship in a Woman-Friendly Polity." *Signs* 15, no. 4 (Summer): 781–812.

Jones, Mack H. 1972. "A Frame of Reference for Black Politics." In *Black Political Life in the United States: A Fist as the Pendulum*, ed. Lenneal J. Henderson, Jr., 7–20. San Francisco: Chandler.

Jordan, Judith V., Alexandra G. Kaplan, Jean Baker Miller, Irene P. Stiver, and Janet L. Surrey, eds. 1991. *Women's Growth in Connection: Writings from the Stone Center*. New York: Guilford Press.

Karnig, Albert K., and B. Oliver Walter. 1976. "Elections of Women to City Councils." *Social Science Quarterly* 56, no. 4 (March): 605–613.

Kathlene, Lyn. 1989. "Uncovering the Political Impacts of Gender: An Exploratory Study." *Western Political Quarterly* 42, no. 2 (June): 397–421.

Kelly, Rita Mae, and Jayne Burgess. 1989. "Gender and the Meaning of Power and Politics." *Women and Politics* 9, no. 1 (Winter): 47–82.

Kennedy, Marie, Mauricio Gaston, and Chris Tilly. 1990. "Roxbury: Capital Investment or Community Development." In *Fire in the Hearth: The Radical Politics of Place in America*, ed. Mike Davis, Steven Hiatt, Marie Kennedy, Susan Ruddick, and Michael Sprinker, 97–136. New York: Verso.

Kennedy, Marie, and Chris Tilly, with Mauricio Gaston. 1990. "Transformative Populism and the Development of a Community of Color." In *Dilemmas of Activism: Class, Community, and the Politics of Local Mobilization*, ed. Joseph M. Kling and Prudence S. Posner, 302–324. Philadelphia: Temple University Press.

Kernstock, Elwyn Nicholas. 1972. "How New Migrants Behave Politically: The Puerto Ricans in Hartford, 1970." Ph.D. diss., University of Connecticut.

Kimball, Penn. 1972. *The Disconnected*. New York: Columbia University Press.

Klein, Ethel. 1984. *Gender Politics: From Consciousness to Mass Politics*. Cambridge, Mass.: Harvard University Press.

Lane, Robert E. 1959. *Political Life: Why People Get Involved in Politics*. Glencoe, Ill.: Free Press.

———. 1962. *Political Ideology: Why the American Common Man Believes What He Does*. New York: Free Press.

———. 1969. *Political Thinking and Consciousness: The Private Life of the Political Mind*. Chicago: Markham.

———. 1972. *Political Man*. New York: Free Press.

Letelier, Isabel Morel. 1989. "Women's Action in Chile." *Women's Studies International Forum* 12, no. 1: 125–127.

Lipset, Seymour M. 1963. *Political Man*. New York: Anchor Books.

Luker, Kristin. 1984. *Abortion and the Politics of Motherhood*. California Series on Social Choice and Political Economy. Berkeley: University of California Press.

Lukes, Steven. 1974. *Power: A Radical View*. London: Macmillan.

MacManus, Susan A., Charles S. Bullock, III, and Barbara P. Grothe. 1986. "A Longitudinal Examination of Political Participation Rates of Mexican

American Females." *Social Science Quarterly* 67, no. 3 (September): 604–612.

MacManus, Susan A., and Carol A. Cassel. 1988. "Mexican-Americans in City Politics: Participation, Representation, and Policy Preferences." In *Latinos and the Political System*, ed. F. Chris Garcia, 201–212. Notre Dame, Ind.: University of Notre Dame Press.

Mansbridge, Jane J. 1983. *Beyond Adversary Democracy.* Chicago: University of Chicago Press.

———, ed. 1990. Preface to *Beyond Self-interest*, ix–xiii. Chicago: University of Chicago Press.

Marable, Manning. 1983. *How Capitalism Underdeveloped Black America: Problems of Race, Political Economy and Society.* Boston: South End Press.

Martin, Margaret. 1989. "Arresting Violence." Ph.D. diss., Brandeis University.

Melville, Margarita B., ed. 1980. *Twice a Minority: Mexican American Women.* St. Louis, Mo.: Mosby.

Merton, Robert K. 1957. *Social Theory and Social Structure.* Glencoe, Ill.: Free Press.

Milbrath, Lester W., and Madan Lal Goel. 1977. *Political Participation: How and Why Do People Get Involved in Politics?* 2d ed. Chicago: Rand McNally.

Miller, Beth. 1992. "Private Welfare: The Distribution Equity of Family Benefits." Ph.D. diss., Brandeis University.

Miller, Jean Baker. 1983. "Women and Power." *Social Policy* 13, no. 4 (Spring): 3–6.

———. 1991. "Women and Power." In *Women's Growth in Connection*, ed. Judith V. Jordan, Alexandra G. Kaplan, Jean Baker Miller, Irene P. Stiver, and Janet L. Surrey, 197–205. New York: Guilford Press.

Mirandé, Alfredo, and Evangelina Enríquez. 1979. *La Chicana: The Mexican American Woman.* Chicago: University of Chicago Press.

Miyares, Marcelino. 1974. "Models of Political Participation of Hispanic-Americans." Ph.D. diss., Northwestern University.

Morgen, Sandra, and Ann Bookman. 1988. "Rethinking Women and Politics: An Introductory Essay." In *Women and the Politics of Empowerment*, ed. Ann Bookman and Sandra Morgen, 3–29. Philadelphia: Temple University Press.

Morone, James A. 1990. *The Democratic Wish: Popular Participation and the Limits of American Government.* New York: Basic Books.

Morris, Aldon D., Shirley J. Hatchett, and Ronald E. Brown. 1989. "The Civil Rights Movement and Black Political Socialization." In *Political Learning in Adulthood*, ed. Roberta S. Sigel, 272–305. Chicago: University of Chicago Press.

Morrison, Minion K. C. 1987. *Black Political Mobilization: Leadership, Power and Mass Behavior.* SUNY Series in Afro-American Studies. Albany: State University of New York Press.

Mota, Vivian M. 1976. "Politics and Feminism in the Dominican Republic: 1931–1945 and 1966–1974." In *Sex and Class in Latin America*, ed. June Nash and Helen Safa, 265–278. New York: Praeger.

Nelson, Dale. 1979. "Ethnicity and Socioeconomic Status as Sources of Participation: The Case for Ethnic Political Culture." *American Political Science Review* 73, no. 4 (December): 1024–1038.

Neruda, Pablo. 1966 (inferred date). "Versainograma a Santo Domingo." Broadside (hoja volante, desde Isla Negra [Chile] en febrero 1966). Valparaiso, Chile: Ediciones Faramalla.

Office of the Secretary of the Commonwealth Elections Division. 1990a. "Candidates for Nomination, State Primary 1990 (Democratic, Republican)." Boston: Office of the Secretary of the Commonwealth.

———. 1990b. *The Official Massachusetts Information for Voters.* Boston, Mass.: Office of the Secretary of the Commonwealth.

———. 1990c. Telephone conversation with Jackie Ladd, Office of the Secretary of the Commonwealth, 1 October.

Orum, Anthony M., Roberta S. Cohen, Sherri Grasmuck, and Amy W. Orum. 1974. "Sex, Socialization and Politics." *American Political Science Review* 39, no. 2 (April): 197–209.

Osterman, Paul. 1992, March. "Latinos in the Midst of Plenty." In *Latinos in Boston: Confronting Poverty, Building Community*, by Miren Uriarte, Paul Osterman, Carol Hardy-Fanta, and Edwin Meléndez, 37–71. A background paper for the Boston Persistent Poverty Project. Boston: Boston Foundation.

Pachon, Harry P. 1981. "An Overview of National Hispanic Political Participation." Paper presented at the Congressional Hispanic Caucus National Symposium, September, Washington, D.C.

———. 1985. "Political Mobilization in the Mexican-American Community." In *Mexican-Americans in Comparative Perspective*, ed. Walker Connor, 245–256. Washington, D.C.: Urban Institute.

———. 1987. "An Overview of Hispanic Elected Officials in 1987." In *1987 National Roster of Hispanic Elected Officials*, iv–xxvi. Washington, D.C.: National Association of Latino Elected and Appointed Officials (NALEO).

Pachon, Harry P., and Louis DeSipio. 1988. "The Latino Vote in 1988." NALEO background paper no. 7. Washington, D.C.: National Association of Latino Elected and Appointed Officials (NALEO) Education Fund.

Padilla, Felix M. 1985. *Latino Ethnic Consciousness: The Case of Mexican Americans and Puerto Ricans in Chicago.* Notre Dame, Ind.: University of Notre Dame Press.

———. 1987. *Puerto Rican Chicago.* Notre Dame, Ind.: University of Notre Dame Press.

Pantoja, Antonia, and Esperanza Martell. 1989–90. "Mi gente." *Centro de Estudios Puertorriqueños Bulletin* 2, no. 7 (Winter): 48–55.

Pardo, Mary. 1990. "Mexican American Women Grassroots Community Activists: 'Mothers of East Los Angeles.'" *Frontiers* 11, no. 1:1–7.

Pateman, Carole. 1970. *Participation and Democratic Theory.* Cambridge: Cambridge University Press.

———. 1980. "The Civic Culture: A Philosophic Critique." In *The Civic Culture Revisited: An Analytic Study,* ed. Gabriel Almond and Sidney Verba, 57–102. Boston: Little, Brown.

———. 1989. *The Disorder of Women.* Stanford, Calif.: Stanford University Press.

Pierce, Neal R., and Jerry Hagstrom. 1988. "The Hispanic Community—a Growing Force to Be Reckoned With." In *Latinos and the Political System,* ed. F. Chris Garcia, 11–27. Notre Dame, Ind.: University of Notre Dame Press.

Piven, Frances Fox, and Richard A. Cloward. 1971. *Regulating the Poor: The Functions of Public Welfare.* New York: Pantheon Books.

———. 1979. *Poor People's Movements: Why They Succeed, How They Fail.* New York: Vintage Books; first published Random House, 1977.

———. 1989. *Why Americans Don't Vote.* New York: Pantheon; first published Random House, 1988.

Pomper, Gerald. 1975. *Voter's Choice.* New York: Dodd, Mead.

Portes, Alejandro, and Robert Bach. 1985. *Latin Journey: Cuban and Mexican Immigrants in the United States.* Berkeley: University of California Press.

Portes, Alejandro, and Cynthia Truelove. 1987. "Making Sense of Diversity: Recent Research on Hispanic Minorities in the United States." *Annual Review of Sociology* 13:359–385.

Portuondo, María Luisa Wilson. 1990. Personal conversation, 17 December.

Powell, Lynda Watts, with Clifford W. Brown and Roman B. Hedges. 1981. "Male and Female Differences in Elite Political Participation: An Examination of the Effects of Socioeconomic and Familial Variables." *Western Political Quarterly* 34, no. 1 (March): 31–45.

Randall, Vicky. 1987. *Women and Politics: An International Perspective.* 2d ed. Chicago: University of Chicago Press.

Riker, William H., and Peter C. Ordeshook. 1968. "A Theory of the Calculus of Voting." *American Political Science Review* 62, no. 1 (March): 25–42.

Rinehart, Sue Tolleson. 1986. "Toward Women's Political Resocialization: Patterns of Predisposition in the Learning of Feminist Attitudes." In *Gender and Socialization to Power and Politics,* ed. Rita Mae Kelly, 11–26. New York: Haworth Press.

Riordon, William L. 1963. *Plunkitt of Tammany Hall.* New York: Dutton.

Rivera, Monte. 1984. "Organizational Politics of the East Harlem Barrio in the 1970s." In *Puerto Rican Politics in Urban America,* ed. James Jennings and Monte Rivera, 61–72. Westport, Conn.: Greenwood Press.

Rivera, Ralph. 1991. *Latinos in Massachusetts and the 1990 U.S. Census: Growth and Geographical Distribution.* Boston: Mauricio Gastón Institute for Latino Community Development and Public Policy, University of Massachusetts—Boston.

Rogler, Lloyd H. 1974. "The Changing Role of a Political Boss in a Puerto Rican Migrant Community." *American Sociological Review* 39, no. 1 (February): 57–67.

Rose, Margaret. 1990. "Traditional and Nontraditional Patterns of Female Activism in the United Farm Workers of America, 1962 to 1980." *Frontiers* 11, no. 1:26–32.

Rule, Wilma. 1981. "Why Women Don't Run: The Critical Contextual Factors in Women's Legislative Recruitment." *Western Political Quarterly* 34, no. 1 (March): 60–77.

Sacks, Karen. 1988. "Gender and Grassroots Leadership." In *Women and the Politics of Empowerment*, ed. Ann Bookman and Sandra Morgen, 77–94. Philadelphia: Temple University Press.

Salamon, Lester M., and Stephen Evera. 1973. "Fear, Apathy, and Discrimination: A Test of Three Explanations of Political Participation." *American Political Science Review* 67, no. 4 (December): 1288–1306.

Sánchez Korrol, Virginia. 1983. *From Colonia to Community: The History of Puerto Ricans in New York City, 1917–1948.* Westport, Conn.: Greenwood Press.

Santillan, Richard. 1988a. "The Latino Community in State and Congressional Redistricting: 1961–1985." In *Latinos and the Political System*, ed. F. Chris Garcia, 328–348. Notre Dame, Ind.: University of Notre Dame Press.

———. 1988b. "Latino Politics in the Midwestern United States: 1915–1986." In *Latinos and the Political System*, ed. F. Chris Garcia, 99–118. Notre Dame, Ind.: University of Notre Dame Press.

———. 1988c. "Styles and Strategies." In *Latinos and the Political System*, ed. F. Chris Garcia, 467–479. Notre Dame, Ind.: University of Notre Dame Press.

Sapiro, Virginia. 1983. *The Political Integration of Women: Roles, Socialization and Politics.* Urbana: University of Illinois Press.

Sartori, Giovanni. 1962. *Democratic Theory.* 2d ed. Detroit, Mich.: Wayne State University Press.

Schattschneider, E. E. 1975. *The Semisovereign People.* Hinsdale, Ill.: Dryden Press; first published, 1960.

Schuck, Peter H., and Rogers M. Smith. 1985. *Citizenship Without Consent: Illegal Aliens in the American Polity.* New Haven, Conn.: Yale University Press.

Schumpeter, Joseph A. 1943. *Capitalism, Socialism and Democracy.* London: Allen and Unwin.

Scott, James C. 1985. *Weapons of the Weak: Everyday Forms of Peasant Resistance.* New Haven, Conn.: Yale University Press.

Shaffer, Stephen D. 1981. "A Multivariate Explanation of Decreasing Turnout in Presidential Elections, 1960–1976." *American Journal of Political Science* 25, no. 1 (February): 68–95.

Shingles, Richard. 1981. "Black Consciousness and Political Participation: The Missing Link." *American Political Science Review* 75, no. 1 (March): 76–91.

Sigel, Roberta S., ed. 1989. *Political Learning in Adulthood.* Chicago: University of Chicago Press.

Stern, Philip. 1988. *The Best Congress Money Can Buy.* New York: Pantheon.

Stone, Deborah. 1987. Lecture, Brandeis University, 8 September.

———. 1989. Conversation with author.

Surrey, Janet L. 1991. "Relationship and Empowerment." In *Women's Growth in Connection,* ed. Judith V. Jordan, Alexandra G. Kaplan, Jean Baker Miller, Irene P. Stiver, and Janet L. Surrey, 162–180. New York: Guilford Press.

Tannen, Deborah. 1990. *You Just Don't Understand: Women and Men in Conversation.* New York: Morrow; Ballantine ed., 1991 (page references are to Ballantine edition).

Tate, Katherine. 1992. "Invisible Woman." *American Prospect,* no. 8 (Winter): 74–81.

Teaford, Jon C. 1982. "Finis for Tweed and Steffans: Rewriting the History of Urban Rule." *Reviews in American History* 10, no. 4 (December): 133–149.

Tolchin, Susan, and Martin Tolchin. 1976. *Clout—Womanpower and Politics.* New York: Capricorn Books.

Torres, María de los Angeles. 1991. Letter to author.

Torres-Gil, Fernando. 1976. "Political Behavior: A Study of Political Attitudes and Political Participation Among Older Mexican-Americans." Ph.D. diss., Brandeis University.

Travis, Toni-Michelle C. 1990. "Boston: The Unfinished Agenda." In *Racial Politics in American Cities,* ed. Rufus P. Browning, Dale Rogers Marshall, and David H. Tabb, 108–121. New York: Longman.

Uriarte, Miren. 1992. "Contra viento y marea (Against All Odds): Latinos Build Community in Boston." In *Latinos in Boston: Confronting Poverty, Building Community,* by Miren Uriarte, Paul Osterman, Carol Hardy-Fanta, and Edwin Meléndez, 3–34. A background paper for the Boston Persistent Poverty Project. Boston: Boston Foundation.

Uriarte, Miren B., and Nelson Merced. 1985. "Social Service Agencies in Boston's Latino Community: Notes on Institutionalization." *Catalyst* 5, nos. 17/18:21–34.

Uriarte-Gaston, Miren. 1988. "Organizing for Survival: The Emergence of a Puerto Rican Community." Ph.D. diss., Boston University.

U.S. Bureau of the Census. 1988. *The Hispanic Population in the United States: March 1988 (Advance Report),* Current Population Reports, Series P-20, No. 431. Washington, D.C.: U.S. Government Printing Office.

———. 1989. *Voting and Registration in the Election of November 1988,* Current Population Reports, Series P-20, No. 440. Washington, D.C.: U.S. Government Printing Office.

———. 1991. *Voting and Registration in the Election of November 1990,* Current Population Reports, Series P-20, No. 453. Washington, D.C.: U.S. Government Printing Office.

Vecoli, Rudolph J. 1972. "European Americans: From Immigrants to Ethnics." *International Migration Review* 6, no. 6 (Winter): 403–434.

Verba, Sidney, and Norman Nie. 1972. *Participation in America: Political Democracy and Social Equality.* New York: Harper and Row.

Vigil, Maurilio E. 1987. *Hispanics in American Politics: The Search for Political Power.* Lanham, Md: University Press of America.

Villarreal, Roberto E., Norma G. Hernandez, and Howard D. Neighbor. 1988. *Latino Empowerment: Progress, Problems, and Prospects.* Westport, Conn.: Greenwood Press.

Walton, Hanes. 1985. *Invisible Politics: Black Political Behavior.* SUNY Series in Afro-American Society. Albany: State University of New York Press.

Walzer, Michael. 1983. *Spheres of Justice: A Defense of Pluralism and Equality.* New York: Basic Books.

Warren, Kay Barbara, and Susan C. Bourque. 1985. "Gender, Power, and Communication: Women's Responses to Political Muting in the Andes." In *Women Living Change,* ed. Susan C. Bourque and Donna Robinson Divine, 255–286. Philadelphia: Temple University Press.

Watson, James B., and Julian Samora. 1954. "Subordinate Leadership in a Bicultural Community: An Analysis." *American Sociological Review* 19, no. 4 (August): 413–421.

Weiss, Penny. 1991. "Feminist Reflections on Community." Paper presented at the annual meeting of the American Political Science Association, 29 August–1 September, Washington, D.C.

Welch, Susan, and Philip Secret. 1981. "Sex, Race and Political Participation." *Western Political Quarterly* 34, no. 1 (March): 5–16.

Willis, Garry. 1988. "'New Votuhs.'" *New York Review of Books* 35, no. 13 (18 August): 3–5.

Wilson, James Q., and Edward C. Banfield. 1971. "Political Ethos Revisited." *American Political Science Review* 65, no. 4 (December): 1048–1062.

Young, Eva, and Mariwilda Padilla. 1990. "Mujeres Unidas en Acción: A Popular Education Process." *Harvard Educational Review* 60, no. 1 (February): 1–18.

Young, Iris Marion. 1990. "Polity and Group Differences: A Critique of the Ideal of Universal Citizenship." In *Feminism and Political Theory,* ed. Cass R. Sunstein, 117–141. Chicago: University of Chicago Press.

Index

Carrillo, Jesús (*cont.*):
leadership issues, 90–94; political activities of, 1, 3–4, 48; on structural constraints of Latino agencies, 162; redistricting politics and, 111–14; views on concept of power, 51–52
census (Boston city), as barrier to voter registration, 171–72
"centerwomen" concept, 206n.31
Central America, politics in, 185–87, 221nn.30–31
Centro Presente, 121–22
"chain-of-command" politics, 81–83
Chamorro, Violeta, 156
change: development of political consciousness and, 128; exclusion of men from forces of, in feminist movement, 158–59; Latina women's emphasis on, 52–53; as political power, 30–31
charity work, as politics, 131–32
charlas: adult resocialization and, 143, 147; held by Mujeres Unidas en Acción, 96–97
Chavez, Linda, 202n.6
Chelsea, Massachusetts, 110, 213n.9
Chicana women: as political leaders, 21; connection-based politics of, 30; voter registration and participation, 25. *See also* Mexican Americans
childhood, political socialization in, 137–40, 216n.11, 217n.22
la chispa que prende, 137–38, 189
church, political activism of, 103
circular migration, 177–79
citizenship: changes in birthright law, 219n.20; community and, 101–102, 118–20, 123; definitions of, 99–101; feminist theories of, 100–101; lack of, as barrier to participation, 118, 214nn.17–19; Latino community, 214n.19; participatory politics and, 124–26; voter registration requirements and, 171–72
City Council (Boston), 12
civil rights movement: interpersonal relationships and, 61–62; political socialization and, 137–38, 216n.12
civil service provisions, as barrier to participation, in Boston, 184
class structure: feminism and, 216n.17; hierarchy and leadership issues, 90–91, 212n.19; Latina-Latino politics

and, 190–93; *personalismo* and, 60–62, 193–97; political education and, 134; racism and sexism and, 157–59; survival politics and, 46
clientelist model of community service, 165–66
coalition politics, Latino community and, 107–108
Colina, Edwin: bilingual education, 116–17; community activism, 164; connection-based politics of, 39; electoral politics and, 105; family background and political socialization, 138–39; gender differences and electoral politics, 69–70, 115; on hierarchy and leadership issues, 91; male politicization and, 150–51; on *personalismo* value, 56–57
collective organization and methods: community organizations and, 97–98; gender-differentiated preferences for, 79–81; Latina-Latino political theory and, 190–93; Latina women's preference for, 95; party politics and, 184–85; political participation fostered by, 76–79, 95–97
Comité de Familias Latinas de Boston, 2, 56–57, 77, 164; cultural-gender interplay at, 62; suppression of political participation and, 85–87; as research source, xiii–xiv
Comité de Mujeres-Miriam López Pérez, 156
Comité de Padres Pro Defensa de la Educación Bilingüe, 116–17
communication styles: gender-based differences in, 48–50; race relations and, 156–59
community: definitions of, 99–101; political activism in, constraints on, 163–68, 218n.10
community organizations: bilingual education, 115–18; citizenship and, 101–102; collective structure and, 77–79, 97–98; Latina women in, 25, 42, 104; male dominance of leadership in, 92–94; political consciousness and, 130; as research source, xiii, 199n.4, 200n.5; staff of, as political resource, 42; structural constraints on, 162–68
compromiso formal, 62
Comunidad Boricua en Acción, 77–79,

81–83, 104; structural constraints on, 163
Concilio Latino, 124, 165
connection-based politics: city hall connections and, 65–68; culture and political mobilization, 53–62; defined, 3–5, 37–38; effectiveness of, 27; feminist theory and machine politics, 68–74; gender differences in Latino politics and, 45–46, 69–70; Josefina Ortega as example of, 28–30; Latina women's role in, 17–23, 26–27; Latina-Latino political theory and, 46–51, 190–93; María Luisa Soto as example of, 42–48; mobilization of illegal aliens with, 122–23; *personalismo* value and, 62–65; vs. position and status-based politics, 40–42; power and, 30–31, 51–53, 204nn.20–21
constituent strategies, in mainland vs. island Puerto Rican politics, 182–83, 221n.28
Contreras, Pedro, 164
Correa, Marta, x, xii; connection-based politics, 18, 46; culture and politics and, 197; family background and political socialization, 140; machine politics and, 72–74; on political consciousness, 130, 147–48, 215n.3
Council of Administrators of Hispanic Agencies (CAHA), 218n.8
Cruzada de Amor, 131–32, 215n.4
Cuadrado, Luz, 81, 104, 163
Cuba, U.S. intervention in, 38
Cuban Americans, political activism of, 35, 77
culture: impact of structure on, 178–87, 220n.23; interactive politics and, 193–97; *personalismo* and, 62–65, 209n.30; political participation and, 12–14, 31–36, 53–62; *venir y averigüar* concept, 58–60; voter participation and, 31–36, 204nn.24–25

del Valle, Andrea: on definition of politics, 2–3; on hierarchy and leadership issues, 91; on Latina women in Puerto Rican politics, 156–57; on limits of hierarchical organizations, 84; on political consciousness of Latina women, 19–20, 133
Democratic Party: gender differences

and electoral politics, 115; grassroots politics and, 104–105; Latina women's participation in, 28–29, 72; Latino relations with, 33, 174, 181
Democratic Wish, 205n.28
"designated leaders," political dilemmas of, 89
Despierta Boricua! slogan, 103, 213n.3
"divisible" political benefits: concrete benefits, 194–95; Latino politics and, 71, 209n.31
doctrine of separation, in Anglo culture, 53–54
Domínguez, Isabel, 58
Dominican Republic: Cruzada de Amor in, 131–32, 215n.4; machine politics and, 176; U.S. intervention in, 9–10
Dominicans: home ties and political participation, 178–79; influence of noncitizens on voter participation, 205n.24; noncitizen political participation and, 121; personal-public relationships among, 53–54, 208n.17; political participation of, 178–79, 183–85, 220n.25, 221n.29; *venir y averigüar* concept and, 59–60, 208n.20; women's political activism, 59–60, 208n.20
Dorchester area (Boston), selection of interviewees from, xii–xiii
Dukakis, Michael, 47, 66, 167

economic conditions: community-based political activism and, 166–68; impact on voter participation, 33–34; Latino politics and, 7–12
educational issues: participatory politics and, 85–87, 211n.9. *See also* bilingual education
El Centro Católico, xiii
El Salvador, 179
elderly, community programs for, 28
electoral politics: gender differences regarding, 114–15; Latina women's participation in, 16–23; Latino political participation and, 46–48, 105–106, 192–93; links with alternative politics, 29–30; *personalismo* and, 54–56, 207n.18; structural barriers to, for Latinos, 169–73; voter participation rates and, 31–36, 205nn.24–25

Index

Emergency Tenants Council (ETC), 103–104
encuentro, 133
English as second language (ESL) courses: Mujeres Unidas programs, 96; voter participation and, 169–70
envidia concept: gender, hierarchy, and leadership, 92; political participation and, 87, 211n.10
Ethnograph, The, xv

family traditions: as catalyst for political consciousness, 138–40; connection-based politics and, 38; gender differences and socialization in, 140–41
fear and danger: in Central American politics, 185–87, 221nn.30–31; as suppression of political participation, 33–34, 179
federal government, political mobilization of minorities and, 165–66, 219n.12
feminist movement: Latina women and, 155–59; political socialization and, 61, 208n.25
feminist theory: adult resocialization and, 142–43; citizenship and, 100–101, 119–20; connection-based politics and, 68–74; gender-defined world view, 26–27; Latina-Latino politics and, 30, 190–93; political ideology and, 24–25, 203n.14; public vs. private politics and, 132–33, 204n.19; racism and, 155–59; social construction of, 204n.14
Fitzgerald, Kevin, 106
Flynn, Mayor Ray, 18, 47, 66
Fonseca, Juanita, 27, 104; on connection-based politics, 52; on economic conditions, 11; family and socialization, 139, 141; on Latino political activism, 35; on politics in Puerto Rico, 180; party politics and, 16
foreign policy: impact of, on connection-based politics, 209n.30; Latino politics and, 9–10, 38–39
formal political structure: gender-differentiated preferences for, 79–81; Latino men's preference for, 62–65; vs. collective organizations, 77–79. *See also* compromiso formal
Freire, Paolo, 97, 135, 212n.21

funding constraints, community-based political activism and, 163–68, 218n.11

García, Carlos, x, 177
García, Frieda, 104, 107
Gardner, Carla, 3; survival politics and, 45–46
Gastón, Mauricio, 115, 214n.14
gender differences: childhood political socialization and, 138–40, 216n.22; community and citizenship, 101–102; definition of politics as connection, 2–5, 41; definition of politics as elections, 105; family and socialization, 140–41; hierarchy and leadership issues, 90–94; interactive politics and, 195–97; in Latino politics, 69–70, 189–92; leadership dilemmas and, 89–90; male politicization and, 151; participation and political consciousness, 151–52; participatory politics and, 2–5, 12–14, 20–23, 30–31, 203nn.9–11; *personalismo* and, 62–65; political theory and, 23–27; quantitative measures of, 206n.3, 206n.6, 207n.16, 208n.25, 209nn.33–34, 212n.2, 212n.18, 213n.5, 213n.10, 214n.13, 215n.5, 216n.19, 219n.22; survival politics and, 45–46, 206.6
generation gap, in Latina women, 29
la gente del pueblo: adult resocialization and, 142–43; Anglo institutions and, 90, 212n.18; citizenship among, 101–102, 214n.18; connection-based politics of, 39–40; defined, x–xii, 199n.1; electoral politics and, 17, 70, 107; grassroots organization of, 102–105, 212n.2; information dissemination among, 133–35, 215n.5; interactive politics and, 194–97; interview methods with, xiii–xiv; limits of hierarchical structure for, 85–87; machine politics and, 175–76; male politicization and, 150–51; marriage and political consciousness, 148, 217n.28; Morales as example of, 65–68; *personalismo* and, 56, 63–65; political consciousness and, 129–35, 215n.2; *venir yaverigüar* concept, 58–60; voter participation rates among, 32

242

King, Mel, 12, 25, 107–108, 167

labor organization: risks of, in Central America, 185–86, 221n.31; role of Latina women in, 203nn.9–10
Lam, Diana, 16, 110–11, 201n.1
language: culture and, 209n.30; as structural barrier to voting, 169–70
"language constructs experience," 116
Latin American countries, personal-public relationships in, 54, 208n.17
Latin Journey, 21–22
Latina, definition of, 5
Latina women: adult resocialization, 141–43; as staff in hierarchical organizations, 83, 211n.7; connection-based politics and differences from Latino men, 48–51; marriage and political consciousness, 148, 217n.28; political mobilization of noncitizens and, 120–22; preference for collective organizations, 79–81; traditional political roles of, 16–23. *See also* Latina women *under other entries*
Latino community: ethnic diversity of, 5–12; frequent job moves of leaders, 166–67, 196–97; gender and hierarchical structure, 90–94; leadership in, community distrust of, 87–90; male dominance of, 92–94; residential dispersion, in Boston, 7–9, 201n.7; sociopolitical context of, 5–12; terminology of, 6–7
Latino Democratic Committee, 117–18, 162, 216n.8; gender differences and electoral politics, 114; grassroots politics and, 104–105; male politicization and, 151; party politics and, 16
Latino men: access to position and status, importance of, 46–48; electoral politics preferred by, 105–18. 213n.5; hierarchical structure preferred by, 79–81; political differences with Latina women, 48–51; politicization of, 3–5, 149–51, 217n.40; redistricting politics and, 111–14. *See also* subhead Latino men under specific topics
Latino Network, 218n.8
Latino Political Action Committee (Latino PAC), 112, 117–18
Lawyers' Committee on Civil Rights, 112

leadership: gender and, of Latino agencies, 90; hierarchy and, 90–94, political dilemmas of Latino, 88–89
leases on apartments, as barrier to voter registration, 170–71, 219n.16
"liaison leaders," political dilemmas of, 89
listening, as component of participatory politics, 65, 86–87, 209n.27
lobbying activities: collective methods for, 78–79; noncitizen political participation and, 120–21
López, Rosa: on economic conditions, 11; gender differences and electoral politics, 114; on hierarchy and leadership issues, 91; on political corruption, 87; on political power, 30–31; political activism and, 16–17
loyalty, Latino political activism and, 71–72, 167–68

machine politics civil service in Boston and, 184; vs. connection-based politics, 68–74; decline of, 173–76; in Dominican Republic, 184; in Puerto Rico, 180–83, 220n.26; Latina women's politics as, 70–74; Latino men's preference for, 82–83
Maldonado, Juan, 3; on community activism, 214n.16; connection-based politics and, 39; electoral politics discussed by, 47–48, 105; on hierarchical organizations, 82; lack of job stability among Latino leaders, 166–67, 196–97; redistricting politics and, 111–14
marianismo, as source of oppression, for Latina women, 19
marriage, politicization of Latina women and, 148, 217n.28
Martínez, Inez, x, xii; on culture and politics, 197; home ties with Mexico and, 177; and noncitizen participation, 120; political activism of, 1, 73–74, 120, 148, 160–62
Marxist feminism, political ideology and, 203n.14
mass movements, decline in, 109–10, 213n.8
Massachusetts Commission Against Discrimination (MCAD), 47, 105, 207n.10

participatory politics (*cont.*): pression of, 83–87, 211n.8; home-country politics and, 176–87, 219n.22; Latina-Latino political theory and, 191–93; Latina women's embrace of, 24–27, 51–53, 188, 203nn.12–14; Latino leadership issues and, 87–94; limitations of, 153–54, 159; mobilization of illegal aliens, 120–23; *personalismo* value and, 56–58; political power and, 31, 204n.20; self-perception and, 129–35; vs. representative democracy theory, 34–35

party politics: decline of, 173–76; in Dominican Republic, 183–85, 221n.30; in Puerto Rico, 180–83, 220n.26; Latina women's participation in, 16–17

patriarchal structures, Latina-Latino political theory and, 191

Pérez, Angel, 63

Pena, Marisela, 146

personal development: Julia Santiago's experience in, 143–48; Latina-Latino political theory and, 189–90; political consciousness and, 127–29; self-perception and, 129–35

personal relationships: connection-based politics, 40–42; *personalismo* and, 54, 56–58; political power and, 26–27, 30–31, 50–51, 204n.21, 207n.14; voter registration and, 60–62, 208n.24

personalismo: cultural value of, 53–62; electoral politics and, 54–56, 207n.18; gender differences and, 62–65; human needs and, 60–62; interactive politics and, 193–97; Morales as example of, 65–68; personal relationships and, 56–58

Petillo, Pablo, 139

Petra, Doña, 67–68

las pioneras, x

Pola, Carmen, 16, 105–106, 112, 213n.11, 216n.8

political apathy: supposed prevalence of, among Latinos, ix; Eurocentric cultural bias regarding, 33–34; representative democracy and, 34–35; voter participation rates as measure of, 32–33

political consciousness: adult resocialization and, 142–43; "becoming politi-

cal," 137–38; gender differences in, 137–38, 151–52, 189, 216n.19; Latino men and, 149–51, 217n.30; marriage for Latina women and, 148, 217n.28; personal development and, 127–29; political education and, 133–35; public vs. private politics and, 132–33; role of family in, 138–40; self-perception and, 129–35; sources of, 138–41

political corruption: in Dominican Republic, 183–84, 208n.21; personal-public relationships and, 54, 208n.17

political-culture research, biases in, 32–33

political elite, in Latino community, x

political ethos theory, 20, 203n.11

"political muting," hierarchical organizations and, 84–85

political participation, gender differences in definition of, ix, 2–5, 12–14, 23–24, 153–54, 192–97; structural constraints on Latino agencies and, 162–63

political socialization, defined, 138; role of family in, 138–41; gender differences in, 140–41

population growth: Latino, in Boston, 5–6; Latino, in U.S., 13

portavoces, 17

Portuondo, María Luisa Wilson, 182–83

position and status-based politics: barriers to, for Latina women, 69–70; vs. connection-based politics, 3–4, 40–42, 206n.1; importance of, for Latino men, 26–27, 46–48; limitations of, for Latina women, 70

Pouncy, Hillard, 206n.1

poverty rates, Latino, in Boston, 10; in U.S., 201n.10

power: connection-based vs. machine politics and, 73–74; gender differences in, 30–31, 49–53, 207n.16; Latina-Latino political theory and, 189–90; participatory politics and, 192–93; political socialization and, 137; public vs. private politics and, 132–33

presidential candidates, Latina women's role as, 204n.16

private politics, vs. public politics, 27, 132–33

Index

Rodríguez, Ivelisse (*cont.*): cation, 134; on *venir y averigüar* concept, 59

·Rojas, Antonio, 88; electoral politics and, x, 105; ethnic diversity of Latino community, 6

Rojas, Julio: connection-based politics and, 40; grassroots political activity of, 25; on Latino leadership, 87–88, 91–93; on *personalismo*, 64–65; on Soto's political success, 44–45

Romero, Grace, 16, 106

Romero, Jaime, x, 61, 105

Rosa, Marta: electoral campaign of, x, 2, 110–11; family background and political socialization, 140; on hierarchy and leadership issues, 91; *personalismo* value in electoral politics and, 54–55; on voter registration, 17, 172

Rosie Jiménez Committee, 218n.5

Ruiz, Dalia, x; on collective methods, 75–76, 79; on family as source of political socialization, 139

Salamanca, Francisco, x, 121; on politics, for Dominican men, 183–84

sampling techniques, for Latino community research, xii

Sánchez, Manuel, 124–25; on community-based politics, 165; family background and political socialization, 139; male politicization and, 150–51

Santiago, Julia: adult resocialization of, 143–48; coalition politics of, 108; on collective organizational structure, 97; on connection-based politics, 37–38, 45, 73; culture and politics and, 197; on *personalismo*, 58; political consciousness and, 4, 134–35, 143–48

school dropout prevention programs, 56–57, 85

Schoolman, Blanca, 91, 134

sexism, political consciousness and, 154–59, 186–87

social conditioning, Latina women's political activity and, 5–12, 69–70

Soto, María Luisa, x–xii; connection-based politics of, 3, 42–46; culture and politics and, 197; machine politics and, 16, 72–74; *personalismo* style of,

63; political activities of, 1, 128–29, 141

South End area (Boston), political activism in, 102–104; selection of interviewees from, xii–xiii

Spanish-language voting machines, 169–70, 219n.15

stereotypes, in Latina research, 18–19

Strong Democracy, 27

"strong women" tradition, in Latina community, 19

subsistence politics, defined, 46, 207n.7

survival politics: Latina women's focus on, 45–46, 206n.6; structural constraints of Latino agencies and, 162–68; Villa Victoria project, 103–105

teenage pregnancy, as Latina issue, 29

Torres, Catalina, 70; family and socialization, 140–41; on connection-based politics, 41, 53–54; on Latino leadership, 87, 91–92

Torrijos, Marta, 57–58, 121

"transformation" process, 145–46

translations: limits of, 78, 210nn.4–6, 217n.25, 219n.18; use of Spanish quotes, xiv–xv

Travelers Aid Society, Latino challenges to, 4–5

Trujillo regime, in Dominican Republic, 59–60, 131–32, 208n.21

United Farm Workers movement, 25

Uriarte, Miren, 103–104, 213n.3

Vázquez, Juan: on *personalismo*, 64–65; on sexism and Latina women, 155; on voter registration, 172

Velez, Ramon, 176

venir y averigüar concept, 58–60

Villa Victoria project, 81–82, 102–105, 160–62, 214n.16

villas y castillos concept, 182

voter participation: class-based aspects of, 60–61; community-based political activism and, 165–68; culture-based differences, 31–36, 204nn.24–25; decline in, 109–10, 167–73, 219nn.14–15; decline of party and machine politics, 173–76; gender differences and, 18, 114–15, 202n.7; impact of home ties on, 178–87, 220n.24; influence of

DATE DUE